EVANGELICAL ETHICS

LIBRARY OF THEOLOGICAL ETHICS

Other books in this series

Basic Christian Ethics, by Paul Ramsey
Christ and the Moral Life, by James M. Gustafson
Christianity and the Social Crisis, by Walter Rauschenbusch
Conscience and Its Problems, by Kenneth E. Kirk
Economic Justice: Selections from Distributive Justice *and* A Living Wage,
    by John A. Ryan
Ethics in a Christian Context, by Paul L. Lehmann
Feminist Theological Ethics: A Reader, edited by Lois K. Daly
Georgia Harkness: The Remaking of a Liberal Theologian, edited by Rebekah Miles
The Holy Spirit and the Christian Life: The Theological Basis of Ethics, by Karl Barth
Love and Justice: Selections from the Shorter Writings of Reinhold Niebuhr, edited
    by D. B. Robertson
The Meaning of Revelation, by H. Richard Niebuhr
Morality and Beyond, by Paul Tillich
Moral Discernment in the Christian Life: Essays in Theological Ethics, edited by James M.
    Gustafson
Moral Man and Immoral Society, by Reinhold Niebuhr
The Nature and Destiny of Man: A Christian Interpretation (2 vols.),
    by Reinhold Niebuhr
Radical Monotheism and Western Culture: With Supplementary Essays,
    by H. Richard Niebuhr
Reconstructing Christian Ethics: Selected Writings, by F. D. Maurice
Religious Liberty: Catholic Struggles with Pluralism, by John Courtney Murray
"The Responsibility of the Church for Society" and Other Essays by H. Richard Niebuhr,
    edited and with an introduction by Kristine A. Culp
The Responsible Self: An Essay in Christian Moral Philosophy, by H. Richard Niebuhr
Selections from Friedrich Schleiermacher's Christian Ethics, edited by James M. Brandt
Situation Ethics: The New Morality, by Joseph Fletcher
The Social Teaching of the Christian Churches (2 vols.), by Ernst Troeltsch
The Structure of Christian Ethics, by Joseph Sittler
The Ten Commandments, edited by William P. Brown
A Theology for the Social Gospel, by Walter Rauschenbusch
Treasure in Earthen Vessels: The Church as Human Community, by James M. Gustafson
War in the Twentieth Century: Sources in Theological Ethics, edited by Richard B. Miller
Womanist Theological Ethics: A Reader, edited by Katie Geneva Cannon, Emilie M.
    Townes, and Angela D. Sims

EVANGELICAL ETHICS

A Reader

Edited by
David P. Gushee and Isaac B. Sharp

WJK WESTMINSTER
JOHN KNOX PRESS
LOUISVILLE · KENTUCKY

First edition
Published by Westminster John Knox Press
Louisville, Kentucky

15 16 17 18 19 20 21 22 23 24—10 9 8 7 6 5 4 3 2 1

Book design by Sharon Adams
Cover design by Lisa Buckley Design
Cover art: © David Chmielewski & James Mclaughlin/Getty Images

Library of Congress Cataloging-in-Publication Data

Evangelical ethics : a reader / David P. Gushee and Isaac B. Sharp, editors. -- First edition.
    pages cm. -- (Library of theological ethics)
    Includes index.
    ISBN 978-0-664-25959-4 (acid-free paper) -- ISBN 0-664-25959-6 1. Christian ethics. 2. Evangelicalism. I. Gushee, David P., 1962- II. Sharp, Isaac B.
    BJ1275.E93 2015
    241'.0404--dc23

                                         2014049532

For the next generation

Contents

Acknowledgments

These pages constitute a continuation of the copyright page. Grateful acknowledgment for permission to republish articles and chapters that first appeared elsewhere is hereby noted:

Chapter 1: "The Evangelical 'Formula of Protest'" and "The Dawn of a New Reformation" were previously published in Carl F. H. Henry, *The Uneasy Conscience of Modern Fundamentalism* (Grand Rapids: Wm. B. Eerdmans Publishing Co., 1947), pp. 75–89. Reprinted by permission of the publisher; all rights reserved.

Chapter 2: "The Otherness of the Church," was previously published in John Howard Yoder, *The Royal Priesthood* (Grand Rapids: Wm. B. Eerdmans Publishing Co., 1994), pp. 54–64. Reprinted by permission of the publisher; all rights reserved. Original publication date: 1960.

Chapter 3: William E. Pannell, "The Evangelical Christian and Black History," was previously published in *Fides et Historia* 2, no. 2 (Spring 1970): 4–14. Used with permission from *Fides et Historia*.

Chapter 4: "Our Society" was previously published in Francis Schaeffer, *How Should We Then Live: The Rise and Decline of Western Thought and Culture* (Wheaton, IL: Crossway, 1976), pp. 205–27. Used by permission of Crossway, a publishing ministry of Good News Publishers, Wheaton, IL 60187, www.crossway.org.

Chapter 5: "A Billion Hungry Neighbors" and "The Affluent Minority" were previously published in Ron Sider, *Rich Christians in an Age of Hunger* (Nashville: Thomas Nelson, Inc., 2005), pp. 31–56. Used by permission. All rights reserved.

Chapter 6: "The Call" was previously published in Jim Wallis, *The Call to Conversion* (San Francisco: Harper & Row, 1981, revised 2005), pp. 1–17. Reprinted by permission of HarperCollins Publishers.

Chapter 7: "Love Is Stronger than Hate" and "The Reconciled Community" were previously published in John Perkins, *With Justice for All* (Ventura, CA: Regal Books, 1982), pp. 97–112. Used by permission from Baker Books, a division of Baker Publishing Group.

Chapter 8: "Biblical Faith and the Reality of Social Evil" was previously published in Stephen Charles Mott, *Biblical Ethics and Social Change* (New York: Oxford University Press, 1982, 2011), pp. 3–17. Used by permission from Oxford University Press, USA.

Chapter 9: "World-Formative Christianity" was previously published in Nicholas Wolterstorff, *Until Justice and Peace Embrace* (Grand Rapids: Wm. B. Eerdmans Publishing Co., 1983), pp. 3–22. Reprinted by permission of the publisher; all rights reserved.

Chapter 10: "Toward an Hispanic American Pentecostal Social Ethic" was previously published in Eldin Villafañe, *The Liberating Spirit: Toward an Hispanic American Pentecostal Social Ethic* (Grand Rapids: Wm. B. Eerdmans Publishing Co., 1993), pp. 193–222. Used with permission from Dr. Eldin Villafañe.

Chapter 11: "A Continuing Theocratic Tradition" was previously published in Allen Verhey, *Remembering Jesus: Christian Community, Scripture, and the Moral Life* (Grand Rapids: Wm. B. Eerdmans Publishing Co., 2002), pp. 456–86. Reprinted by permission of the publisher; all rights reserved.

Chapter 12: "Politics: Toward a Christian Social Ethic of Salt, Light and Deeds" was previously published in Glen H. Stassen and David P. Gushee, *Kingdom Ethics: Following Jesus in Contemporary Context* (Downers Grove, IL: InterVarsity Press, 2003), pp. 473–83. Used by permission of InterVarsity Press, P. O. Box 1400, Downers Grove, IL 60515, USA. www.ivpress.com.

Chapter 13: "Racism: The Residue of Western, White Cultural Captivity" was previously published in Soong-Chan Rah, *The Next Evangelicalism: Freeing the Church from Western Cultural Captivity* (Downers Grove, IL: InterVarsity Press, 2009), pp. 64–87. Used in an abbreviated form by permission of InterVarsity Press, P. O. Box 1400, Downers Grove, IL 60515, USA. www.ivpress.com.

Chapter 14: "Concrete Implications of an Ecclesial Witness Based on Repentance" was previously published in Jennifer McBride, *The Church for the World: A Theology of Public Witness* (New York: Oxford University Press, 2012), pp. 206–14. Used by permission from Oxford University Press, USA.

Chapter 15: Gabriel Salguero's "The Cross" was previously published in Bruce Ellis Benson, Malinda Elizabeth Berry, and Peter Goodwin Heltzel, ed., *Prophetic Evangelicals: Envisioning a Just and Peaceable Kingdom* (Grand Rapids: Wm. B. Eerdmans Publishing Co., 2012), pp. 130–38. Reprinted by permission of the publisher; all rights reserved.

Chapter 16: Helene Slessarev-Jamir's "Justice" was previously published in Bruce Ellis Benson, Malinda Elizabeth Berry, and Peter Goodwin Heltzel, ed., *Prophetic Evangelicals: Envisioning a Just and Peaceable Kingdom* (Grand Rapids: Wm. B. Eerdmans Publishing Co., 2012), pp. 77–85. Reprinted by permission of the publisher; all rights reserved.

Library of Theological Ethics

General Editors' Introduction

The field of theological ethics possesses in its literature an abundant inheritance concerning religious convictions and the moral life, critical issues, methods, and moral problems. The Library of Theological Ethics is designed to present a selection of important texts that would otherwise be unavailable for scholarly purposes and classroom use. The series engages the question of what it means to think theologically and ethically. It is offered in the conviction that sustained dialogue with our predecessors serves the interests of responsible contemporary reflection. Our more immediate aim in offering it, however, is to enable scholars and teachers to make more extensive use of classic texts as they train new generations of theologians, ethicists, and ministers.

The volumes included in the Library comprise a variety of types. Some make available English-language texts and translations that have fallen out of print; others present new translations of texts previously unavailable in English. Still others offer anthologies or collections of significant statements about problems and themes of special importance. We hope that each volume will encourage contemporary theological ethicists to remain in conversation with the rich and diverse heritage of their discipline.

ROBIN LOVIN
DOUGLAS F. OTTATI
WILLIAM SCHWEIKER

Introduction

WHO ARE THE EVANGELICALS?

Evangelicalism is notoriously difficult to define. *Everything* within the post-modern academy suffers from contestation *ad nauseam,* but evangelicalism has proven time and again a *particularly* thorny concept. Even if we choose to focus exclusively on evangelicalism within the United States, and almost entirely restrict the conversation to the post-World War II period, as we will do here, there is much to contest.

Due to the multiplicities of meaning associated with the descriptor and the attempts, time and again, to offer a concise definition for a group that defies easy categorization, some scholars have suggested that we jettison the term *evangelical* altogether.[1] Feeling that the broader cultural association of the term with a particularly narrow political agenda—an anti-gay and anti-abortion agenda—has left the label unredeemable, some within the evangelical community itself are today choosing to self-disassociate with evangelicalism and are using terms like "post-evangelical" or even "ex-evangelical."[2] In this sense a particular

---

1. See, especially, Donald W. Dayton's provocative suggestion that "evangelical" has lost its usefulness as a category, Donald W. Dayton, "Some Doubts about the Usefulness of the Category 'Evangelical,'" in *The Variety of American Evangelicalism,* ed. Donald W. Dayton and Robert K. Johnston (Downers Grove: InterVarsity Press, 1991), 245–51.

2. This move is more prevalent among popular authors and sometimes gains steam in widely circulated internet blogs and stories. See articles such as Scot McKnight, "The Ironic Faith of Emergents," *Christianity Today,* September 26, 2008, http://www.christianitytoday.com/ct/2008/september/39.62.html?start=1. And others including Leonardo Blair, "Ex-Evangelical Pastor Jerry Dewitt to Host Atheist Church Service in Louisianna," *The Christian Post,* June 13, 2013, http://www.christianpost.com/news/ex-evangelical-pastor-jerry-dewitt-to-host-atheist-church-service-in-louisiana-97963/ and Rachel Held Evans, "What Now?" (blog), http://rachelheldevans.com/blog/what-now-world-vision.

social-political theological ethic within a sector of evangelicalism is undercutting evangelicalism itself. But that gets ahead of our story.

If no one can agree on anything else about evangelicalism there is, at least, a consensus among those who know it best that evangelicalism is a slippery term. Some scholars approach the study of evangelicalism through a sociological lens and then disagree about who counts as an evangelical. Others define the movement in terms of religious history and then disagree about when and from whence it came. Still others view evangelicalism in terms of theological beliefs: a lens most often chosen by those "on the inside" and frequently deployed in times of hottest disagreement in order to decide who is still in and, more importantly, who is now out. Evangelicals, in part due to a distinctive historical journey we are about to describe, do an awful lot of arguing about who counts as an evangelical and who does not.

Still, we must make the definitional effort. Let's try a few theological definitions to get started. Among the most widely employed theological definitions of evangelicalism comes from British church historian David W. Bebbington in his famous "Bebbington Quadrilateral." He says evangelicals offer: 1. A stress on *conversion*; 2. A focus on *evangelism* and/or *activism*; 3. A sincere reverence for *the Bible*; 4. *Crucicentrism*: a view of the *cross* as absolutely central.[3]

In another attempt at enumerating evangelical theological characteristics, evangelical historian George Marsden includes the five following "essential evangelical beliefs": 1. Harkening ever back to the Protestant Reformation, evangelicals maintain the "final authority of the Bible"; 2. the belief that Scripture records the real historical narrative of "God's saving work"; 3. redemption through the salvific work of Jesus Christ and yielding eternal life; 4. "the importance of evangelism and missions"; 5. the necessity "of a spiritually transformed life."[4]

Union Seminary professor Gary Dorrien, contra Donald Dayton's suggestion that the term *evangelical* has lost its usefulness, instead agrees with Marsden and further quips about his "favorite definition of an evangelical, which is 'anyone who likes Billy Graham.'"[5] This quip is revelatory of a *sociological* reality about evangelicalism; it has often produced hugely visible and charismatic figures ranging from Aimee Semple Macpherson to Billy Sunday to Billy Graham to Jerry Falwell to Rick Warren to John Piper to Jim Wallis to Rob Bell to . . . whoever comes next. An "evangelical" in this sense would be someone who knows who these evangelical icons are and who takes as authoritative one, some, or all of them.

---

3. David W. Bebbington, "Evangelicalism in Its Settings: The British and American Movements since 1940," in *Evangelicalism*, ed. Mark A. Noll, David W. Bebbington, George A. Rawlyk (New York: Oxford University Press, 1994), 365–88.

4. George M. Marsden, *Understanding Fundamentalism and Evangelicalism* (Grand Rapids: Wm. B. Eerdmans Publishing Co., 1991), 4–5.

5. Gary Dorrien, *The Remaking of Evangelical Theology* (Louisville, KY: Westminster John Knox Press, 1998), 9.

Noting the importance of the *denominational and confessional diversity* of evangelicalism, evangelical church historian Timothy Weber sees evangelicalism as "a large extended family" with four main branches including: 1. *classical*: loyalists to the Reformation, with a tendency toward creedalism and away from the value of religious experience 2. *pietistic*: also within the Reformation stream but including an emphasis on religious experience and including both pietism and Puritanism; 3. *fundamentalist*: defined as opposing "liberal, critical, and evolutionary teaching" but also including "their 'neo-evangelical' offspring"; 4. *progressive*: including those who attempt to reconcile modernity with a variety of evangelical beliefs.[6] This sophisticated and helpful definition points already at sociological diversities within evangelicalism.

Or we could just go back to the *etymological origins* of the word *evangelical*, which at least are clear. The English word *evangelical* and associated words like *evangelism* come from the Greek word εὐαγγέλιον (*euangelion*). Every definition of these terms must, therefore, reckon with their original meaning: "good news."[7] (Evangelicals themselves will sometimes argue about which versions of our faith still represent "good news" to a suffering and unjust world and thus still merit the term "evangelical.") And as traced by Mark Noll—who is evangelicalism's foremost historian—the use of the term evangelical as an adjective dates back at least to the Middle Ages, when writers used it to describe the prophet Isaiah or the followers of St. Francis.[8]

More history helps us gain some clarity. The term *evangelical* began taking on its modern shape during the sixteenth century with the advent of the Protestant Reformation, at which point it began to be used as a synonym for Protestant—as is still the case in Germany today, where *Evangelische* means Protestant and especially Lutheran.[9] The movement that would become what we are describing when we say evangelicalism, however, offers a particular flavor of Christian faith that neither includes all Protestants nor is limited solely to Reformation-descended Protestantism. As we will see, though, the *reformist impulse*, implanted at its birth, continues to impact evangelicalism even now. This impulse has at times focused on *doctrine* and therefore on renewing theological seriousness or offering resistance to theological (or ethical) liberalism. Some of evangelicalism's greatest contributions to Christianity, however, have been about the renewal of *passion* in

6. Timothy P. Weber, "Premillenialism and the Branches of Evangelicalism," in *The Variety of American Evangelicalism*, ed. Donald W. Dayton and Robert K. Johnston (Downers Grove: InterVarsity Press, 1991), 5–21.

7. Mark A. Noll, "What Is Evangelical," in *The Oxford Handbook of Evangelical Theology*, ed. Gerald R. McDermott (New York: Oxford University Press, 2010), 19–34.

8. Ibid., 21.

9. Ibid. Noll importantly notes that the German language has maintained this original meaning of their word *evangelisch*, describing Lutheranism, and developed the term *Evangelikal* as a descriptor for the "movement" described in this volume. For a far more thorough account of the broader history of Evangelicalism, see InterVarsity Press's extensive five-volume series, A History of Evangelicalism, edited by David W. Bebbington and Mark A. Noll.

moribund Christianity and the drive to move people back toward devout "biblical" Christianity.

The first "modern" evangelicals were born when some newly minted Protestants were insultingly called "evangelicals" and chose to accept the label. The ensuing religious foment of sixteenth- through eighteenth-century Europe and the fledgling American colonies then gave rise to several more movements varyingly described as evangelical including Puritanism, Pietism, and the revival movements of the first American "Great Awakening." Formed for a variety of activist and evangelistic goals, evangelical "associations" then began taking root in the fertile, more disestablished religious soil of nineteenth-century North America.[10] Evangelicalism as a movement was always multi-denominational and multi-confessional, including Calvinists (but also Arminians), Wesleyans, Anabaptists, Baptists, Methodists, Presbyterians, Holiness, and eventually charismatics, Pentecostals, and others. There are even evangelical Episcopalians, now often called Anglicans in the U.S. setting, and some speak of evangelical Catholics. The historic black churches are almost all evangelical by any theological definition, though they have often not been institutionally close to predominantly white evangelical bodies due to the tortured history of race in America. Evangelicalism has never been confined to official denominational structures—sometimes evangelicals are a minority within a broader denomination while at other times they dominate a particular denomination—thus there are self-identified evangelicals in the mainline Presbyterian and Methodist denominations while the Southern Baptist Convention as a whole is normally viewed as evangelical. Meanwhile, evangelicals have tended to produce a lush crop of parachurch organizations for various mission and activist purposes. So evangelicals include groups ranging from the Salvation Army to the Vineyard churches to the World Relief and World Vision social ministries. In some ways the leaders of these groups act as each era's current evangelical gatekeepers, an unofficial house of bishops for a decentralized evangelicalism attempting to retain its vitality and identity.

These evangelical institutions—some old and some new, including churches, colleges, publishing houses, and parachurch groups—continue to help define and shape the evangelical subculture. If you know Wheaton, Gordon, and Azusa Pacific universities; if you have heard of *Books & Culture*, *Relevant*, and *Charisma* magazines; if you read books published by Thomas Nelson, Baker, and Zondervan publishing houses; if you participated in Campus Crusade, RUF, or Intervarsity Christian Fellowship while in college; if you sang worship songs from Hillsong or have attended the Passion conference held in Atlanta each year—you probably are, or were, an evangelical. Each nation with a strong evangelical presence could tell its own version of the same story; meanwhile, there are

10. David P. Gushee and Dennis P. Hollinger, "Toward an Evangelical Ethical Methodology," in *Toward an Evangelical Public Policy: Political Strategies for the Health of the Nation*, ed. Ronald J. Sider and Diane Knippers (Grand Rapids: Baker, 2005), 117–39.

institutions of global evangelicalism, such as the World Evangelical Fellowship and the Lausanne Movement.

AMERICAN EVANGELICALISM AND ITS SOCIAL ETHICS

But now let us focus more tightly on the trajectory of American evangelicalism and its social ethics. The waves of religious and cultural change cresting around the turn of the twentieth century left an indelible imprint on all aspects of American Christianity, including what became American evangelicalism. American Christian approaches to social-political theology and ethics were especially affected by the events during this period. For American evangelical social ethics and political theology, the most important and influential of these events was the advent of *fundamentalism*, which we understand here to be a particularly reactionary variant of older, less reactionary forms of evangelical Christianity in America.

Developing largely in reaction to the encroachment of European Protestant theological liberalism on American Christianity, fundamentalism and the "fundamentalist-modernist" controversies of the late nineteenth and early twentieth century set much of the trajectory of what later became evangelical political theology.[11] Fundamentalists, almost by definition, were those who opposed the encroachments of modernity, especially modern science, on traditional Christian faith. Their problem was not just biological and evolutionary science, which remains a site of conflict even today, but also the literary sciences, which cast doubt on many long-held Christian beliefs about the Bible and its contents. Fundamentalists held tightly to the divine inspiration, authority, and truthfulness of the Bible (sometimes heightening these claims to infallibility and inerrancy). They struggled to assimilate claims such as the four-source theory for the authorship of the Pentateuch (rather than sole Mosaic authorship) or the idea that Jesus' incarnation, miracles, and resurrection as described in the New Testament were perhaps something other than the kinds of factual observations one might read in a newspaper. When some of these ideas began to be integrated into the teachings of the major North American Christian denominations and their key scholarly leaders, fundamentalists recoiled in horror. Where possible they separated institutionally and certainly intellectually from these "modernist" or "liberal" groups, setting the groundwork for the long-standing split between what became known as "mainline Protestantism" on the more liberal side and fundamentalism on the conservative side.

This context also contributed to a tendency toward at least a selective anti-intellectualism in fundamentalism, because it was the liberal intellectuals who had betrayed Christianity. This has contributed to a populist strand in

11. Ibid.

fundamentalism that continues to this day, where religious leader-experts do not necessarily have or need much formal education. Yet some fundamentalists, at least, wanted to joust with their adversaries on equal terms, which required developing alternative, sometimes rigorous educational institutions and credentialing. Fundamentalists and their evangelical successors focused special intellectual effort on biblical/textual/language scholarship in keeping with their high view of the authority of the Bible. This remains with us to this day in both fundamentalism and evangelicalism, along with the tendency to believe that all theological and ethical questions for Christians can simply be resolved by more biblical study and expertise.

If Christian leaders and long-standing denominations could succumb to heretical liberalism (so it was thought), then the broader world was an even more threatening place. The fundamentalist posture toward the world became a hunkered-down separatism. The response to the question, "What does Christ have to do with culture?" became: "Not much." Fundamentalism's agenda became saving a few souls for heaven from a dying world while protecting their own doctrinal and moral purity.

Eschewing the culturally reformist and activist strands of previous generations of American evangelicals, which had motivated social crusades on issues ranging from abolition to Sabbath to urban poverty to temperance, the fundamentalists of that era began to see nothing redeemable in the broader American culture and were often led by this burgeoning cultural pessimism to a strictly sectarian understanding of the role of Christians in society. (This is to be distinguished from the more deeply rooted theological "sectarianism" found among the Anabaptists, which had European origins going back to the Reformation, so different as to hardly merit the same label.) Forming their own schools and publishing houses, organizations and denominations, fundamentalists saw cultural withdrawal as the only appropriate response for the American Christian in light of the increasingly evil and assuredly hell-bound broader society.

But after World War II, a new generation of leaders emerged with a very different approach. These leaders proclaimed themselves unsatisfied with the political theology of the *culturally-declinist* fundamentalists, some of whom had also picked up hysterical yet quasi-scientific apocalyptic end-times scenarios that reinforced their cultural withdrawal.[12] Maintaining that they were in fact in agreement with fundamentalism's core *theological commitments* but drawing on an older wellspring of culturally engaged evangelicalism, leaders such as Carl F. H. Henry began to challenge fundamentalism's separatism. Though most of these post-fundamentalists opted for (re)claiming the older label *evangelical*, some historians have chosen to use Harold Ockenga's designation of choice,

---

12. For an excellent analysis of the cultural pessimism displayed by twentieth-century evangelical leadership see James A. Patterson, "Cultural Pessimism in Modern Evangelical Thought: Francis Schaeffer, Carl Henry, and Charles Colson," *Journal of the Evangelical Theological Society* 49, no. 4 (December 2006): 807–20.

neo-evangelical, to describe this culturally reengaging movement just after World War II.[13] Either way, the shadow of these leaders and their influence on twentieth-century postfundamentalist evangelicalism looms large and long, along with the flagship institutions they founded, such as Fuller Theological Seminary, *Christianity Today* magazine, and the National Association of Evangelicals—still major evangelical institutions today.

The initial message of Carl Henry can be found in his seminal work, *The Uneasy Conscience of Modern Fundamentalism*.[14] Robust, confident, even somewhat arrogant in tone, Henry and other early neo-evangelicals sound certain not only that the world needs Jesus Christ but that soon the world itself will see that. Evangelism and personal conversion are the bottom line; biblical authority is unquestioned, and little allowance is made for others who do not share that theological presupposition. Evangelicals must not give an inch on their theological commitments but should in fact now join the broader global community as it works to rebuild the postwar world; such social reform partnerships are permissible as long as evangelicals *always* make clear that reforms of social and political structures alone will never be sufficient. People need personal conversion above all, from which most needed social changes will flow.

Though it must be reiterated that postwar American evangelicalism was not monolithic, the most prominent *public presence* of evangelicalism from 1945 until at least 2000 was represented by dynamic leaders such as Henry, emerging from this neo-evangelical stream—and sometimes from a stream more reminiscent of fundamentalism itself. The dominant and prototypical public face of evangelicalism during this period was theologically conservative if not fundamentalist, usually culturally engaged and/or reformist, and also predominantly white and male. Indeed, evangelicalism continued to put forward an almost exclusively conservative white male visage into the public arena long after other sectors of American culture and religion became less monochromatic.

The social revolutions of the 1960s evoked a fatefully bifurcated response among these white evangelicals, with effects lingering to this day in evangelical political theology. All evangelicals who stayed evangelicals rejected the "free love" version of the sexual revolution, and most later rejected abortion rights. Some, like the towering evangelical figure Francis Schaeffer, studied the 1960s radicals pretty closely and found ways to affirm some of what they were protesting but not how they were protesting or the solutions they were reaching.[15] The 1960s Schaeffer was, well, kind of groovy; he was an evangelical who was not confined by a narrow fundamentalist reading list but instead attempted a broad intellectual/cultural critique of what had gone wrong in Western culture since

---

13. Gushee and Hollinger, "Toward an Evangelical Ethical Methodology."

14. Carl Henry, *The Uneasy Conscience of Modern Fundamentalism* (Grand Rapids: Wm. B. Eerdmans, 1947).

15. See especially Francis Schaeffer, *How Should We Then Live?* (Wheaton, IL: Crossway Books, 1976).

the Enlightenment, not just since Kennedy. At this early stage Schaeffer did not treat the West as irredeemable. Schaeffer was one of several key neo-Calvinist evangelicals working on philosophical efforts to define and defend a "Christian world- and life-view" against secular and liberal alternatives. He was equipping evangelical Christians to meet the culture well armed for conversionist and intellectual engagements.

Other contemporaries, however, slipped back into the old fundamentalist default setting of cultural reaction in a mood that again became increasingly apocalyptic by the 1970s and '80s—signaled by the resurfacing of the end-times scenarios in best-selling books by authors like Hal Lindsey. (The fear of nuclear war played a part in this, as did recurrent Middle East wars.) As their hope for mass Christian conversion, intellectual argument-winning, and consequent social transformation declined, evangelical cultural pessimism increased. Claims that the "barbarians are at the gate" with their pitchforks and flaming torches became more common—and ever more hysterical.[16] Often evangelical voices waxed nostalgic over the supposed virtues of an earlier America—before the 1960s, before everything went off the rails. Now aging, Henry and Schaeffer aligned with and encouraged the voices we now think of as representing the (in) famous Christian right of the 1970s through the 1990s: Jerry Falwell, James Dobson, Pat Robertson, etc. In our view, this was a sad decline from their more creative work as younger men. As they aged, they became culture warriors, their books an increasingly dreary and repetitive set of jeremiads.

Even before the full-blown birth of the Christian right in the late 1970s there were already very different white evangelical voices. Consider John Howard Yoder, the sophisticated polymath Anabaptist (though, we now know, sadly guilty of sexual misconduct that hurt women and stained his reputation); Ron Sider, the Canadian Mennonite historian trained at Yale who settled in gritty urban Philadelphia and lamented "rich Christians in an age of hunger"; Jim Wallis, the most politically savvy of the bunch, who settled in Washington, first in a radical evangelical commune and still today serving as a kind of evangelical senator in Washington and around the world; and Glen Stassen, a progressive Baptist evangelical from Minnesota who became the leading peace theorist and peacemaker of the group. All represented some version of an Anabaptist position. Sider, Wallis, Stassen, and others in their camp clearly were affected by U.S. developments (including the Vietnam War and the broader Cold War). But they also represented that earlier, less conservative, more nineteenth-century strand of evangelical social engagement, especially its non-Calvinist variants. Sider was particularly self-conscious about the effort to connect his own work to the nineteenth-century "holistic mission" approaches of people like evangelist and abolitionist Charles Finney.

16. A trope employed by Carl Henry in his *Twilight of a Great Civilization* (Westchester, PA: Crossway Books, 1988) and echoed by Charles Colson in *Against the Night* (Ann Arbor, MI: Vine Books, 1989).

Bitter American fights over racial justice and integration motivated the emergence of new black evangelical voices. These voices, like Bill Pannell, Tom Skinner, and John Perkins, simply could not join so many white conservatives in uncritically applauding the supposedly glorious Christian past of our slaveholding, Jim Crow, lynching, segregationist, quasi-apartheid white American heritage. And they were bitterly critical of evidence that white evangelical cultural pessimism was in part triggered by advances for black civil rights in America. These men were evangelicals, but they were black evangelicals, and they had something quite striking to say to their white counterparts—and to America.[17]

From the 1970s through today a split emerges between two types of evangelical political theology. One is the evangelical right, an overwhelmingly white evangelical political theology of cultural pessimism, periodically alternating between triumphalist take-back-America-now confidence and despairing America-is-going-to-hell apocalyptic, steadfastly opposed to almost all social changes since the 1960s, including the areas of gender, U.S. patriotism, sexuality, and sometimes race. The other is an evangelical left, a multihued alternative evangelicalism offering much internal critique of white reaction and its overidentification of Christianity/evangelicalism with the older white segregationist America, often emerging from Anabaptist, Wesleyan, and Holiness strands. Then there is perhaps an evangelical center drawn from many evangelical quadrants and not fully convinced by either right or left.[18]

White male hegemony over the evangelical conversation began to collapse by the late 1990s if not before, not that you could always know that by the makeup of Christian right gatherings. Early evangelical feminists surfaced, critiquing evangelical patriarchalism and contributing to dramatic change in the churches while accepting dramatic changes in culture that their male counterparts often decried.[19] More and more African American evangelical voices emerged as the deep bench of theologically conservative but politically progressive black evangelicals began to get a chance to take the field.[20] Native American, Latino/a,[21] Asian American,[22] and other new nonwhite evangelical voices got a platform while critical evangelical voices from abroad helped in critiquing white American blind spots.

17. See, for example, William E. Pannell, "The Evangelical Christian and Black History," *Fides et Historia* 2, no. 2 (Spring 1970): 4–14; John Perkins, *With Justice for All* (Ventura, CA: Regal Books, 1982); Tom Skinner, *Words of Revolution* (Grand Rapids: Zondervan, 1970).

18. David P. Gushee, *The Future of Faith in American Politics: The Public Witness of the Evangelical Center* (Waco: Baylor University Press, 2008).

19. Including: Gretchen Gaebelein Hull, Aida Besancon Spencer, Letha Scanzoni, and Nancy Hardesty and later, ethicist Christine Pohl and others.

20. Such as Daryl Trimiew, Reggie Williams, and womanist thinkers like Emilie Townes.

21. Leaders like Gabriel Salguero and Eldin Villafane.

22. For example, Soong Chan-Rah and Amos Yong.

Along the way there were and still are scholarly voices working out of one or another deeper stream of political theology to offer an alternative perspective.[23] These have provided more substance and ballast for evangelical political theology and social ethics and at times have actually had influence at the evangelical grassroots level as well. None could be described as right-wing, but neither do they fall easily into the left.

Evangelical social ethics during this period has been defined by its simultaneous convergences and divergences. The major convergence: *the clearest recurring motif in evangelical Christian social ethics during this period has been a critical and conversionary stance toward culture, aimed both more broadly at American society and at times specifically at American Christians.* Evangelicals continue to seek conversion! The major divergence: post-1960s ideological polarization drove a politically/demographically familiar split in which a group consisting almost entirely of white (usually but not always male) evangelicals hypervalorized a mythic American Christian past and critiqued American culture in stark, sometimes apocalyptic terms for abandoning Christ and Christian morality and risking divine judgment, moral collapse, and barbarism. These leaders tended to offer reflexive opposition to all broader culturally progressive movements, beginning with those of the 1960s but continuing to the present day. This reactionary posture shut down much meaningful engagement with critiques either of America or evangelical religion in terms of race, gender, LGBT inclusion, and so on. After a while this essentially reactionary posture began to lose more and more credibility, first in American culture and eventually in evangelicalism itself. White evangelical hysterics over U.S. cultural decline began to be seen as thinly veiled fears of dwindling white straight male conservative religious cultural dominance. Meanwhile another group of evangelicals, much more diverse, saw the mottled grays of American Christian history and critiqued American culture for different things—racism, militarism, sexism, consumerism. This group offered a much more pointed critique of American Christianity itself. Far more often their critiques were directed at the evangelical subculture and its white male leadership.

This split clearly demonstrated that the diagnosis of what used to be called "the social problem" looks very different from the underside of social and religious power structures than it does from a position of dominance. Evangelicals cannot avoid the epistemological problem we all face: we all see through lenses provided by our social location even when we are claiming, as evangelicals so often do, to merely be reading the Bible and reporting what it says.

Despite their profound differences, just about all evangelical political theologians/social ethicists/activists/writers represent that evangelical *impulse for renewal,* even conversion, that goes back into evangelicalism's DNA, its very

---

23. Such as Stephen Charles Mott, David P. Gushee, Glen Stassen, Richard Mouw, Nicholas Wolterstorff, Eldin Villafañe, Amos Yong, and Jennifer McBride, representing, respectively, Wesleyan, Baptist, Calvinist, Pentecostal, and Bonhoefferian.

marrow. But the various parties within evangelical political and social ethics were seeking to reform dramatically different things. This remains the case today.

INTO THE FUTURE

There can be little doubt that self-identified evangelicals have exerted massive cultural influence in the United States, both in previous eras and in the past half century or so. Though numbers alone don't necessarily equate with size of influence, in a liberal democratic setting head-counts *matter*, and evangelicals continue to have the numbers:

- The extensive Pew Forum on Religion and Public Life "U.S. Religious Landscape Survey" estimates that 26.3 percent of Americans belong to a Protestant evangelical church as opposed to the 18.1 percent of Americans who belong to a Protestant mainline church and the 23.9 percent who are Catholic.[24]
- Gallup, between 1991 and 2005, conducted a poll asking Americans some version of the question, "Would you describe yourself as a 'born again' or evangelical?" Those who answered yes varied between the low of 35 percent in 1996 and the high of 47 percent in 2005.[25]
- Larry Eskridge of the Institute for the Study of American Evangelicals at Wheaton College, while acknowledging the inherent difficulties associated with such surveys, draws on multiple sources to suggest:

    In summary, when one lays a number of different studies side-by-side and considers the fact that many Americans could be described as "cultural evangelicals" (particularly within the African-American and Southern white populations), a general estimate of the nation's evangelicals could safely be said to range somewhere between 30–35% of the population, or about 90–100 million Americans.[26]

So it is inarguable that a large slice of the American population fits somewhere under the larger taxonomic umbrella of evangelicalism. And as attested every time an election year rolls around, evangelicals have the numbers—so in the American context, evangelicals matter.

Therefore it really does matter whether evangelical public engagement and working social ethics look more like early Carl Henry or late Carl Henry, early Francis Schaeffer or late Francis Schaeffer; or more like Ron Sider and Jim Wallis

---

24. "Religious Landscape Survey," *The Pew Research Center*, The Pew Forum on Religion & Public Life, February 2008, religions.pewforum.org/pdf/report-religious-landscape-study-full.pdf.

25. Frank Newport and Joseph Carroll, "Another Look at Evangelicals in America Today," *Gallup*, December 2005, www.gallup.com/poll/20242/another-look-evangelicals-america-today.aspx.

26. Larry Eskridge, "Defining Evangelicalism," Institute for the Study of American Evangelicals, Wheaton College, 2012, www.wheaton.edu/ISAE/Defining-Evangelicalism/How-Many-Are-There.

or Jerry Falwell and Chuck Colson; or Soong Chan Rah or Helene Slessarev-Jamir; or Gabriel Salguero or John Perkins. It matters whether evangelicalism defines its public witness as culturally reactionary, and white reactionary at that; or instead as culturally liberal; or as some hybrid that doesn't quite fit any of our contemporary political polarities. It matters whether evangelicalism stretches to include voices reflecting its full gender, linguistic, racial, and sexual orientation diversity or whether it remains dominated by (straight) white English-speaking American males. Where evangelicalism is simply white cultural reaction dressed up in religion, it fuels cultural division and white resentment of emerging multicultural America by turbocharging it with "biblical" fuel. Where evangelicalism leads with its love-based, soft-hearted "evangelical-like-Saint-Francis" compassion for those on the margins, it fuels countercultural campaigns for ending mass incarceration, feeding hungry kids, and advancing humane immigration reform—some of which involve creating strikingly broad evangelical coalitions that bring even our own warring tribes together.

At the moment of the composition of this essay, American evangelicalism is less confident than it was a generation ago. Numerical flattening, or decline, is hitting us too. Our own internal theological and ideological polarities are tearing us up. The LGBT issue is a new battlefront that looks likely to stay with us for the next generation as it has the mainline in the prior one, with polling revealing that many younger evangelicals are jumping ship over the issue. The Christian right is weaker than ever culturally, but ironically a sense of cultural embattlement is contributing to a stronger grip of that often-reactionary spirit, at least in much of mainstream evangelicalism. The latest battlefront is defined as preserving religious liberty for evangelicals in a hostile culture; adversaries view it as preserving space for faith-based discrimination. Voices of dissent within evangelicalism often get pushed out to the margins or out of evangelicalism in an oddly passive-aggressive, quasi-unofficial way, while some wash their hands of evangelicalism preemptively. The Christian right has made a generational succession while the evangelical left has only just begun to do so, leading perhaps to a modest change in tone on the right but little change in message—so far.

The journey continues. No one but God knows how it will end. But this much is sure—where there are evangelicals, they will be trying to convert somebody, maybe beginning with themselves. As demonstrated in this volume, this impulse is at the very heart of evangelical Christian social ethics.

CONCLUSION: ABOUT THE COLLECTION

We intend to let the authors contained herein speak for themselves. We have not edited them except for space and have sought and received appropriate consent for the edited version we present here. The choices about which authors and selections to include were sometimes agonizingly difficult. In the end we have sought to represent the breadth of evangelical thinking across confessional, gender, racial, and other lines. The collection is arranged chronologically, from the earliest (Henry, 1947) to the most recent (Salguero and Slessarev-Jamir, 2012). As a courtesy to the intrepid reader, we will close with some brief notes pointing to key themes and contextual clues about each chapter.

Chapter 1: Carl F. H. Henry (1947). Everyone agrees that Henry's *Uneasy Conscience of Fundamentalism* was foundational for modern evangelicalism. The selection here calls the new evangelicals to serious social engagement addressing the rebuilding of the shattered postwar world alongside others of good will but emphasizes that evangelicals committed to Christian truth understand social problems and their real solutions better than their cobelligerents do. Evangelical cooperation on addressing major social ills must always include the articulated caveat that the ultimate solution to such problems is Jesus Christ.

Chapter 2: John Howard Yoder (1960). This early Yoder gem originally written for a European audience offers an important statement of his principled Anabaptist position as well as his analysis of what went wrong in and with historic Christendom. Yoder became a highly influential wellspring of Anabaptist thinking in scholarly evangelical Christian social ethics and beyond.

Chapter 3: William E. Pannell (1970). This essay, originally a paper presented to an evangelical Christian historical society, is one of the very earliest statements of a distinctive black evangelical social ethic. Note Pannell's fluency with contemporary white evangelical thought but his pointed critique of its blindness in relation to race.

Chapter 4: Francis Schaeffer (1976). This characteristic Schaeffer travelogue over the political, moral, and cultural landscape of 1960s/early 70s Western culture, including an examination of its intellectual background, offers a declinist account of what has gone wrong that feels more like an elegy than an attack. This selection offers a very early focus on the abortion issue that became so central in conservative evangelical politics after 1976 or so.

Chapter 5: Ron Sider (1977). This excerpt from the opening to the very first edition of Sider's famous *Rich Christians in an Age of Hunger* offers a glimpse into a hugely transformative work in contemporary evangelical social ethics at a semipopular level. While the conservative evangelicals were sharpening their swords on a cultural decline narrative and take-back-America political agenda, Sider was among the first to offer a very different kind of conversionist project— this was to convert America's Christians from their greed and consumerism and toward serving a world with "a billion hungry neighbors."

Chapter 6: Jim Wallis (1981). This opening chapter from Wallis's seminal *Call to Conversion* was a remarkably ahead-of-its-time treatment of the aims of the ministry of Jesus as holistic conversion toward the kingdom of God. We also wanted to include but had to cut his next chapter, which describes quite pungently the betrayal of the mission of Jesus by evangelical cultural captivity in America.

Chapter 7: John Perkins (1982). This excerpt from Perkins's autobiographical work *With Justice for All* tells his story of attempting to live in dignity as a black man in Mississippi during the civil rights years. The harrowing brutality Perkins experienced in his flesh at the hands of white police officers became the crucible that forged his holistic message of justice and reconciliation. The excerpt tells that story as well as describing the early days of his effort to build intentional interracial Christian community in Mississippi.

Chapter 8: Stephen Charles Mott (1982). This excerpt from Mott's classic work offers a richly biblical and scholarly treatment of evangelical social engagement rooted in a Wesleyan evangelical tradition. Mott was among the first evangelicals to undertake serious analysis of the way the New Testament addresses systemic social evil. This Oxford University Press book was a major contribution to early evangelical social ethics.

Chapter 9: Nicholas Wolterstorff (1983). *Until Justice and Peace Embrace* offered many things, including a justice- and peace-oriented Reformed social ethical vision—rather than the more conservative neo-Calvinist vision being offered by Henry and Schaeffer by this stage. In this excerpt Wolterstorff offers an exposition of the way early Calvinism especially prepared its adherents to view the world as an arena for restless, active, creative social change efforts.

Chapter 10: Eldin Villafañe (1993). This work offered, in the author's words, a "Hispanic American Pentecostal Social Ethic." The book offers outstanding evidence of the creative possibilities unleashed when new voices began to be heard in the evangelical conversation. In this excerpt we catch a glimpse of how the New Testament is read by a Pentecostal, with much heightened emphasis on the power of the Holy Spirit in the ministry of Jesus and the church, and by a Hispanic American, with much greater attention to the struggles and learnings of those on this particular margin of American society.

Chapter 11: Allen Verhey (2002). This sprawling work, the author's magnum opus, offers a deeply scholarly treatment of Christian social ethics from a version of the Calvinist strand that sounds neither quite like Henry nor quite like Wolterstorff. The excerpt we have selected offers an important counterperspective to Yoder on the same controverted questions of what to make of church and world under and beyond Constantine and Christendom.

Chapter 12: Glen H. Stassen and David P. Gushee (2003). This excerpt comes from *Kingdom Ethics: Following Jesus in Contemporary Context*, probably the most widely used evangelical Christian ethics textbook of the early twentieth century. It offers a rendering of Christian political ethics focused on service and ministry rather than Christian cultural domination.

Chapter 13: Soong-Chan Rah (2009). The author is a professor of church growth and evangelism and one of the leading younger voices on the progressive wing of U.S. evangelicalism. The excerpt offers a scathing critique of what Rah calls the "white captivity of the church," moving into a sophisticated discussion of the origins and nature of racism. Rah is an important voice, not least because his work reflects the growing significance of Asian and Asian American evangelicalism.

Chapter 14: Jennifer McBride (2012). McBride's *The Church for the World: A Theology of Public Witness* is a hidden gem at the intersection of Bonhoeffer studies and Christian social ethics. The author, a product of southern evangelical Christianity, finds in Dietrich Bonhoeffer (an evangelical favorite) dramatically helpful resources for developing a nontriumphalist version of social engagement. The excerpt included here discusses the work of two ministries McBride studied intensively in part because they seemed already to represent this posttriumphalist way of incarnating Christian social ethics.

Chapter 15: Gabriel Salguero (2012). The collection *Prophetic Evangelicals: Envisioning a Just and Peaceable Kingdom,* edited by Peter Heltzel of New York Theological Seminary—an important voice in his own right—provides the final two excerpts in this collection. Gabriel Salguero, a scholar, pastor, and activist representing one of the leading Latino/a Christian activist organizations in the country, offers a riveting and deeply biblical and contextual exposition of the meaning of the cross. Note how postcolonial theology, including reflection on the meaning of empire, has affected this particular essay.

Chapter 16: Helene Slessarev-Jamir (2012). The author reflects on her move out of the evangelical subculture and with that newfound freedom offers a scathing critique of mainstream "triumphalistic, fearful, border-guarding" evangelicalism.

Chapter 1

"The Evangelical 'Formula of Protest'" and "The Dawn of a New Reformation"

1947

Carl F. H. Henry

The future kingdom in evangelical thought . . . does not displace an interim world program. That contemporary program in evangelicalism is (1) predicated upon an all-inclusive redemptive context for its assault upon global ills; (2) involves total opposition to all moral evils, whether societal or personal; (3) offers not only a higher ethical standard than any other system of thought, but provides also in Christ a dynamic lift to humanity to its highest level of moral achievement.

But the spearhead of the current attack on moral evils is not directed . . . by evangelical forces. Rather, the non-evangelical humanistic movements are heading up the agitation for a new and better world. The social program is, by and large, projected constructively today by non-evangelical groups.

Yet the non-evangelical camp has been plunged into considerable confusion, at the moment, by the collapse of its vision for an utopian world. The convictions of non-evangelicals are on the move; liberals are moving upward toward neo-supernaturalism or downward toward humanism, and some humanists are moving downward toward pessimism, while some others are impatiently marking time.

This creates the most favorable opportunity evangelicalism has had since its embarrassing divorce from a world social program, to recapture its rightful leadership in pressing for a new world order. Any conviction of foredoomed failure does not automatically cancel the missionary obligation. The futility of trying to win all does not mean that it is futile to try to win some areas of influence and life. An evangelical world program has its timeliest opportunity at the present hour.[1]

But a difficult problem is projected by the fact that evangelicals are found in fellowships which often seek eliminations of social evils in a context which is not specifically redemptive, and often hostile to supernatural redemptionism. Since the evangelicals are convinced that a non-redemptive attack on any problem is sentenced to failure, what would be a consistent attitude in such circumstances? This is not an easy question to answer, and the writer does not pretend to offer more than preliminary reflection with regard to it. But it is a problem which confronted the apostolic church, and with the desupernaturalization of western culture it again looms large. The best evangelical thought may well occupy itself with the query in the immediate present. The spirit of the evangelical seminaries and colleges may largely determine the interpretation of social need which crystallized during this post-war crisis period among Fundamentalist leaders. No framework is really relevant today unless it has an answer to the problem of sin and death in every area of human activity. Confronted by this problem, the evangelical mind will have to work out a satisfactory solution proportionate to its conviction of evangelical relevance.

The statement of a few pertinent considerations, however preliminary, may contribute to the ultimate solution, whether by action or reaction. Surely Christianity ought not to oppose any needed social reform. It ought, indeed, to be in the forefront of reformative attack. And it ought, if it has a historical consciousness, to press its attack on a redemption foundation, convinced that every other foundation for betterment, because of inherent weaknesses, cannot sustain itself.

While the evangelical will resist the non-evangelical formulas for solution, he assuredly ought not on that account to desist from battle against world evils. Just because his ideology is unalterably opposed to such evils, the evangelical should be counted upon not only to "go along" with all worthy reform movement, but to give them a proper leadership. He must give unlimited expression to his condemnation of all social evils, coupled with an insistence that a self-sustaining solution can be found only on a redemptive foundation. More vigorously than the humanists and religious modernists press their battle, the evangelical ought to be counted upon in the war against aggressive conflict, political naturalism, racial intolerance, the liquor traffic, labor-management inequities, and every wrong. And as vigorously as the evangelical presses his battle, he ought to be

---

1. The difficulty of relating the Christian social imperative to concrete decisions is acknowledged by spokesmen for higher liberalism also. John C. Bennett suggests some of the problems in *Christian Ethics and Social Policy*, chapter two. But difficulty is no excuse for indifference.

counted upon to point to the redemption that is in Christ Jesus as the only adequate solution. This appears to the writer to be the true evangelical methodology; to fill this form with content, in its application, is the difficult task which remains undone.

Evangelical action is not complicated within movements or organisms composed entirely of historic Christian theists, who, therefore, are united not only on the need for a social program, but also on the context within which such world renewal is a possibility. And yet only minimal effort has been made in such circles, to articulate the Christian message in its social challenge. There are here and there conservative denominational groups, like the Reformed movements and the great Southern Baptist Convention, which have maintained or are beginning to reflect a vigorous social interest. But to capture for the church all of the social zeal through redemptive categories, would involve even here a considerable change.

But the problem of social reform is more complicated when projected in great assemblies, often religious in nature, in which the membership is composed on inclusive lines, so that evangelicals, liberals, and humanists must act together. The evangelical voice in such a group cannot maintain silence when evils are condemned by others. But neither can it yield to a non-evangelical framework. Therefore, the path of evangelical action seems to be an eagerness to condemn all social evils, no less vigorously than any other group, and a determination (1) when evangelicals are in the majority, to couple such condemnation with the redemptive Christian message as the only true solution; (2) when evangelicals are in the minority, to express their opposition to evils in a "formula of protest," concurring heartily in the assault on social wrongs, but insisting upon the regenerative context as alone able to secure a permanent rectification of such wrongs. Thus evangelicals will take their stand against evil, and against it in the name of Jesus Christ the deliverer, both within their own groups and within other groups. To do this, is to recapture the evangelical spirit. Just how to express such protest in a positive rather than negative way, beyond a minority committee report, remains to be studied. Every provision of democratic parliamentary procedure must be graciously employed, rather than to misrepresent evangelical conviction at this point. Fundamentalists, uneasy about ecclesiastical bondage, are usually more alert to what they oppose, than to what they propose.

There are Fundamentalists who will insist immediately that no evangelical has a right to unite with non-evangelicals in any reform. It is not [my] task . . . to evaluate the possibility or impossibility of evangelical loyalty to Christ within large modern denominations, each differing somewhat in organization and condition. Assuredly, no demand for loyalty can be recognized by the evangelical as higher than that by Christ Jesus, and each evangelical must settle, to the satisfaction of his own conscience, whether such loyalty is best served, or is impeded by loyalty within his denomination. But unrestricted loyalty to Christ cannot be interpreted as consistent with a tacit condonement of great world evils.

Apart from denominational problems, it remains true that the evangelical, in the very proportion that the culture in which he lives is not actually Christian, must unite with non-evangelicals for social betterment if it is to be achieved at all, simply because the evangelical forces do not predominate. To say that evangelicalism should not voice its convictions in a non-evangelical environment is simply to rob evangelicalism of its missionary vision.

It will be impossible for the evangelical to cooperate for social betterment with any group only when that group clearly rules out a redemptive reference as a live option for the achievement of good ends. If evangelicals in such groups are not accorded the democratic parliamentary right of minority action, there remains no recourse but that of independent action. Action there must be if evangelicalism is to recapture the spirit of its evangel. In non-evangelical groups, the evangelical must have opportunity to witness to the redemptive power of Jesus. Because of his convictions, he ought never to vote for something lower than his position except with an accompanying protest. This is a far truer road of expression for his convictions than to decline to support an attack on admitted evils—because the latter course tacitly withdraws his opposition to that which the Redeemer would unhesitatingly condemn.

In point of fact, those movements for a "pure evangelicalism," which have come out of larger denominational groups, have not infrequently done so with a sacrifice of social vision and a concentration on redemptive rescue of individuals from an environment conceded to be increasingly hostile. The point here is not that they needed to become socially indifferent as a consequence of a rupture with denominationalism, but rather that such movements so frequently sacrifice an evangelical ecumenicity, and replace a world view with a fragmentary isolationism that "breaks through" its adverse environment with atomistic missionary effort, at home and abroad, with whatever heroic and genuine sacrifices.

It cannot be held then that the social indifference of evangelicals is attributable to organic denominational associations with liberalism. For Fundamentalist churches in no liberal associations whatever are often as socially inactive as others. Curiously, some Fundamentalist churches in liberal associations have had more ecumenical awareness by far than many churches in purely evangelical environments.

Any yet it remains true that evangelical convictions need a united voice; the force of the redemptive message will not break with apostolic power upon the modern scene unless the American Council of Churches and the National Association of Evangelicals meet at some modern Antioch, and Peter and Paul are face to face in a spirit of mutual love and compassion. If, as is often remarked, the Federal Council of Churches is the voice of Protestant liberalism in America, Protestant evangelicalism too needs a single voice. When such a unity comes, the present competitive spirit of evangelical groups shall be overruled to the glory of God, and the furtherance of the Gospel witness. If this does not come, groups most responsible will inevitably wither . . .

The need for a vital evangelicalism is proportionate to the world need. The days are as hectic as Nero's Rome, and they demand attention as immediate as Luke's Macedonia.

The cries of suffering humanity today are many. No evangelicalism which ignores the totality of man's condition dares respond in the name of Christianity. Though the modern crisis is not basically political, economic or social—fundamentally it is religious—yet evangelicalism must be armed to declare the implications of its proposed religious solution for the politico-economic and sociological context for modern life.

However marred, the world vessel of clay is not without some of the influence of the Master Molder. God has not left Himself entirely without witness in the global calamity; He discloses Himself in the tragedies as well as the triumphs of history. He works in history as well as above history. There is a universal confrontation of men and women by the divine Spirit, invading all cultures and all individual lives. There is a constructive work of God in history, even where the redemptive Gospel does not do a recreating work. The evangelical missionary message cannot be measured for success by the number of converts only. The Christian message has a salting effect upon the earth. It aims at a re-created society; where it is resisted, it often encourages the displacement of a low ideology by one relatively higher. Democratic humanitarianism furnishes a better context for human existence than political naturalism, except as it degenerates to the latter.

Modern evangelicalism need not substitute as its primary aim the building of "relatively higher civilizations." To do that is to fall into the error of yesterday's liberalism. Its supreme aim is the proclamation of redeeming grace to sinful humanity; there is no need for Fundamentalism to embrace liberalism's defunct social gospel. The divine order involves a supernatural principle, a creative force that enters society from outside its natural sources of uplift, and regenerates humanity. In that divine reversal of the self-defeating sinfulness of man is the only real answer to our problems—of whatever political, economic, or sociological nature. Is there political unrest? Seek first, not a Republican victory, or a labor victory, but the kingdom of God and His righteousness. Then there will be added—not necessarily a Republican or labor victory, but—political rest. Is there economic unrest? Seek first, not an increase of labor wages coupled with shorter hours, with its probable dog-eat-dog resultant of increased commodity cost, but the divine righteousness; this latter norm will involve fairness for both labor and management. But there will be added not only the solution of the problems of the economic man, but also those of the spiritual man. There is no satisfying rest for modern civilization if it is found in a context of spiritual unrest. This is but another way of declaring that the Gospel of redemption is the most pertinent message for our modern weariness, and that many of our other so-called solutions are quite impertinent, to say the least.

But that does not mean that we cannot cooperate in securing relatively higher goods, when this is the loftiest commitment we can evoke from humanity, providing we do so with appropriate warning of the inadequacy and instability of such solutions. The supernatural regenerative grace of God, proffered to the regenerate, does not prevent His natural grace to all men, regenerate and unregenerate alike. Because He brings rivers of living water to the redeemed, He does not on that account withhold the rain from the unjust and just alike. The realm of special grace does not preclude the realm of common grace. Just so, without minimizing the redemptive message, the church ministers by its message to those who stop short of commitment, as well as to regenerate believers.

The implications of this for evangelicalism seem clear. The battle against evil in all its forms must be pressed unsparingly; we must pursue the enemy, in politics, in economics, in science, in ethics—everywhere, in every field, we must pursue relentlessly. But when we have singled out the enemy—when we have disentangled him from those whose company he has kept and whom he has misled—we must meet the foe head-on, girt in the Gospel armor. Others may resist him with inadequate weapons; they do not understand aright the nature of the foe, nor the requirements for victory. We join with them in battle, seeking all the while more clearly to delineate the enemy, and more precisely to state the redemptive formula.

These sub-Christian environments which result from an intermingling of Christian and non-Christian elements, however much they fail to satisfy the absolute demand of God, are for the arena of life more satisfactory than an atmosphere almost entirely devoid of its redemptive aspects. It is far easier, in an idealistic context, to proclaim the essential Christian message, than it is in a thoroughly naturalistic context. Life means more in a context of idealism, because true meaning evaporates in a context of naturalism; for that reason, the preaching of a more abundant life finds a more favorable climate in the former. Though neither is to be identified with the kingdom of God, Anglo-Saxon democracy is a relatively better atmosphere by far than German totalitarianism was, and what made it better is the trace of Hebrew-Christian ideology that lingers in it.

While it is not the Christian's task to correct social, moral and political conditions as his primary effort apart from a redemptive setting, simply because of his opposition to evils he ought to lend his endorsement to remedial efforts in any context not specifically anti-redemptive, while at the same time decrying the lack of a redemptive solution. In our American environment, the influences of Christian theism are still abroad with enough vigor that the usual solutions are non-redemptive, rather than anti-redemptive, in character. Such cooperation, coupled with the Gospel emphasis, might provide the needed pattern of action for condemning aggressive warfare in concert with the United Nations Organization, while at the same time disputing the frame of reference by which the attempt is made to outlaw such warfare; for condemning racial hatred and intolerance, while at the same time protesting the superficial view of man which overlooks the need of individual regeneration; for condemning the liquor traffic, while insisting that it is impossible by legislation actually to correct the heart of man; for seeking justice for both labor and management in business and industrial problems, while protesting the fallacy that man's deepest need is economic. This is to link the positive Christian message with a redemptive challenge to the world on its bitterest fronts. Christian ethics will always resist any reduction of the good of the community to something divorced from theism and revelation; its conviction that non-evangelical humanism cannot achieve any lasting moral improvements in the world as a whole, because of the lack of an adequate dynamic, will engender the vigorous affirmation of a Christian solution.

Not that evangelical action stops here; this is hardly the beginning of it. One of the fallacies of modern thought, with which non-evangelical groups have been so much taken up in recent years, is that the mere "passing of a resolution" or the "writing of a book" in which the proposed method was set forth, automatically constitutes a long step on the road to deliverance. But too often the action stopped with the resolution or the book. Western culture was flooded with solutions for deliverance, from every sort of idealism and humanism, during the very years that it walked most rapidly to its doom. The same danger attends any evangelical revival.

The evangelical task primarily is the preaching of the Gospel, in the interest of individual regeneration by the supernatural grace of God, in such a way that divine redemption can be recognized as the best solution of our problems, individual and social. This produces within history, through the regenerative work of the Holy Spirit, a divine society that transcends national and international lines. The corporate testimony of believers, in their purity of life, should provide for the world an example of the divine dynamic to overcome evils in every realm. The social problems of our day are much more complex than in apostolic times, but they do not on that account differ in principle. When the twentieth century church begins to "out-live" its environment as the first century church outreached its pagan neighbors, the modern mind, too, will stop casting about for other solutions. The great contemporary problems are moral and spiritual. They demand more than a formula. The evangelicals have a conviction of absoluteness concerning their message, and not to proclaim it, in the assault on social evils, is sheer inconsistency. But the modern mood is far more likely to react first on the level of Christianity as a life view, than at the level of Christianity as a world view. Obviously, from the evangelical viewpoint, the two cannot be divorced. But from the non-evangelical viewpoint, a baptism of pentecostal fire resulting in a world missionary program and a divinely-empowered Christian community would turn the uneasy conscience of modern evangelicalism into a new reformation—this time with ecumenical significance.

Chapter 2

"The Otherness of the Church"

1960

John Howard Yoder

That the "Constantinian era" is coming to an end has become one of the commonplaces of European social analysis. The fact that this breakdown has at some points been anticipated in North America (in the disestablishment of religion) and at other points is evolving differently here (rising church membership) hides from no one the fact that the framework of thought about the church and the world and their mutual interrelations, which for centuries was shared by all mainline Christian theologies, Protestant and Catholic, orthodox and rationalist, has fallen in the last two generations. The assumption that we live in a Christian world no longer holds.

The predominant theological response to this development has been to face the fact without evaluating it. Apart from a few clericalists and monarchists who are still working to restore the past, most thinkers simply make their peace with the new situation as they had with the old, assuming that the total process is of God's doing. For the first three centuries Christians were persecuted by the world; that was as it had to be. For over a millennium Christians ruled the world; that was as it should be. In the modern age the world again faces the church as an autonomous, articulate, partly hostile party; that is as it should be. The Lord gave, the Lord takes away, blessed be the name of the Lord. The early church was right in facing persecution courageously, the church of the fourth century was right in making its peace with the world, the churches of the Middle Ages and the Reformation were right in leaning on the state; and now that that is no longer possible, the church is again right in making the best of a bad deal.

But we can no longer so simply identify the course of history with Providence. We have learned that history reveals as much of Antichrist as of Christ. We are no longer sure that we are edging upwards at the top of a progression of which every preceding step must have been right for its time, since it has led us to this pinnacle. Above all we have learned to ask if it can really be the will of the Lord of history that his church should be limping after history, always attempting to adapt to a new situation that it assumes to be providential, always a half-step behind in the effort to conform, being made by history instead of making history. We, therefore, cannot say whether the deconstantinizing of the church—be it in the form of possible disestablishment in East Germany, in that of defecting membership in Western Europe, or more complex forms taken by post-Christian paganism elsewhere—is a bane or a boon, until we have sought on a deeper level an understanding of the roots of modem secularism, of the *Mündigkeit,* the coming-of-age of the world. In this search we shall expect no new answers but shall attempt to illuminate some old answers with a modified question.

We begin by seeking to isolate the concepts "church" and "world" in their pre-Constantinian significance. "World" *(aion houtos* in Paul, *kosmos* in John) signifies in this connection not creation or nature or the universe but rather the fallen form of the same, no longer conformed to the creative intent. The state, which for present purposes may be considered as typical for the world, belongs with the other *exousiai* in this realm. Over against this "world" the church is visible; identified by baptism, discipline, morality, and martyrdom. It is self-evident for the early centuries as a part of this visibility of the fellowship of disciples that the church's members do not normally belong in the service of the world and a fortiori in that of the pagan state.

But behind or above this visible dichotomy there is a believed unity. All evidence to the contrary notwithstanding, the church believed that its Lord was also Lord over the world. The explicit paganism of state, art, economics, and learning did not keep the church from confessing their subordination to him who sits at the right hand of God. This belief in Christ's lordship over the *exousiai* enabled the church, in and in spite of its distinctness from the world, to speak to the world in God's name, not only in evangelism but in ethical judgment as well. The church could take on a prophetic responsibility for civil ethics without baptizing the state or the statesman. The justice the church demanded of the state was not Christian righteousness but human *iustitia;* this it could demand from pagans, not because of any belief in a universal, innate moral sense, but because of its faith in the Lord. Thus the visible distinctiveness of church and world was not an insouciant irresponsibility; it was a particular, structurally appropriate way, and the most effective way, to be responsible. This attitude was meaningful for the church because it believed that the state was not the ultimately determinative force in history. It ascribed to the state at best a preservative function in the midst of an essentially rebellious world, whereas the true sense of history was to be sought elsewhere, namely in the work of the church. This high estimation of the church's own vocation explains both its visible distinctiveness from the world and the demands it addressed to the world. The depth of the church's conviction that its own task was the most necessary enabled it to leave other functions in society to pagans: the church's faith in Christ's lordship enabled it to do so without feeling that it was abandoning them to Satan.

It follows from the "already, but not yet" nature of Christ's lordship over the powers that there is no one tangible, definable quantity that we can call "world." The *aion houtos* is at the same time chaos and a kingdom. The "world" of politics, the "world" of economics, the "world" of the theater, the "world" of sports, the under-"world," and a host of others—each is a demonic blend of order and revolt. The world "as such" has no intrinsic ontological dignity. It is creaturely order in the state of rebellion; rebellion is, however, for the creature estrangement from what it "really is"; therefore, we cannot ask what the world "really is," somehow "in itself." This observation is borne out by the New Testament's use of a multiplicity of terms, most of them in the plural, when speaking of the world. All that the Powers have in common is their revolt, and revolt is not a principle of unity. Since the Prince of the Power of the Air is a liar from the beginning, he cannot even lie consistently. Only the lordship of Christ holds this chaos of idolatrous "worlds" together.

We have seen that for the early church, "church" and "world" were visibly distinct yet affirmed in faith to have one and the same Lord. This pair of affirmations is what the so-called Constantinian transformation changes (I here use the name of Constantine merely as a label for this transformation, which began before A.D. 200 and took over 200 years; the use of his name does not mean an evaluation of his person or work). The most pertinent fact about the new state of things after Constantine and Augustine is not that Christians were no longer persecuted and began to be privileged, nor that emperors built churches and presided over ecumenical deliberations about the Trinity; what matters is that the two visible realities, church and world, were fused. There is no longer anything to call "world"; state, economy, art, rhetoric, superstition, and war have all been baptized.

It is not always recognized in what structural connection this change, in itself self-evident, stands with a new distinction that now arose. It was perfectly clear to men like Augustine that the world had not become Christian through its compulsory baptism. Therefore, the doctrine of the invisibility of "the true church" sprang up in order to permit the affirmation that on some level somewhere the difference between belief and unbelief, i.e., between church and world, still existed. But this distinction had become invisible, like faith itself. Previously Christians had known as a fact of experience that the church existed but had to believe against appearances that Christ ruled over the world. After Constantine one knew as a fact of experience that Christ was ruling over the world but had to believe against the evidence that there existed "a believing church." Thus the order of redemption was subordinated to that of preservation, and the Christian hope turned inside out.

The practical outworkings of this reversal were unavoidable. Since the church has been filled with people in whom repentance and faith, the presuppositions of discipleship, are absent, the ethical requirements set by the church must be adapted to the achievement level of respectable unbelief. Yet a more significant reason for moral dilution lies in the other direction. The statesman, who a century earlier would have been proud to declare that his profession was unchristian by nature, now wants to be told the opposite. What he does is the same as before, if not worse. Yet since there are no more heathen to do the work (correction: of course there are heathen; everyone knows with Augustine that most of the population is unbelieving, but unbelief has become invisible, like the church), since there are no more confessing heathen, every profession must be declared Christian. Since Christian norms for the exercise of some professions are difficult to find, the norms of pagan *iustitia* will be declared to define the content of Christian love. The autonomy of the state and of the other realms of culture is not brought concretely under the lordship of Christ, with the total revision of form and content which that would involve: it has been baptized while retaining its former content. An excellent example is Ambrose's rephrasing of Cicero's political ethics.

And yet the medieval church maintained significant elements of otherness in structure as in piety, which are generally underestimated. When under the influence of men like Troeltsch we speak of the "medieval synthesis" and of a fusion of church and world such that the salt had lost *all* its savor, the risk of caricature is great. Whatever was wrong with the basic confusion we have just described, the church in the Middle Ages retained a more than vestigial consciousness of its distinctness from the world. The higher level of morality asked of the clergy, the international character of the hierarchy, the visibility of the hierarchy in opposition to the princes, the gradual moral education of barbarians into monogamy and legality, foreign missions, apocalypticism and mysticism—all of these preserved an awareness, however distorted and polluted, of the strangeness of God's people in a rebellious world. Will the Reformation unearth and fan into new flame these smoldering coals, or will it bury them for good?

Despite many insights and initiatives which could have led in another direction, the Reformation, deciding between 1522 and 1525 in favor of political conservatism, decided at the same time not to challenge the Constantinian compromise. The Reformers knew very well of the "fall of the church"; but they dated this fall not in the fourth century but rather in the sixth and seventh. They did not see that the signs of fallenness to which they objected—papacy, Pelagianism, hagiolatry, sacramentalism—were largely fruits of the earlier confusion of church and world.

For this reason there remains a fundamental inconsistency in the work of the Reformers. They decided in favor of the Middle Ages. They wanted nothing other than the renewal and purification of the *corpus christianum*. And yet they were driven, for reasons partly of tactics, partly of principle, to shatter that unity which they sought to restore. We have already noted that the hierarchy, the higher ethical commitment of the orders, the missionary and international character of the Roman Church, had preserved, even though in a distorted form, a residual awareness of the visible otherness of the church. All of these dimensions of specificity were abandoned by the Reformation.

In the face of monasticism the Reformation affirmed the ethical value of the secular vocation. Through the imprecision of their terms this affirmation, right in itself, amounted to the claim, as wrong as the other was right, that every calling is its own norm, thereby heightening immeasurably (and unintentionally) the autonomy of the several realms of culture. Proper behavior in a given vocation is decided not by Christ but by the inherent norms of the vocation itself, known by reason, from creation, despite the Fall. The Reformers did not intend thereby to secularize the vocations and declare the order of creation independent of Christ; this is demonstrated by their continued efforts to give instructions to statesmen and by their claim that certain professions are unchristian (not those of prince, mercenary, and hangman, but those of monk, usurer, and prostitute); nevertheless the autonomy of state and vocation was mightily furthered by what they said, so that even today many German Lutherans will argue that faithfulness to Luther demands that they let the state be master in its own house.

When the church of the fourth century wished to honor Constantine, it interpreted him in the light of its eschatology. For Eusebius, the Christian *Imperator* stood immediately under *Christos Pantokrator;* the state was unequivocally in the realm of redemption. The Reformation, however, placed the state in the realm of creation. Theoretically this meant decreasing the state's dignity; practically it meant increasing its autonomy. The prince in the sixteenth century is a Christian, the noblest and most honored member of the church; but the work he does as prince is a purely rational one, finding its norms not in Christ but in the divinely fixed structure of society; it is a work a reasonable Turk could do as well.

Further: the Reformers did not call on "the state" abstractly, on the state as such, or on the state *universal* (Charles V), but on the *territorial* state—on the Elector of Saxony and Milords of Zürich—to carry through the Reformation. The territorial state was thereby loosed from the network of imponderable political and ecclesiastical forces and counterforces, which in their complex entirety had formed and held together the *corpus christianum* and given an immediate, unequivocal, uncontrollable divine imperative, subject to no higher earthly authority. Previously political action in God's name had been possible only in the name of "the Church Universal"; now religiously motivated political struggle is possible between Christian peoples. The Thirty Years' War was the last crusade—on both sides.

The conviction that the center of the meaning of history is in the work of the church, which had been central in the pre-Constantinian church and remained half alive in the Middle Ages, is now expressly rejected. The prince is not only a Christian, not only a prominent Christian; he is now the bishop. True faith and "the true church" being invisible, the only valid aims of innerworldly effort are those that take the total secular society of a given area as the object of responsibility. The prince wields not only the sword but all other powers as well. The church confesses in deed and sometimes in word that not it but the state has the last word and incarnates the ultimate values in God's work in the world. What is called "church" is an administrative branch of the state on the same level with the army or the post office. Church discipline is applied by the civil courts and police. It is assumed that there is nothing wrong with this since the true church, being invisible, is not affected.

It cannot be said that this turn of events was desired by the Reformers. Their uniform intention was a renewal of the visible, faithful body of believers. But the forces to which they appealed for support, namely the drives toward autonomy that exist in the state and the other realms of culture, were too strong to be controlled once they had been let loose.

In the context in which the Reformers made this decision there is much that we can understand and even approve. Their faith in the all-powerful Word of God, which will not return void if it but be rightly preached, and their awareness of the divine ordination of the secular order, which were their conscious points of departure, were true in themselves. But they did not succeed in bringing up for examination the Constantinian synthesis itself. Thus their decisions, which in their minds were conservative, reveal themselves in a broader socio-historical perspective to have been inconsistent and revolutionary. The order of creation, in which they placed the state and the vocations, could with a turn of the hand become the deistic order of nature or the atheistic order of reason without any change in its inner structure. The right of the local government to administer the church in the interest of the Reformation could become a right of the state to use the church for its own purposes, and there was no court of appeal. The divine obligation of Zürich or Saxony to shatter the superstructure of the Holy Roman Empire could flip over—especially after the Thirty Years' War had discredited confessionalism as a moral imperative—and appear as the absolute *raison d'etat*. It was, therefore, precisely the attempt of the Reformers to maintain the medieval ideal and to lay claim on the autonomous dynamics of state and profession that led to the secularization that defines the modern period. Fully to accept the Constantinian synthesis is to explode it. The Reformers created modern secularism; not, as the liberalism of two generations ago boasted, intentionally, by glorifying the individual, but unintentionally, through the inner contradictions of their conservatism.

The Constantinian approach has thereby shown itself to be incapable, not accidentally but constitutionally, of making visible Christ's lordship over church and world. The attempt to reverse the New Testament relationship of church and world, making faith invisible and the Christianization of the world a historic achievement with the institutional forms, was undertaken in good faith but has backfired, having had the sole effect of raising the autonomy of unbelief to a higher power. Islam, Marxism, secular Humanism, and Fascism—in short, all the major adversaries of the Christian faith in the Occident and the strongest adversaries in the Orient as well—are not nature- or culture-religions but bastard faiths, all of them the progeny of Christianity's infidelity, the spiritual miscegenation involved in trying to make a culture-religion out of faith in Jesus Christ. As religious adversaries in our day, these hybrid faiths are more formidable than any of the pagan alternatives faced by Paul, by Francis Xavier, or by Livingstone. Those who have refused to learn from the New Testament must now learn from history; the church's responsibility to and for the world is first and always to be the church. The short-circuited means used to "Christianize" "responsibly" the world in some easier way than by the gospel have had the effect of dechristianizing the Occident and demonizing paganism.

What then should be the path of the church in our time? We must first of all confess—if we believe it—that the meaning of history lies not in the acquisition and defense of the culture and the freedoms of the West, not in the aggrandizement of material comforts and political sovereignty, but in the calling together "for God saints from every tribe and language and people and nation," a "people of his own who are zealous for good deeds." The basic theological issue is not between right and left, not between Bultmann and Barth, not between the sacramental and the prophetic emphases, nor between the Hebraic and Greek mentalities, but between those for whom the church is a reality and those for whom it is the institutional reaction of the good and bad conscience, of the insights, the self-encouragement—in short, of the religion of a society.

If with the apostles we confess the Holy Spirit and the church, we must further recognize that unbelief also incarnates itself. The "world" must return in our theology to the place that God's patience has given it in history. The "world" is neither all nature nor all humanity nor all "culture"; it is *structured unbelief,* rebellion taking with it a fragment of what should have been the Order of the Kingdom. It is not just an "attitude," as is supposed by the shallow interiorization of attempts to locate "worldliness" in the mind alone. Nor is it to be shallowly exteriorized and equated with certain cataloged, forbidden, leisure-time occupations. There are acts and institutions that are by their nature—and not solely by an accident of context or motivation—denials of faith in Christ . . .

. . . The awareness of the visible reality of the world leads to two scandalous conclusions. The first is that Christian ethics is for Christians. Since Augustine this has been denied; the first criterion for an ethical ideal for the laity is its generalizability. From Kant's rigorous formulation of this criterion to the lay application in questions like, "What would happen if we were all pacifists like you?" the presupposition is universal that the right will have to apply as a simple performable possibility for a whole society. Thus the choice is between demanding of everyone a level of obedience and selflessness that only faith and forgiveness make meaningful (the "puritan" alternative) and lowering the requirements for everyone to the level where faith and forgiveness will not be needed (the medieval alternative). This dilemma is *not* part of the historical situation; it is an artificial construction springing from a failure to recognize the reality of the world.

The second scandalous conclusion is that there may well be certain functions in a given society which that society in its unbelief considers necessary, and which the unbelief renders necessary, in which Christians will not be called to participate. This was self-evident in the early Christian view of the state; that it had to be rejected later becomes less and less self-evident the longer we live and learn.

This view of the church commends itself exegetically and theologically. Contrary to the opposing view, it refuses to accept pragmatic grounds for deciding how Christians should relate themselves to the world. And yet after saying this we observe that this biblical approach is in fact the most effective. The moral renewal of England in the eighteenth century was the fruit not of the Anglican establishment but of the Wesleyan revival. The Christianization of Germanic Europe in the Middle Ages was not achieved by the "state church" structure, with an incompetent priest in every village and an incontinent Christian on every throne, but by the orders, with the voluntaristic base, the demanding discipline, the mobility, and the selectivity as to tasks that characterize the "free-church" pattern. What moral tone there is in today's Germany is due not to the state-allied church and the church-allied political parties but to the bootleg *Brüderschaften* of the Barmen Confession.

This makes it clear that the current vogue of the phrase "responsible society" in ecumenical circles is a most irresponsible use of terms. Even if we let pass the intentional ambiguity that makes society both the subject and the object of the responsibility, and the further confusion caused by the hypostatising of "society," there remains a fundamental misdefinition, furthered by a misreading of socio-ethical history. It continues to work with the Constantinian formulation of the problem, as if the alternatives were "responsibility" and "withdrawal." The body of thought being disseminated under this slogan is a translation into modern terms of the two ancient axioms: that the most effective way for the church to be responsible for society is for it to lose its visible specificity while leavening the lump; and that each vocation bears in itself adequately knowable inherent norms. Thus we are invited to repeat the mistake of the Reformation, and that just as the time when the younger churches, themselves in an essentially pre-Constantinian position, need to be helped to think in other terms than those of the *corpus christianum* framework that has already dechristianized Europe.

Christ's victory over the world is to be dated not A.D. 311 or 312 but A.D. 29 or 30. That church will partake most truly of his triumph that follows him most faithfully in that warfare whose weapons are not carnal but mighty. The church will be most effective where it abandons effectiveness and intelligence for the foolish weakness of the cross in which are the wisdom and the power of God. The church will be most deeply and lastingly responsible for those in the valley of the shadow if it is the city set on the hill. The true church is the *free* church.

How then do we face deconstantinization? If we meet it as just another turn of the inscrutable screw of providence, just one more chance to state the Constantinian position in new terms, then the judgment that has already begun will sweep us along in the collapse of the culture for which we boast that we are responsible. But if we have an ear to hear what the Spirit says to the churches, if we let ourselves be led out of the inferiority complex that the theologies of the Reformation have thus far imposed on free church thought, if we discover as brethren in a common cause the catacomb churches of East Germany and the *Brüderschaften* of West Germany, if we puncture the "American dream" and discover that even in the land of the God-trusting post office and the Bible-believing chaplaincy we are in the same essentially missionary situation, the same minority status as the church in Sri Lanka or Colombia; if we believe that the free church, and not the "free world," is the primary bearer of God's banner, the fullness of the One who fills all in all, if we face deconstantinization not as just another dirty trick of destiny but as the overdue providential unveiling of a pernicious error; then it may be given to us, even in the twentieth century, to be the church. For what more could we ask?

Chapter 3

"The Evangelical Christian and Black History"

1970

William E. Pannell

On an occasion like this I could wish myself to be an historian. But I am not an historian, I am a preacher—a fact that you would probably deduce in thirty seconds. I have spent a great deal of time in the last few years trying to find out what an evangelical is. In fact most of my problems in the last few years have grown up out of the fact that I have professed to be a "Negro evangelical Christian," whatever those words mean. I think it is possible to give you a theological definition of "evangelical," but theological definitions have a way of being woefully inadequate in the mileau of contemporary American life. My birth certificate says that I am "black," and that will give you the considered opinion of that hospital staff, to say nothing of their eyesight. I am willing to accept that definition because it fits in pretty much with the general thinking of white America with respect to what constitutes blackness.

I have been thinking for some months about whether or not the study of the past has any practical significance in helping us understand what in the world is going on in the present. I am aware that studies of whatever nature have great value whether or not they have any utilitarian significance, although there are some of us in America who feel that this is a luxury that we can ill afford. Perhaps you have seen William M. Wiecek's review of Martin Duberman's book

17

in the current issue of *Saturday Review*.[1] Duberman says: "For those among the young, historians and otherwise, who are chiefly interested in changing the present I can only say speaking from my own experience that they doom themselves to bitter disappointment if they seek their guides to action in the study of the past. Though I have tried to make it otherwise, I have found that a life in history has given me very limited information or perspective with which to understand the central concerns of my own life and my own times." I suppose an evangelical response to this statement might be that those who hold such a view need a biblical eschatology or a biblical interpretation of history. I know some conservatives who simply write Duberman off and say he needs to be saved.

However, my contact with certain areas of the black community these days, especially the younger people, indicates that there is absolutely no question in their mind about the value of the study of history. I think black people have a sneaking suspicion, sometimes rather unsophisticated, that in the study of history they are going to find the key to their own desperate search for meaning, manhood, and identity in America. So when you mention history, whether it be Afro-American or Black or whatever designation you give it, it can elicit a very immediate response, particularly from black youth. Black people are beginning to understand, or at least they think they do, that American history has emasculated them by a cruelly calculated omission of their contributions and thoughts. Black people tend to think that history has been taught as propaganda, and that there is no place for black people when white men promote American myths. They have learned (or think they have) and more are discovering every day (or think they are) that history was distorted not only by what it said but perhaps more especially by what it did not say: by its inclusion of certain folk heroes and significant omission of others.

I can recall my own study of history when I was growing up and going through school. Like perhaps most of you, I learned of only three black people in all of my history. One of them was called "Sambo." And whether he was black or not, he at least was colored, and that in a white man's world is still bad news. As I have mentioned, I am black according to my birth certificate and like many of my race, I have spent most of my life, consciously or otherwise, trying either to escape that fact or to find out what it means in order to make whatever adjustments were necessary. I did not know until the last few years just how committed white Americans were to "whiteness" as the official race of this so-called "melting-pot" country. I think Garry Wills is right in his book *The Second Civil War*. He suggests that Americans do not think of their country as "white," but they are very careful to keep it that way. I think that is the significance of the recent elections in Los Angeles, Detroit and Minneapolis, and accounts for the presence of the Nixon administration in Washington. One of the reasons black America is strangely silent these days in the fact of an almost unbelievable

1. William M. Wiecek, *The Saturday Review*, January 3, 1970, p.24.

administration insensitivity to continued outrages is because black people predicted this kind of leadership. Black people have a rather unsophisticated way of saying it. They say: "Blessed is the black man who expects nothing from the Nixonians. When it comes, they shall not be disappointed."

Black people correctly understood that as it has always been, so it is now; that if push comes to shove and someone needs to be sacrificed on the altar of expedient politics, it will be the black man. We have reached the beginning of the end of our second reconstruction period and the banner over us is called "Law and Order." The black man, especially the black youth, understands William Wiecek's research, that: "We cannot know who we are, how we came to be, where we are, or where we are going without knowing whence we came. Man is, in part at least, what he has been. He cannot escape or ignore his past, but he may overcome it. The past has shaped our present and will continue to shape the future."[2] The old Talmudic phrase is no less relevant: "If I do not see myself as a man, who else will?" And this, of course, lays a struggling people open to all kinds of excesses, and I strongly suspect that in an attempt either to rewrite history, to re-interpret history, or to force historians to be more objective in their speech with regard to history, there are all kinds of very interesting and subtle nuances. I have a lot of fun visiting some of the black bookstores these days. Talk about propaganda in the name of history, it is a rather interesting study to say the least.

I would like to suggest several things that black people think they have learned about history as they have been exposed to it and perhaps add a couple of thoughts about what it means for us who are evangelicals. Black people, for instance, have learned, or think they have learned, that when Rap Brown and Stokely Carmichael and some of the brothers talk about black people building this country, this is not mere rhetoric. Black people did build this country! If your ancestors were not slaves you might not understand the significance of that. I get a big bang out of listening to some of these angry young black men assert their manhood with references to the past contributions of their slave forefathers. Not long ago, these same people would have been embarrassed even to admit that their forefathers were slaves. No doubt this is threatening to most of white America and the temptation, even in educational circles, is to write them off as black racists who deal in myths. I was interested in David Brion Davis's book, *The Problem of Slavery in Western Culture*, where he asserts that what these angry young blacks have been saying is true although he does not refer to them by name. And his concluding suggestion is this: "Without exaggerating the economic significance of Negro slavery, we may safely conclude that it played a major role in the early development of the New World and the growth of commercial capitalism. Given the lack of an alternate labor supply, it is difficult to see how European nations could have settled America and exploited its resources

2. Ibid.

without the aid of African slaves."[3] The history of the black man is inextricably bound with that of white America though it is questionable that the founders of this nation intended that black men be Americans. Black people believe, at least some of them, especially the more radical, that they have every right in the world to burn this country down because they built it.

A second lesson that black people think they have learned from history is that violence, according to the words of that great American H. Rap Brown, is "as American as apple pie." As a result of a careful reading of history, black people have begun to suspect that when white Americans talk about making effective change or accomplishing their desired ends through due process, they quite frequently have resorted to violence in order to achieve "due process." Black people, for instance, are getting a lot of mileage out of Patrick Henry these days. They discovered that Patrick had a lot of soul, baby! When he said, "Give me liberty or give me death," he was telling it like it is. But black people also have learned that white people who eulogize Henry never intended that black men say those same words in Washington, D. C. or Hough, or Watts, or Twelfth Street in Detroit. I have to chuckle about some of the reports on violence that have been coming out through government agencies which make Rap Brown sound like a prophet. Much more sophisticated research has been done, but the message is the same. This is not necessarily a "land of the free and the home of the brave," particularly if you happen to be an Indian brave.

The third lesson that black people think they have learned from history is that somehow or another, inextricably bound up with this society and its developments, is that nebulous thing called Christianity. Black kids to whom I have been exposed, spend an awful lot of time and shed an awful lot of heat telling us preachers that "Jesus" was a name on the side of at least one slave ship, and that phrases like the "grace of God" also graced the sides of slave ships, and that, perhaps, some of those slaves on that middle passage heard about Jesus and the Christian thing from the lips of slave captains. And so Christianity, whatever it is in the minds of black people today in America, is looked upon as that body of thought which has tended to support, buttress, and indeed, promote the physical and psychological slavery of black people in America. And I suppose no other more contemporary evidence of that, or at least giving it certain credibility is the fact of the racially divided church in America today. Now this is a tough one to counter, and believe me, I try. For if the failure of America is its capitulation to secularism and a lot of other "isms," then it seems to me that the failure of the church is its capitulation to America. The church *is* America. One can scarcely tell where piety leaves off and patriotism begins.

I was impressed by something Carl F. H. Henry said the other day when speaking at a seminary convocation. He said: "Institutional Christianity has muffled the call for a new humanity and in doing so forfeits a mighty spiritual

3. David Brion Davis, *The Problem of Slavery in Western Culture* (Ithaca, N.Y.: Cornell University Press, 1966), p.10

opportunity at the crossroads of modern history. The organized church, which ought to have been burdened for the evangelization of the earth, has been too busy with powdering her nose to present an attractive public image, or powdering the reactionaries and revolutionaries who need rather to be made in Christ's image." And I assume, though I did not see the whole printed text, that that particular critique is levelled at the so-called liberal church. I think the practical fact, however, is that it also aptly fits the contemporary evangelical church in many aspects as well. If the National Council has sold itself to revolutionaries and reactionaries, some of us black people get the impression that the National Association of Evangelicals has sold itself to patriotism, conservative politics, and the preservation of the good old American way.

I am not so sure, gentlemen, that from an historical point of view you can support the idea that Jesus Christ was an American, much less an evangelical. A recent column in *Christianity Today* by a layman warned evangelicals against over-involvement in social action, which was at least ill-timed, if not presumptuous. It was a great piece—for *Christian Century*. I think our sin as a church in America today is not that we are un-American or not even that we are just pro-American, but simply that we are more American than Christian! Now if we don't know this, if WE don't know this, black Americans do! Whether we listen, or whether we admit to it, or whether we take any action in the light of what others are saying about us in this regard, will largely determine our future effectiveness as agents of God's reconciliation.

A fourth lesson of history now not being lost on black people is that if there ever was such a thing as "rugged individualism" it is either dead or irrelevant today. Blacks think that they have learned that people survived in America as groups and that you spell survival in America: P-O-W-E-R. They have learned that a minority group is a reference to that group's powerlessness not to its numerical strength. The black man knows now what other great black leaders meant when they talked in former years about black power, black pride, black self-determination. I suppose that this is what Marcus Garvey was talking about, and W. E. B. DuBois, and even Booker T. Washington in his own way. Sherwood Wirt in his helpful volume *The Social Conscience of an Evangelical* states it well: "For today mankind is being forced to learn another lesson. In an interlocking society individualism is not enough. Men are still born alone, they still die alone, and they still come to Jesus Christ alone. But the modern world is forcing them to live most of their waking moments together. Interdependence has supplanted independence as a rule of life." And even though I take a certain amount of encouragement from that, I would even question the fact that men come to Jesus Christ alone. I doubt that! I doubt that! Most of the people I have ever seen come to Jesus Christ were brought by somebody, in one way or another. Black America is beginning to understand that in order to survive in America where white power has always been assumed, black power is inevitable. I am kind of excited about that. Someone has suggested that we have moved in our lifetime from a geopolitical to a psycho-political world view which makes it possible for a black American in Harlem to understand an American Indian in the Southwest or an Eskimo in Alaska who is just beginning to realize that he has been "had" by Big Daddy. (Especially if oil has been discovered behind his igloo.) Someone will get to him. You had better believe it! . . .

As Christian men in history, we have, I think, an especially significant role to play. In the first place, we are committed to truth, and in the second place, we are committed to a certain detached objectivity regarding our place as pilgrims in a culture such as ours which desperately needs some kind of objective pilgrim prophetic witness. Our insights into history certainly ought to be much more significant because they are imbued with a much sharper specificity concerning what we believe, where history is going and so forth.

Most black students today do not have the faintest notion that there is such a thing as a Christian interpretation of history. Most black students do not even know what Christianity really is. And I am not saying that black students have a monopoly at that point. Somehow or another, in the name of history, we must de-mythologize the thing, or to use a cruder word, we must "de-honkify" history, which is not the same as saying we must blacken it. But we certainly have a lot of work to do in interpreting and presenting history with some of the outstanding myths removed therefrom if we are going to win the right to communicate with a whole new generation of black people. Somehow or another as Christians, we also with greater honesty must present biblical insights supported by all kinds of history to show that a man, simply because he is an American, is not automatically some kind of saint removed far beyond and out of the reach of all the carnalities to which other men are subject. I think a great commentary on our society, perhaps even greater than that of the suggested credibility gap of the Johnson Administration, has to do with our successful moon shots and our other successful shots in that little Vietnamese village over in the other part of the world. On the one hand our technology is able to plant the feet of white men on the moon and on the other hand, with amazing detachment, we are able to exterminate people in the name of war, or what? Our technology has far outstripped our humanity, and we have kidded ourselves that because we are Americans we simply could not have perpetrated My Lai. Black people will tell you differently—from 300 years experience. What happened over there? What do we have to say to the present generation about the fact of violence in American history? We have to say something about it, both as to its cause and to its possible cure, with integrity in the name of our God, if we are going to win a sympathetic ear from many people today.

And lastly, somehow or another, we have to rap with our kids, both white and black, about those very real, positive, courageous contributions which Christians have made as they have hurled themselves against terrible odds in an effort to tear down the horrible barriers to humanity and to human fulfillment. Have Christians really made contributions? Have evangelical Christians made efforts in the past to help take the burden off the backs of black people? Have evangelicals done this, not because they were Americans, but because they were Christians? If they have, then it ought to be said and we must find a way to say it with integrity and with sound scholarship. We must find a way to say it. I know it has been said. I have a couple of these books in my library. But black men will little note nor long remember what men wrote in their theses or doctoral dissertations for Ph.D. degrees. Great day in the morning! Kids in my neighborhood including my own son, unless I pass it down to them, will never know what contributions we made in history, unless somehow or another we find ways to communicate this. We must find that way!

Chapter 4

"Our Society"

1976

Francis Schaeffer

Gradually, that which had become the basic thought form of modern people became the almost totally accepted viewpoint, an almost monolithic consensus. And as it came to the majority of people through art, music, drama, theology, and the mass media, values died. As the more Christian-dominated consensus weakened, the majority of people adopted two impoverished values: *personal peace* and *affluence.*

Personal peace means just to be let alone, not to be troubled by the troubles of other people, whether across the world or across the city—to live one's life with minimal possibilities of being personally disturbed. Personal peace means wanting to have my personal life pattern undisturbed in my lifetime, regardless of what the result will be in the lifetimes of my children and grandchildren. Affluence means an overwhelming and ever-increasing prosperity—a life made up of things, things, and more things—a success judged by an ever-higher level of material abundance.

For several generations the fragmented concept of knowledge and life which had become dominant was taught to the young by many of the professors in universities around the world. All too often when the students of the early sixties asked their parents and others, "Why be educated?" they were told, in words if not by implication, "Because statistically an educated man makes so much more money a year." And when they asked, "Why make more money?" they were told, "So that you can send *your* children to the university." According to this kind of spoken or implied answer, there was no meaning for man, and no meaning for education.

Much of the mass media popularized these concepts, pouring them out in an endless stream so that a whole generation from its birth has been injected with the teaching that reason leads to pessimism in regard to a meaning of life and with reference to any fixed values. This had been that generation's atmosphere. It had no personal memory of the days when Christianity had more influence on the consensus. Those in the universities saw themselves as little computers controlled by the larger computer of the university, which in turn was controlled by the still-larger computer of the state.

The work ethic, which had meaning within the Christian framework, now became ugly as the Christian base was removed. Work became an end in itself— with no reason to work and no values to determine what to do with the products of one's work. And suddenly, in 1964 at the University of California at Berkeley, the students carried these ideas about the meaninglessness of man out into the streets. Why should anybody have been surprised? Many of the teachers taught the ultimate meaninglessness of man and the absence of absolutes, but they themselves lived inconsistently by depending on the memory of the past. Was it not natural that one generation would begin to live on the basis of what they had been taught? And at Berkeley in 1964 the results were visible, full blast.

Because the only hope of meaning had been placed in the area of non-reason, drugs were brought into the picture. Drugs had been around a long time, but, following Aldous Huxley's ideas, many students now approached drug taking as an ideology, and some, as a religion. They hoped that drugs would provide meaning "inside one's head," in contrast to objective truth, concerning which they had given up hope. Psychologist Timothy Leary, Gary Snyder, author-philosopher Alan Watts, and poet Allen Ginsberg were all influential in making drugs an ideology. Timothy Leary, for example, said that drugs were the sacraments for the new religion. Of course . . . this drug taking was really only one more leap, an attempt to find meaning in the area of non-reason. Charles Slack, writing of his long relationship with Leary, reported . . . that Leary had said to him, "Death to the mind, that is the goal you must have. Nothing else will do."

The utopian dream of the turned-on world was that if enough people were on drugs, the problems of modern civilization would be solved. With this in mind there was talk of introducing LSD into the drinking water of the cities. This was not vicious, for the people suggesting it really believed that drugs were the door to Paradise. In 1964 and for some years after, the hippie world really believed this ideological answer.

At Berkeley the Free Speech Movement arose simultaneously with the hippie world of drugs. At first it was politically neither left nor right, but rather a call for the freedom to express any political views on Sproul Plaza. Then soon the

Free Speech Movement became the Dirty Speech Movement, in which freedom was seen as shouting four-letter words into a mike. Soon after, it became the platform for the political New Left which followed the teaching of Herbert Marcuse . . .

For some time, young people were fighting against their parents' impoverished values of personal peace and affluence—whether their way of fighting was through Marcuse's New Left or through taking drugs as an ideology. The young people wanted more to life than personal peace and affluence. They were right in their analysis of the problem, but they were mistaken in their solutions.

The peak of the drug culture of the hippie movement was well symbolized by . . . Woodstock . . . a rock festival held in northeastern United States in the summer of 1969 . . . Many young people thought that Woodstock was the beginning of a new and wonderful age . . . But the drug world was already ugly, and it was approaching the end of its optimism, although the young people did not yet know it. Jimi Hendrix himself was soon to become a symbol of the end. Black, extremely talented, inhumanly exploited, he overdosed in September 1970 and drowned in his own vomit, soon after the claim that the culture of which he was a symbol was a new beginning. In the late sixties the ideological hopes based on drug taking died . . .

Unhappily, the result was not that fewer people were taking drugs. As the sixties drew to a close and the seventies began, probably more people were taking some form of drug, and at an ever-younger age. But taking drugs was no longer an ideology. That was finished. Drugs simply became the escape which they had been traditionally in many places in the past.

In the United States the New Left also slowly ground down, losing favor because of the excesses of the bombings, especially in the bombing of the University of Wisconsin lab in 1970, where a graduate student was killed. This was not the last bomb that was or will be planted in the United States. Hard-core groups of radicals still remain and are active, and could become more active, but the violence which the New Left produced as its natural heritage (as it also had in Europe) caused the majority of young people in the United States no longer to see it as a hope. So some young people began in 1964 to challenge the false values of personal peace and affluence, and we must admire them for this. Humanism, man beginning only from himself, had destroyed the old basis of values, and could find no way to generate with certainty any new values. In the resulting vacuum the impoverished values of personal peace and affluence had come to stand supreme. And now, for the majority of the young people, after the passing of the false hopes of drugs as an ideology and the fading of the New Left, what remained? Only *apathy* was left. In the United States by the beginning of the seventies, *apathy* was almost complete. In contrast to the political activists of the sixties, not many of the young even went to the polls to vote, even though the national voting age was lowered to eighteen. Hope was gone.

After the turmoil of the sixties, many people thought that it was so much better when the universities quieted down in the early seventies. I could have wept. The young people had been right in their analysis, though wrong in their solutions. How much worse when many gave up hope and simply accepted the same values as their parents—personal peace and affluence. Now drugs remain, but only in parallel to the older generation's alcohol, and an excessive use of alcohol has become a problem among the young people as well. Promiscuous sex and bisexuality remain, but only in parallel to the older generation's adultery. In other words, as the young people revolted against their parents, they came around in a big circle—and often ended an inch lower—with only the same two impoverished values: their own kind of personal peace and their own kind of affluence.

In some places the Marxist-Leninist line or the Maoist line took over. This was not so true in the United States, but these ideologies have become a major factor in Europe, South America, and other parts of the world. But Marxist-Leninism is another leap into the area of non-reason—as idealistic as drug taking was in its early days. The young followed Marxism in spite of clear evidence that oppression was not an excess of Stalin, but was and is an integral part of the system of communism. No one has made this more clear than Alexander Solzhenitsyn in *The Gulag Archipelago* (Vol. I, 1974). He takes great pains to point out that the foundations of lawless expediency were firmly established by Lenin. Summarizing the trials up through 1922 and looking ahead to the famous "showcase trials" of 1937, Solzhenitsyn asks, "What, then, were they surprised at in 1937? Hadn't all the foundations of lawlessness been laid?" But if this preceded Stalin, it is clear that it also survived him. Solzhenitsyn says that the salamander, by which he means the prison-camp network, is still alive. In *The Gulag Archipelago* (Vol. II, 1975) he says that the prison camps held up to fifteen million inmates at a time, and he estimated that from the Revolution to 1959 a total of sixty-six million prisoners died.

Even if this salamander is not so obviously voracious now, Solzhenitsyn is not appeased. He correctly identifies the root cause of the lawless expediency as the willingness to assure internal security at any cost. And he sees that when his contemporaries now urge him to "let bygones be bygones" they are making the same choice. "Dwell on the past and you'll lose an eye," they say. Solzhenitsyn adds, "But the proverb goes on to say: 'Forget the past and you'll lose both eyes.'"

Tellingly, he compares the West German effort since World War II to track down and punish major, known Nazi criminals (of which 86,000 had been convicted by 1966) with the total absence of such a procedure both in East Germany as regards Nazis and in Russia as regards the active agents of the officially condemned crimes of Stalin. He selects Molotov as a symbol of this mentality—a man who lives on comfortably, "a man who has learned nothing at all, even now, though he is saturated with our blood and nobly crosses the sidewalk to seat himself in his long, wide automobile." Reflecting upon these facts, Solzhenitsyn writes, "From the most ancient times justice has been a two-part concept: virtue triumphs and vice is punished." In contrast, Solzhenitsyn concludes about Russia, "Young people are acquiring the conviction that foul deeds are never punished on earth, that they always bring prosperity." He then adds, "It is going to be uncomfortable, horrible, to live in such a country!" And this is the case not only in Russia but wherever communism has attained power. China probably has less internal freedom than Russia . . .

How romantic, in a negative sense, is the leap into the area of non-reason to Marxist-Leninism! It is a different kind of leap from that of the existentialist . . . but it, too, is without a base in reason. Materialism, the philosophic base for Marxist-Leninism, gives no basis for the dignity or rights of man. Where Marxist-Leninism is not in power it attracts and converts by talking much of dignity and rights, but its materialistic base gives no basis for the dignity or rights of man. Yet it attracts by its constant talk of idealism.

To understand this phenomenon we must understand that Marx reached over to that for which Christianity *does* give a base—the dignity of man—and took the words as words of his own. The only understanding of idealistic sounding Marxist-Leninism is that it is (in this sense) a Christian heresy. Not having the Christian base, until it comes to power it uses the words for which Christianity does give a base. But wherever Marxist-Leninism has had power, it has at no place in history shown where it has not brought forth oppression. As soon as they have had the power, the desire of the majority has become a concept without meaning . . .

Countries which have a different base, for example, a Christian one (or at least one with the memory of a Christian foundation) may indeed act most inconsistently and horribly. But when a state with a materialistic base acts arbitrarily and gives no dignity to man, internally or externally, it is being consistent to its basic presuppositions and principles. To accept Marxist-Leninism is indeed a leap into the area of non-reason. It is its own kind of Nietzsche game plan, a setting of limits as to what one will observe, and a refusal to look outside of these boundaries lest the system be brought down like a house of cards . . .

In the United States many other practical problems developed as man's desire to be autonomous from God's revelation—in the Bible and through Christ— increasingly reached its natural conclusions. Sociologically, *law is king* (Samuel Rutherford's *Lex Rex*) was no longer the base whereby one could be ruled by law rather than the arbitrary judgments of men and whereby there could be wide freedoms without chaos. Any ways in which the system is still working is largely due to the sheer inertia of the continuation of the past principles. But this borrowing cannot go on forever.

. . . There is a danger that without a sufficient base modern science will become *sociological science*; so civil law has moved toward being *sociological law*. Distinguished jurist and Supreme Court Justice Oliver Wendell Holmes, Jr. took a long step in this direction. In *The Common Law* (1881) Holmes said that law is based on experience. Daniel H. Benson, assistant professor of law at the Texas Tech University School of Law quotes Holmes: "Truth is the majority vote of that nation that could lick all others." In a 1926 letter to John C. H.

Wu, Holmes wrote, "So when it comes to the development of a *corpus juris* the ultimate question is what do the dominant forces of the community want and do they want it hard enough to disregard whatever inhibitions may stand in the way." This is very different from Samuel Rutherford's biblical base and from Paul Robert's painting in which Justice points to "The Word of God."

Frederick Moore Vinson, former Chief Justice of the United States Supreme Court, spelled out this problem by saying, "Nothing is more certain in modern society than the principle that there are no absolutes." All is relative; all is experience. In passing, we should note this curious mark of our age: The only absolute allowed is the absolute insistence that there is no absolute.

Roscoe Pound wrote in *Jurisprudence* (1959): "The Greek philosophers sought to find some assured basis of social control other than tradition and the habit of obedience on the one hand, or the will of the politically supreme for the moment on the other hand. They conceived they had found such a basis in the analogy of the constant and universal phenomena of physical nature." In the days of Rousseau, Goethe, and Constable, when nature was being venerated, there was a concerted attempt to make nature the base for law. It is called Natural Law or the Law-of-Nature School of Jurisprudence. Roscoe Pound writes about the men identified with this approach: "Jurists of the 18th century Law-of-Nature School conceived that a complete and perfect system of law might be constructed upon principles of natural (i.e., ideal) law which were discoverable by reason." This was a part of Enlightenment optimism.

But, as we have seen, nature provides no sufficient base for either morals or law, because nature is both cruel and noncruel. Gradually, the hope that nature would give a fixed value in law was abandoned, and instead (as Pound quotes French jurist and legal philosopher Joseph Charmont) by the start of the twentieth century, law rooted in nature only had a variable content. A Jewish-Christian lawyer once wrote to me that, as he considered the serious meaning of the Nuremberg war-crimes trials, "I knew then that no moral law was written on a blade of grass, in a drop of water, or even in the stars. I realized the necessity of the Divine Immutable Law as set forth in the Sacred Torah, consisting of definite commandments, statutes, ordinances and judgments."

Man has failed to build only from himself autonomously and to find a solid basis in nature for law, and we are left today with Oliver Wendell Holmes's "experience" and Frederick Moore Vinson's statement that nothing is more certain in modern society than that there are no absolutes. Law has only a variable content. Much modern law is not even based on precedent; that is, it does not necessarily hold fast to a continuity with the legal decisions of the past. Thus, within a wide range, the Constitution of the United States can be made to say what the courts of the present want it to say—based on a court's decision as to what the court feels is sociologically helpful at the moment. At times this brings forth happy results, at least temporarily; but once the door is opened, anything can become law and the arbitrary judgments of men are king. Law is now freewheeling, and the courts not only interpret the laws which legislators have made, but make law. *Lex Rex* has become *Rex Lex*. Arbitrary judgment concerning current sociological good is *king*.

As arbitrary absolutes characterize communistic rule, so there is a drift in this direction on our side of the Iron Curtain as well. *This means that tremendous changes of direction can be made and the majority of the people tend to accept them without question—no matter how arbitrary the changes are or how big a break they make with past law or past consensus.*

It is worth considering at length, as an example, the United States Supreme Court ruling concerning the human fetus, the unborn baby. On January 22, 1973, the United States Supreme Court ruled that every woman in the United States has the right to an abortion during the first three months of pregnancy, with no discussion. In the second three months abortion is allowed if the state agrees it is healthy for the mother to have the abortion. During the second three months, as in the first three months, the fetus does not enter into consideration. Even during the last three months the fetus does not have effective protection under the law, because the word *health* (of the mother) has been given a very wide meaning.

To quote Joseph P. Witherspoon, professor of jurisprudence at the University of Texas School of Law, in the *Texas Tech Law Review*, Volume six, 1974–1975: "In this 1973 decision the Court . . . held that the unborn child is not a person within the meaning and protection of the term 'person' utilized in the fourteenth amendment so as to strip all unborn children of all constitutional protection for their lives, liberty, and property." In Britain the law allows pregnancies to be terminated up to the twenty-eighth week. There are several things to notice here.

This is a totally arbitrary absolute. First, it is *medically* arbitrary. *Our Future Inheritance: Choice or Chance?* (1974) is a book put out in England to inform the public about the questions of genetics which are immediately before us at this point of history. It is based on a series of working papers produced with the cooperation of scientists in a number of fields, including some scientists from the United States. It is in favor of abortion. However, the book says that the question about when human life begins is open: "It [abortion] can be carried out before the foetus becomes 'viable'—although when that is, is in itself an arguable point." It further states that "a biologist might say that human life started at the moment of fertilization when the sperm and the ovum merge."

The arbitrary nature of the decision *medically* is underlined by the fact that one section of the book accepts the destruction of the fetus by abortion, yet another section focuses on the question of whether it is ethical to fertilize the ovum with a sperm *in vitro* (in the laboratory) when at our present stage of technology it is certain to live for only a very limited number of days. The problem is that after fertilization it has "the full genetic potential for becoming a human being and will become one if implantation [in the womb] and gestation are successful. At what stage of development should the status of a patient be attributed to the embryo or foetus?" Here the question is raised whether the six-day-old fetus should be considered "a patient." In another place the book argues for fertilization in the laboratory on the basis that, since we help a baby who is prematurely born, should we not be willing to help "the complete development of a baby outside the body"? This is preceded by the sentence: "Assistance for the premature baby would, by most, be considered one of the basic duties of society." And in the argument for a total development outside the body the concept of the *premature baby* is carried back to the time of fertilization. What does this make the abortion of a five-and-one-half-month-old baby? It certainly has "the full genetic potential for becoming a human being."

I am making only one point here: Both the ruling by the United States Supreme Court and the British law were purely arbitrary *medically.* They established an arbitrary absolute which affects millions of embryos, when *medically* the matter is so open that the asking of ethical questions about a fertilized ovum of only seven days is considered valid, and when *medically* the question concerning the seven-day-old fertilized ovum rests on the fact that it has "the full genetic potential for becoming a human being." So when the official *Supreme Court Reporter* (Vol. 410) says that the unborn are not recognized in the law as persons, here is a *medical* arbitrary absolute with a vengeance—and at the point of human life.

Second, it is not only arbitrary medically but *legally.* The ruling set up an arbitrary absolute by disregarding the intent of the Thirteenth and Fourteenth Amendments of the Constitution. Quoting Professor Witherspoon again:

> Thus, the failure of the Court in Roe v. Wade [the abortion case] to have examined into the actual purpose and intent of the legislature in framing the fourteenth amendment and the thirteenth amendment to which it was so closely related and supplementary thereof when it was considering the meaning to be assigned to the concept of "person" was a failure to be faithful to the law or to respect the legislature which framed it. Careful research of the history of these two amendments will demonstrate to any impartial investigator that there is overwhelming evidence supporting the proposition that the principal, actual purpose of their framers was to prevent any court, and especially the Supreme Court of the United States, because of its earlier performance in the *Dred Scott* case, or any other institution of government, whether legislative or executive, from ever again defining the concept of person so as to exclude any class of human beings from the protection of the Constitution and the safeguards it established for the fundamental rights of human beings, including slaves, peons, Indians, aliens, women, the poor, the aged, criminals, the mentally ill or retarded, and children, including the unborn from the time of their conception.

Supreme Court Justice White in his dissent to the Court's action stated, "As an exercise of raw judicial power, the Court perhaps has authority to do what it does today; but in my view its judgment is an improvident and extravagant exercise of the power of judicial review that the Constitution extends to this Court." Upon this arbitrary ruling *medically* and *legally,* the Supreme Court invalidated the law on this subject of abortion of almost every one of the states in the Union.

Further, this arbitrary decision is at complete variance with the past Christian consensus. In the pagan Roman Empire, abortion was freely practiced, but Christians took a stand against it. In 314 the Council of Ancyra barred from the taking of the Lord's Supper for ten years all who procured abortions or made drugs to further abortions. Previously the Synod of Elvira (305–306) had specified excommunication till the deathbed for these offenses. The arbitrary absolutes of the Supreme Court are accepted against the previous consensus of centuries, as well as against past law. *And (taking abortion as an example) if this arbitrary absolute by law is accepted by most modern people, bred with the concept of no absolutes but rather relativity, why wouldn't arbitrary absolutes in regard to such matters as authoritarian limitations on freedom be equally accepted as long as they were thought to be sociologically helpful?* We are left with *sociological law* without any certainty of limitation.

By the ruling of the Supreme Court, the unborn baby is not counted as a person. In our day, quite rightly, there has been a hue and cry against some of our ancestors' cruel viewing of the black slave as a non-person. This was horrible indeed—an act of hypocrisy as well as cruelty. But now, by an arbitrary absolute brought in on the humanist flow, millions of unborn babies of every color of skin are equally by law declared non-persons. Surely this, too, must be seen as an act of hypocrisy . . .

As the Christian consensus dies, there are not many sociological alternatives. One possibility is hedonism, in which every man does his own thing. Trying to build a society on hedonism leads to chaos. One man can live on a desert island and do as he wishes within the limits of the form of the universe, but as soon as two men live on the island, if they are to live in peace, they cannot both do simply as they please. Consider two hedonists meeting on a narrow bridge crossing a rushing stream: Each cannot do his own thing.

A second possibility is the absoluteness of the 51-percent vote. In the days of a more Christian culture, a lone individual with the Bible could judge and warn society, regardless of the majority vote, because there was an absolute by which to judge. There was an absolute for both morals and law. But to the extent that the Christian consensus is gone, this absolute is gone as a social force. Let us remember that on the basis of the absoluteness of the 51-percent vote, Hitler was perfectly entitled to do as he wished if he had the popular support. On this basis, law and morals become a matter of averages. And on this basis, if the majority vote supported it, it would become "right" to kill the old, the incurably ill, the insane—and other groups could be declared non-persons. No voice could be raised against it . . .

. . . The Greeks found that society—the *polis*—was not a strong enough final authority to build upon, and it is still not strong enough today. If there are no absolutes, and if we do not like either the chaos of hedonism or the absoluteness of the 51-percent vote, only one other alternative is left: one man or an elite, giving authoritative arbitrary absolutes.

Here is a simple but profound rule: *If there are no absolutes by which to judge society, then society is absolute.* Society is left with one man or an elite filling the vacuum left by the loss of the Christian consensus which originally gave us form and freedom in northern Europe and in the West. In communism, the elite has won its way, and rule is based upon arbitrary absolutes handed down by that elite. Absolutes can be *this* today and *that* tomorrow. If Mao equals the law, then the concept of a continual cultural revolution, "The Great Leap Forward," may be in order one year and very much out of order the next. Arbitrary absolutes can be handed down and there is no absolute by which to judge them . . .

Humanism has led to its natural conclusion. It has ground down to the point Leonardo da Vinci visualized so long ago when he realized that, starting only from man, mathematics leads us only to particulars—and particulars lead only to mechanics. Humanism had no way to find the universal in the areas of meaning and values . . .

There is a death wish inherent in humanism—the impulsive drive to beat to death the base which made our freedoms and our culture possible.

In ancient Israel, when the nation had turned from God and from his truth and commands as given in Scripture, the prophet Jeremiah cried out that there was death in the city. He was speaking not only of physical death in Jerusalem but also a wider death. Because Jewish society of that day had turned away from what God had given them in the Scripture, there was death in the *polis,* that is, death in the total culture and the total society.

In our era, sociologically, man destroyed the base which gave him the possibility of freedoms without chaos. Humanists have been determined to beat to death the knowledge of God and the knowledge that God has not been silent, but has spoken in the Bible and through Christ—and they have been determined to do this even though the death of values has come with the death of that knowledge . . .

Edward Gibbon in his *Decline and Fall of the Roman Empire* (1776–1788) said that the following five attributes marked Rome at its end: first, a mounting love of show and luxury (that is, affluence); second, a widening gap between the very rich and the very poor (this could be among countries in the family of nations as well as in a single nation); third, an obsession with sex; fourth, freakishness in the arts, masquerading as originality, and enthusiasms pretending to be creativity; fifth, an increased desire to live off the state. It all sounds so familiar. We have come a long road . . . and we are back in Rome.

Chapter 5

"A Billion Hungry Neighbors" and "The Affluent Minority"

1977

Ron Sider

"A BILLION HUNGRY NEIGHBORS"

Sometimes I think, "If I die, I won't have to see my children suffering as they are." Sometimes I even think of killing myself. So often I see them crying, hungry; and there I am, without a cent to buy them some bread. I think, "My God, I can't face it! I'll end my life. I don't want to look anymore!"

—Iracema Da silva, resident of a slum in Brazil[1]

What does poverty really mean in daily life?

One way to answer this question is to list what a typical American family would need to give up if they were to adopt the lifestyle of a typical family living among our billion hungry neighbors. Economist Robert Heilbroner has itemized the abandoned "luxuries."

1. "Iracema's Story," *Christian Century,* Nov. 12, 1975, p. 1030.

We begin by invading the house of our imaginary American family to strip it of its furniture. Everything goes: beds, chairs, tables, television set, lamps. We will leave the family with a few old blankets, a kitchen table, a wooden chair. Along with the bureaus go the clothes. Each member of the family may keep in his "wardrobe" his oldest suit or dress, a shirt or blouse. We will permit a pair of shoes for the head of the family, but none for the wife or children.

We move to the kitchen. The appliances have already been taken out, so we turn to the cupboards. . . . The box of matches may stay, a small bag of flour, some sugar and salt. A few moldy potatoes, already in the garbage can, must be hastily rescued, for they will provide much of tonight's meal. We'll leave a handful of onions, and a dish of dried beans. All the rest we take away: the meat, the fresh vegetables, the canned goods, the crackers, the candy.

Now we have stripped the house: the bathroom has been dismantled, the running water shut off, the electric wires taken out. Next we take away the house. The family can move to the toolshed. . . .

Communications must go next. No more newspapers, magazines, books—not that they are missed, since we must take away our family's literacy as well. Instead, in our shantytown we will allow one radio. . . .

Now government services must go. No more postman, no more firemen. There is a school, but it is three miles away and consists of two classrooms. . . . There are, of course, no hospitals or doctors nearby. The nearest clinic is ten miles away and is tended by a midwife. It can be reached by bicycle, provided that the family has a bicycle, which is unlikely. . . .

Finally, money. We will allow our family a cash hoard of five dollars. This will prevent our breadwinner from experiencing the tragedy of an Iranian peasant who went blind because he could not raise the $3.94 which he mistakenly thought he needed to receive admission to a hospital where he could have been cured.[2]

How many of our sisters and brothers confront that kind of grinding poverty today? Hundreds of millions, at the very least, although exact figures are not available. The Sept. 15, 1975 issue of *Newsweek* reported that 900 million persons subsisted on less than $75 a year. The most reliable statistics available are the conservative figures prepared by the United Nations for the World Food Conference in Rome in late 1974. "At least 460 million are actually starving," the U.N.'s *Development Forum* reported. That does not mean that they will die tomorrow . . . But it does mean that they get less than the minimum daily amount of needed calories. When this happens, one becomes listless and the body begins to burn up its own fats, muscles and proteins for energy.

Tragically, even this ghastly figure of 462 million starving persons tells only part of the story. Experts think that another one-half to one and one-half billion persons lack adequate protein even though they eat enough calories. In order to stay on the conservative side, we will use the figure of one-half billion.

2. Robert L. Heilbroner, *The Great Ascent: The Struggle for Economic Development in Our Time* (New York: Harper & Row, 1963), pp. 33–36.

That makes a total of one billion starving and/or malnourished persons suffering today[3] . . .

But what of the other three billion persons alive today? One and one-half billion have an extremely modest but tolerable life. And then there are you and me and our one and one-half billion affluent friends in the rich countries of the Northern Hemisphere. Just how different is our life?

"THE AFFLUENT MINORITY"

I used to think, when I was a child, that Christ might have been exaggerating when he warned about the dangers of wealth. Today I know better. I know how very hard it is to be rich and still keep the milk of human kindness. Money has a dangerous way of putting scales on one's eyes, a dangerous way of freezing people's hands, eyes, lips, and hearts.

—Dom Helder Camara[4]

The north-south division is the most dangerous division in the world today. With one or two exceptions, the rich countries are in the Northern Hemisphere, and the poor countries are in the south. North America, Europe, Russia and Japan are an affluent northern aristocracy. Our standard of living is at least as luxurious in comparison with that of a billion hungry neighbors as was the lifestyle of the medieval aristocracy in comparison with their serfs.

And the chasm widens every year.

A Widening Chasm

The Gross National Product (GNP) provides one standard of comparison. A country's GNP is the sum of all its goods and services produced in a year. If one divides the total GNP by the number of persons in the country, one arrives at a per capita GNP which then can be compared with that of other nations . . . The world's goods are divided in an astoundingly unequal fashion.

. . . There are fifty-five times more goods and services available per person in the United States than in India. If one divides up the world into a rich one-third and a poor two-thirds, then the rich 34 per cent claims 87 per cent of the world's total GNP each year. The poor two-thirds is left with 13 per cent![5]

3. The special supplement to *Development Forum* (n.3) says "half the world's population, 2,000 million, is badly nourished." Georg Borgstrom suggests 1.5 billion lack adequate protein. See Borgstrom, "The Dual Challenge of Health and Hunger—A Global Crisis," Population Reference Bureau, "Selection," No. 31, January, 1970.

4. *Revolution through Peace* (New York: Harper & Row, 1971), p. 142.

5. Figures from the UN (Pearson) Commission on International Development quoted in Arthur Simon, *Bread for the World* (Grand Rapids: Eerdmans; Paramus, NJ: Paulist Press, 1975), p. 43.

Virtually all authorities agree that the chasm will widen greatly by the year 2000. The most widely recognized forecast is that of Professor Bhagwati of the Massachusetts Institute of Technology . . . In 1965 the per capita GNP of all developed countries was twelve times as large as that of developing countries taken as a group. By 2000 the rich will have fifteen times as large a per capita GNP!

Actually, GNP is not an entirely precise tool by which to measure the gap between rich and poor nations. Since GNP includes all goods and services, it includes the cost of things like haircuts. Now obviously one pays much more for a haircut in New York than in an Indian village. But it probably is worth no more. Some specialists have tried to take all such differences into account. A frequently quoted conclusion is that "differences in income per head between the poor and rich countries were around 1:2 at the beginning of the 19th century; they are around 1:40 today in nominal or around 1:20 in real terms."[6]

In 1975 Professor Irving Kravis, specialist in income comparisons at the University of Pennsylvania, published a massive painstaking comparison of total output and real purchasing power in different countries. He concluded that the real income per person in the United States is fourteen times that of India and seventeen times that of Kenya.[7] Even on the conservative calculations of economist Kravis, then, the average American is fourteen times as rich as the average Indian.

A comparison of energy usage simply underscores our affluence. Because of a lengthening list of luxuries—numerous electrical gadgets and toys, large air-conditioned cars, skyscrapers and so on—North Americans consume more than twice as much energy per person as their counterparts in industrialized countries like Germany and England. And we use 351 times as much as the average Ethiopian.[8]

In 1974, while Europeans complained about car-less Sundays and Americans grumbled over long lines at the gas pumps, Indian farmers waited in line for days for a small can of fuel to run their irrigation pumps. And when they returned home empty-handed, they also turned back in despair to earlier, less productive types of farming. If we persist in using so much energy, we will certainly help push up the world price of oil. As a result, poor countries will not be able to afford even the small amounts they so badly need. The result: less food and more starvation. Food specialist Lester Brown confronts us with a stark fact: "The continuous pursuit of superaffluence by some of us in a world of scarce resources can now directly affect the prospects for survival elsewhere."[9]

6. James W. Howe et al., *The U.S. and World Development: Agenda for Action, 1975* (New York: Praeger, 1975), p. 166.

7. *Newsweek,* August 18, 1975, p. 66. Irving B. Kravis, et. al., *A System of International Comparisons of Gross Product and Purchasing Power* (Baltimore: Johns Hopkins University Press, 1975), especially pp. 8–9.

8. See Ron Sider, *Rich Christians in an Age of Hunger* (Nashville: Thomas Nelson, Inc., 2005), chapter 6, p. 149; and Lester R. Brown, *In the Human Interest* (New York: Norton, 1974), pp. 31–32.

9. *Ibid.,* p. 93.

Undoubtedly the most striking measure of the gap between rich and poor is food consumption . . . U.S. citizens consume almost five times as much grain per person as do the people in the developing countries.

The major reason for this glaring difference is that we eat most of our grain indirectly—via grain-fed livestock and fowl. The annual per capita consumption of beef in the U.S. jumped from 55 pounds in 1940 to 116 pounds in 1972[10] . . .

Why is that important? Because it takes many pounds of grain to produce just one pound of beef. According to the Economic Research Service of the U.S. Department of Agriculture, a steer in a feed lot gains one pound of edible meat for every thirteen pounds of grain consumed! But the animal also spends time on the range eating grass . . . The U.S. Department of Agriculture reports that when the total life of the animal is considered, each pound of edible beef represents seven pounds of grain.[11] That means that in addition to all the grass, hay and other food involved, it also took seven pounds of grain to produce a typical pound of beef purchased in the supermarket. Fortunately, the conversion rates for chicken and pork are lower: two or three to one for chicken and three or four to one for pork. Beef is the Cadillac of meat products. Should we move to compacts?

It is because of this high level of meat consumption that the rich minority of the world devours such an unfair share of the world's available food. Whereas we eat most of our grain indirectly via meat, people in the poor countries eat almost all of their grain directly. The United Nations reports that livestock in the rich countries eat as much grain as do all the People of India and China.[12]

The final irony of this injustice is that our high meat consumption is harmful to our health! According to Harvard nutritionist Dr. Jean Mayer, a diet high in saturated fats contributes to heart disease.[13] (Beef, especially choice and prime cuts, pork, eggs and whole milk all contain large amounts of saturated fats.) Diets high in meat and low in roughage are also harmful for the bowel. The National Cancer Institute has indicated that diets high in meat may contribute to colon cancer (the second most common cancer in North America).[14] Dr. Mark Hegsted of the Harvard School of Public Health says that "meat consumption in this country is preposterously high, relative to need, and cannot be justified on a nutritional basis."[15]

10. Brown, p. 44.

11. *Bread for the World Newsletter,* January, 1975, p. 2; and personal conversation with George Allen, U.S. Department of Agriculture on April 9, 1976.

12. "Facts on Food," Supplement to *Development Forum,* Nov., 1974.

13. Jean Mayer, "Heart Disease: Plans for Action," *U.S. Nutrition Policies in the Seventies* (San Francisco: W. H. Freeman and Co., 1973), p. 44.

14. "How Much Is Enough?" *Consumer Reports,* 38, No. 9 (1974), p. 668.

15. Quoted in W. Stanley Mooneyham, *What Do You Say to a Hungry World?* (Waco, Texas: Word Books, 1975), p. 184. For excellent suggestions for more healthy eating patterns, see Doris Longacre, *More With Less Cookbook* (Scottdale, Pa.: Herald Press, 1976) and F. M. Lappé, *Diet for a Small Planet,* Rev. ed. (New York: Ballantine, 1975).

While lack of food destroys millions in poor lands, too much food devastates millions in affluent countries. According to the American Medical Association, 40 per cent of the U.S. population is overweight.[16]

The percentage of disposable income spent on food in different countries provides another stark comparison. In the United States it is a mere 17 per cent. In India 67 per cent. And 17 per cent of $10,000 is $1,700 while 67 per cent of $200 is $134. How would we like to have $134 for food this year?

Agony and anguish are concealed in [some] simple statistics. . . . If one is spending 17 per cent of one's disposable income on food, a 50 per cent increase in food costs is a minor irritation. But if one is already spending 67 percent of one's income on food, a 50 per cent increase means starvation.

The facts are clear. North Americans, Europeans, Russians and Japanese devour an incredibly unjust share of the world's available food. Whether measured in terms of GNP or energy and food consumption, we are many, many times more affluent than the poor majority of our sisters and brothers. And the chasm widens every year.

Poverty at $15,000 a Year?

It was late 1974. Millions were literally dying from starvation. But that was not the concern of Judd Arnett, a syndicated columnist with Knight Newspapers. In a column read (and probably believed) by millions of North Americans, Arnett lamented the fact that people earning $15,000 a year are on the edge or poverty. "One of the great mysteries of life to me is how a family in the $15,000 bracket, before taxes, or even $18,000, can meet all its obligations and still educate its children."[17]

To the vast majority of the world's people, such a statement would be unintelligible—or very dishonest. To be sure, we do need $15,000, $18,000 or more each year if we insist on two cars, an expensively furnished, sprawling suburban home, a $100,000 life insurance policy, new clothes every time fashions change, the most recent "labor saving devices" for home and garden, an annual three-week vacation to travel and so on. Many North Americans have come to expect precisely that. But that is hardly life at the edge of poverty.

By any objective criterion, the 6 per cent of the world's people who live in the United States are an incredibly rich aristocracy living among a vast, hungry proletariat. Surely one of the most astounding things, therefore, about this affluent minority is that we honestly think we barely have enough to survive in modest comfort.

Constant, seductive advertising helps to create this destructive delusion. Advertisers regularly con us into believing that we genuinely need one luxury

16. "Malnutrition and Hunger in the United States," *American Medical Journal*, 213, No. 2 (1970), pp. 272–75.

17. "Middle Class? Not on $15,000 a Year," *Philadelphia Inquirer*, Oct. 28, 1974, p. 9-A.

after another. We are convinced that we must keep up with or even go one better than our neighbors. So we buy another dress, sports jacket or sports car and thereby force up the standard of living. The ever more affluent standard of living is the god of twentieth-century North America and the adman is its prophet.

The purpose of advertising no longer is primarily to inform. It is to create desire. "CREATE MORE DESIRE" shrieked one inch-high headline for an unusually honest ad in the *New York Times.* It continued: "Now, as always, profit and growth stem directly from the ability of salesmanship to create more desire."[18] Luxurious houses in *Better Homes and Gardens* make one's perfectly adequate house shrink by comparison into a dilapidated, tiny cottage in need of immediate renovation. The advertisements for the new fall fashions make our almost new dresses and suits from previous years look shabby and positively old-fashioned.

We are bombarded by costly, manipulative advertising at every turn. The average American teen-ager has watched 350,000 TV commercials before he or she leaves high school![19] We spend more money on advertising than on all our public institutions of higher education. In 1974, $26.5 billion went into advertising "to convince us that Jesus was wrong about the abundance of possessions."[20] . . .

Promises, Promises

Perhaps the most devastating and most demonic part of advertising is that it attempts to persuade us that material possessions will bring joy and fulfillment. "That happiness is to be attained through limitless material acquisition is denied by every religion and philosophy known to man, but is preached incessantly by every American television set."[21] Advertisers promise that their products will satisfy our deepest needs and inner longings for love, acceptance, security and sexual fulfillment. The right deodorant, they promise, will bring acceptance and friendship. The newest toothpaste or shampoo will make one irresistible. A house or bank account will guarantee security and love . . .

If no one paid any attention to these lies, they would be harmless. But that is impossible. Advertising has a powerful affect on all of us. It shapes the values of our children. Many people in our society truly believe that more possessions will bring acceptance and happiness. In its "Life-Style" section, *Newsweek* recently

---

18. *New York Times*, July 12, 1949. Quoted in Jules Henry, *Culture Against Man* (New York: Random House, 1963), p. 19.

19. Robert N. Bellah, *The Broken Covenant* (New York: Seabury Press, 1975), p. 133. See also Wilbur Schramm, Jack Lyle and Edwin B. Parker, *Television in the Lives of Our Children* (Stanford: Stanford University Press, 1961).

20. Richard K. Taylor, "The Imperative of Economic De-Development," *The Other Side*, July-August, 1974, p. 17. For the figures on advertising and education, see U.S. Bureau of the Census, *Statistical Abstract*, 1975, pp. 112, 791.

21. Bellah, *Broken Covenant*, p. 134.

described the craze for $150 belt buckles, $695 rattlesnake belts and exceedingly expensive jewelry. A concluding comment by New York jewelry designer Barry Kieselstein shows how people search for meaning and friendship in things: "A nice piece of jewelry *you can relate to is like having a friend* who's always there."[22] . . .

Theologian Patrick Kerans has recently argued that our society's commitment to a growth economy and an ever-increasing standard of living promoted by constant advertising is really a sell-out to the Enlightenment. During the eighteenth century, Western society decided that the scientific method would shape our relationship to reality. Since only quantitative criteria of truth and value were acceptable, more intangible values such as community, trust and friendship became less important. Unlike friendship and justice, GNP can be measured. The result is our competitive, growth economy where winning and economic success (and they are usually the same) are all-important.[23]

The result, if Kerans is correct, can only be social disintegration. If our basic social structures are built on the heretical suppositions of the Enlightenment that the scientific method is the only way to truth and value, and if Christianity is true, then our society must eventually collapse . . .

How Generous Are We?

The United States is the richest nation in the world . . . the U.S. government ranks fifth from the bottom (in percentage of GNP given) among the major Western donors of foreign aid.[24]

Popular opinion does not reflect this reality. A recent survey discovered that more than two-thirds (69 per cent) of all Americans think that the United States is more generous in foreign aid than other developed nations.[25] Perhaps our illusion of generosity is a necessary protective device. In order to justify our affluence, we foster an image of a generous nation dispensing foreign aid on a grand scale.

The United States did display national generosity at the end of World War 2. At the height of the Marshall Plan (begun in 1947 to rebuild war-torn Europe) we actually gave annually 2.79 per cent of our total Gross National Product for development assistance. By 1975 that figure had plummeted to a mere 0.24 per cent of GNP![26] In those twenty-eight years our total GNP doubled. We were twice as rich in 1975 as in 1949. But we gave only 1/11 as much of our abundance. The richer we have become, the less we care to share with others.

In 1975 the Organization for Economic Cooperation and Development (an organization of rich nations) underlined the contrast between growing wealth

22. *Newsweek*, Oct. 28, 1974, p. 69 (my italics).
23. Patrick Kerans, *Sinful Social Structures* (New York: Paulist Press, 1974), pp. 80–81.
24. Howe, *Agenda for Action, 1975*, p. 258.
25. *Bread for the World Newsletter*, May, 1976, p. 1; Howe, *Agenda for Action, 1975*, p. 258.
26. Paul A. Laudicina, *World Poverty and Development: A Survey of American Opinion* (Washington: Overseas Development Council, 1973), p. 21.

and declining foreign aid. In 1961–62 developed countries as a whole gave 0.52 per cent of total GNP in economic foreign aid. By 1974 it had declined to a mere 0.33 per cent (1/3 of one per cent). But the economies of developed countries grew at an annual rate of 3.5 per cent per year during the past fifteen years. The OECD report concludes with the following statement:

> This means that, at the end of a 10-year period, the resources available per person [in developed countries] had increased by 41 percent. To have reached the 0.7 per cent target [for development aid] from a starting point of 0.5 per cent would have reduced the increase in resources available for other purposes only marginally—from 41 to 40.5 per cent . . . [27]

But developed nations would not spare a mere 1/82 of their *increase*!

A comparison of our expenditures on foreign aid and the military is startling. In 1975 we spent $3.67 billion on foreign aid. But more than half of that aid was military assistance. Only $1.5 billion was economic development. Another $1.3 billion went for food aid although three-quarters of our food aid was given in the form of long-term, low-interest loans.[28] We spent approximately 2 billion dollars on non-military aid in 1975. Forty-two times that much went for U.S. military expenditures. The $85 billion spent by the United States on defense in 1975 is greater than the *total annual income* of the poorest one billion inhabitants of this hungry globe. In fact every one billion dollars we spent on arms would have adequately supplemented the diets of 50 million undernourished children.

The United States devours about $246 million each day for current military purposes—more than the entire annual budget of the UN World Food Program. In 16 hours the US military spends more than the World Health Organization and the Food and Agriculture Organization spend in a year.[29]

Is that the way we want to divide our abundance?

Rationalizing Our Affluence

It would be impossible for the rich minority to live with themselves if they did not invent plausible justifications. These rationalizations take many forms. Analyzing a few of the most common may help us spot each year's new models.

In the last few years concepts such as "triage"[30] and "life-boat ethics" have become increasingly popular. Dr. Garrett Hardin, a distinguished biologist

---

27. Howe, *Agenda for Action, 1975*, p. 258.
28. Simon, *Bread for the World*, pp. 114–15.
29. *Ibid.*, p. 123.
30. Any system used to allocate a scarce commodity, such as medical help or food, only to those whom it may help to survive and not to those who have no chance of surviving or who will survive without assistance.

at the University of California at Santa Barbara, has provoked impassioned, widespread debate with his provocative articles on "lifeboat ethics."[31] He argues that we should not help the poor countries with food or aid. Each rich country is a lifeboat that will survive only if it refuses to waste its very limited resources on the hungry masses swimming in the water around it. If we eat together today, we will all starve together tomorrow. Furthermore, since poor countries "irresponsibly" permit unrestrained population growth, starvation is the only way to check the ever-growing number of hungry mouths. Hence, increased aid merely postpones the day of reckoning. When it comes, our aid will only have preserved even more persons for ultimate starvation. Therefore it is ethically correct to help them learn the hard way—by letting them starve now!

There are fundamental flaws, however, in Hardin's argument. Even though he is preoccupied with overpopulation, Hardin ignores some basic data. The poor countries are not the most densely populated ones. Except for Bangladesh, South Korea and some very tiny lands like Hong Kong, the most densely populated countries are rich Western European nations and Japan. The population density of the Netherlands is almost four times that of China; that of West Germany almost three times that of Indonesia. If overpopulation were the main reason for continuing poverty then England, Japan, Belgium and the Netherlands would be among the poorest countries of the world.

Hardin also ignores recent data which show that poor countries can (and have) cut population growth fairly rapidly if, instead of investing in advanced technology and industrial development, they concentrate on improving the lot of the poor masses. If the poor masses have a secure food supply, access to some (relatively inexpensive) health services and modest educational opportunities population growth tends to decline quickly. Lester Brown summarizes recent findings:

> There is new striking evidence that in an increasing number of poor countries . . . birth rates have dropped sharply *despite relatively low per capita income*. . . . Examination of societies as different as China, Barbados, Sri Lanka, Uruguay, Taiwan, The Indian Punjab, Cuba and South Korea suggests a common factor. In all these countries, a large portion of the population has gained access to modern social and economic services—such as education, employment, and credit systems. . . . There is increasing evidence that the very strategies which cause the greatest improvement in the welfare of the entire population also have the greatest effect on reducing population growth.[32]

31. Garrett Hardin, "Lifeboat Ethics: The Case Against Helping the Poor," *Psychology Today,* 8, No.4 (Sept., 1974), pp. 38ff. See also William and Paul Paddock, *Famine 1975!* (Boston: Little, Brown and Co., 1967). (Reprinted in 1976 under the title *Time of Famines: America and the World Food Crisis*.)

32. Brown, *In the Human Interest,* pp. 113–14 (my italics).

The right kind of aid—focused especially on promoting labor-intensive, agricultural development using intermediate technology[33]—will help check population growth. Hardin's ghastly thesis suggests doing nothing at a time when the right kind of action could probably avoid disaster.

Another omission in Hardin's thesis is even more astonishing. He totally ignores the fact that the ever increasing affluence among the rich minority is one of the fundamental causes of the present crisis. It is simply false to suggest that there is not enough food to feed everyone. There is enough—if it is more evenly distributed. In 1970 the United Nations estimated that it would take only 12 million additional tons of grain per year to provide 260 extra calories per day to the 460 million people suffering from malnutrition. That is only 30 per cent of what we feed our livestock in the United States.[34] In a world where the rich minority feed more grain to their livestock than all the people in India and China eat, it is absurd and immoral to talk of the necessity of letting selected hungry nations starve. The boat in which the rich sail is not an austerely equipped lifeboat. It is a lavishly stocked luxury liner.

Hardin's proposal, of course, is also unrealistic. Hungry nations left to starve would not disappear in submissive silence. India is one of the nations frequently nominated for this dubious honor. As indicated before, a nation with nuclear weapons would certainly not tolerate such a decision![35]

A second rationalization has a pious ring to it. Does not the evangelistic mandate to witness to wealthy persons require that some Christians adopt an affluent lifestyle? Maybe.

But rationalization is dreadfully easy. Garden Grove Community Church in California has a lavish multimillion dollar plant complete with a series of water fountains that begin spraying when the minister touches a button in the pulpit. The pastor, Robert Schuller, defends his luxurious facilities:

> We are trying to make a big, beautiful impression upon the affluent non-religious American who is riding by on this busy freeway. It's obvious that we are not trying to impress the Christians! . . . Nor are we trying to impress the social workers in the County Welfare Department. They would tell us that we ought to be content to remain in the orange Drive-In Theater and give the money to feed the poor. But suppose we had given this money to feed the poor? What would we have today? We would still have hungry, poor people and God would not have this tremendous base of operations which He is using to inspire people to become more successful,

33. Labor-intensive development uses people rather than machines (e.g. dams can be built by 5000 people carrying ground and stones just as well as by two bulldozers and three earthmovers). Advocates of intermediate technology urge developing nations to move from, for example, the hoe to the ox-drawn plough rather than from the hoe to the huge tractor. See E. F. Schumacher, *Small Is Beautiful* (New York: Harper Torchbooks, 1973), especially pp. 161–79.

34. Howe, *Agenda for Action*, 1975, pp. 60–62.

35. For short critiques of triage and lifeboat ethics, see Lester Brown, *The Politics and Responsibility of the North-American Breadbasket*, p. 36; and *Bread for the World Newsletter*, July, 1976.

more affluent, more generous, more genuinely unselfish in their giving of themselves.[36]

Where does valid justification end and rationalization begin? We must avoid simplistic legalism. Christians certainly ought to live in the suburbs as well as the inner city. But those who defend an affluent lifestyle on the basis of a call to witness to the rich must ask themselves hard questions: How much of my affluent lifestyle is directly related to my witnessing to rich neighbors? How much of it could I abandon for the sake of Christ's poor and still be able to witness effectively? Indeed how much of it *must* I abandon in order to faithfully proclaim the biblical Christ who clearly taught that failure to feed the poor entails eternal damnation (Mt. 25:45–46)?

The response of top U.S. leaders to recent proposals by the developing nations shows how rationalization can degenerate into doubletalk. In 1974 there was an historic meeting at the United Nations. The developing nations adopted a document calling for a new international economic order. They insisted on higher prices for their raw materials and other changes in trade patterns and international monetary arrangements that would facilitate their development. The U.S. Secretary of State, Henry Kissinger, and other U.S. leaders charged the large coalition of poor countries with "using" the United Nations. Some highly placed U.S. officials suggested that this "tyranny of the majority" warranted U.S. withdrawal from the UN. Is not the democratic principle of majority rule *our* principle? Is it not dishonest doubletalk to speak of tyranny when the majority use their numbers to demand justice? It would surely be ironic if we would belittle democratic principles in order to defend our affluence!

In the coming decades rationalizations for our affluence will be legion. They will be popular and persuasive. "Truly, I say to you, it will be hard for a rich man to enter the kingdom of heaven" (Mt. 19:23). But all things are possible with God—if we will hear and obey his Word. If there is any ray of hope for the future, it is in the possibility that growing numbers of affluent Christians will dare to allow the Bible to shape their relationship to a billion sons and daughters of poor Lazarus . . .

36. Robert H. Schuller, *Your Church Has Real Possibilities!* (Glendale, Calif.: Regal Books, 1974), p. 117.

Chapter 6

"The Call"

1981

Jim Wallis

The people who sat in darkness have seen a great light, and for those who sat in the region and shadow of death light has dawned. From that time Jesus began to preach, saying, "Repent, for the kingdom of heaven is at hand."

—Matthew 4:16–17 (RSV)

Just as light breaks into the darkness, the kingdom of God has arrived. That is how the prophet Isaiah, quoted here by Matthew, said it would be. The times into which Jesus came were dark indeed. Political domination at the hands of Rome, economic oppression by the rich, and human sinfulness on every side—these were the experiences of the common people. But where there was no light, God's new order would shine for all to see in the person of Jesus Christ. No wonder the word *gospel* means "good news"! The people had been waiting a long time.

Jesus inaugurated a new age, heralded a new order, and called the people to conversion. "Repent!" he said. Why? Because the new order of the kingdom is breaking in upon you and, if you want to be a part of it, you will need to undergo a fundamental transformation. Jesus makes the need for conversion clear from the beginning. God's new order is so radically different from everything we are accustomed to that we must be spiritually remade before we are ready and equipped to participate in it. In his Gospel, John would later refer to the change as a "new birth." No aspect of human existence is safe from this sweeping change—neither the personal, nor the spiritual, social, economic, and

46

political. The kingdom of God has come to change the world and us with it. Our choice is simply whether or not we will offer our allegiance to the kingdom.

> As he walked by the Sea of Galilee, he saw two brothers, Simon who is called Peter and Andrew his brother, casting a net into the sea; for they were fishermen. And he said to them, "Follow me, and I will make you fishers of men." Immediately they left their nets and followed him. And going on from there he saw two other brothers, James the son of Zebedee and John his brother, in the boat with Zebedee their father, mending their nets, and he called them. Immediately they left the boat and their father, and followed him. (Matt. 4:18–22 RSV)

Jesus called people to follow him. The first disciples took him quite literally. They were young Jewish men with established occupations and family responsibilities who nevertheless left everything to follow him. Jesus called them to himself, and he called them to a mission. "Follow me, and I will make you fishers of men." Their calling was not just for their own sake. From the outset, Jesus' disciples were—and are—called for a purpose.

To leave their nets was no light choice for these Galilean fishermen. Their fishing nets were their means of livelihood and the symbol of their identity. Now Peter and the others were leaving not only their most valued possessions; they were leaving their former way of life. That is what it meant to follow Jesus. Old ties were broken, former things left behind. Peter said, "Lo, we have left everything and followed you" (Matt. 19:27 RSV).

Four simple fishermen heard the call of Jesus. They were the first to obey and follow. They would not be the last. Others too would forsake all previous commitments to join Jesus' band. They would become his disciples and share his life. From then on they were bound to Jesus and to his kingdom; nothing would ever be the same for them again. They had made a clear choice with very real consequences. Jesus told potential converts to count the cost:

> As they were going along the road, a man said to him, "I will follow you wherever you go." And Jesus said to him, "Foxes have holes, and birds of the air have nests; but the Son of man has nowhere to lay his head." To another he said, "Follow me." But he said, "Lord, let me first go and bury my father." But he said to him, "Leave the dead to bury their own dead; but as for you, go and proclaim the kingdom of God." Another said, "I will follow you, Lord; but first let me say farewell to those at my home." Jesus said to him, "No one who puts his hand to the plow and looks back is fit for the kingdom of God." (Luke 9:57–62 RSV)

In the Bible, conversion means "turning." "To convert" in the King James Bible is translated "to turn" in the Revised Standard Version.

The Old Testament word for conversion *(shub)* means "to turn, return, bring back, restore." It occurs more than one thousand times and always involves turning from evil and to the Lord.[1] The prophets continually called Israel to turn from its sins and worship of idols and return to Yahweh, the true and living God. This call to conversion was both individual and corporate in the Old Testament. These people of God were much like us, always falling away from their Lord and getting themselves into trouble. Conversion meant to come back, to come home again, to wander no longer in sin, blindness, and idolatry. To convert meant to be again who you really were and to remember to whom you really belonged.

The New Testament words for conversion *(metanoein* and *epistrephein)* mean "to turn around."[2] Turning around involves stopping and proceeding in a new direction. The New Testament stresses the necessity of a radical turnabout and invites us to pursue an entirely different course of life. Thus, fundamental change of direction is central to the meaning of the words. The assumption—from the preaching of John the Baptist through Jesus to the first apostles—is

---

1. See the article on "Conversion" by F. Laubach, J. Goetzmann, and U. Becker, in *The New International Dictionary of the New Testament,* ed. Colin Brown, 3 vols. (Grand Rapids, Mich.: Zondervan, 1975–78), 1:353–362 (hereafter cited as *NIDNT);* and the article on "Strepho" by G. Bertram in the *Theological Dictionary of the New Testament,* ed. Gerhard Friedrich, trans. and ed. Geoffrey W. Bromiley, 10 vols. (Grand Rapids, Mich.: Eerdmans, 1964–1976), 7:714–29 (hereafter cited as *TDNT).* Both of these New Testament dictionaries discuss the Hebrew roots of conversion.

The Hebrew verb *shub* is basically one of motion and preserves much of the real meaning of conversion as an actual turning around, a *reversal from* and a *turning toward* something. The concept of conversion, however, is not exhausted by this one word. Walter Eichrodt shows that there are at least twenty common phrases used to indicate conversion and a return to God, including: to seek God, to humble oneself before God, to soften one's heart, to seek the good and hate the evil, to break up the fallow ground, etc. *Shub,* though, sums up all those other descriptions in a single, pregnant word.

The metaphor was an especially suitable one, for not only did it describe the required behavior as a real act—"to make a turn"—and so preserve the strong personal impact; it also included both the negative element of turning away from the direction taken hitherto and the positive element of turning towards, and so, when combined with prepositions, allowed the rich content of all the many other idioms to be reproduced tersely yet unmistakably *(Theology of the Old Testament,* Vol. 2, trans. J. A. Baker [London: SCM Press, 1967], pp. 465–466).

2. See Laubach, Goetzmann, and Becker, "Conversion," *NIDNT,* 1:353–362; Bertram, "Strepho," *TDNT,* 7:714–29; J. Behm and E. Wurthwein, "Metanoia," *TNDT,* 4:975–1008. The process of conversion is expressed in the New Testament by three primary word groups, which deal with its various aspects: *epistrephein, metamelomai,* and *metanoein.* Since *metamelomai* expresses the feeling of sorrow for sin without necessarily encompassing a turn to God, the other two terms become the predominant word groups that carry the central meaning of conversion in the New Testament. *Strephein* is the root for ten basic terms in the New Testament that refer to conversion and, in different contexts, may mean turn, return, turn around, turn back, be converted, change, turn away from, or conversion. *Metanoia* means conversion or repentance—in verb form, to repent or be converted.

The New Testament is full of other symbols that describe conversion. The fact that these two primary word groups do not occur often in Paul or John does not mean that the idea of conversion is not present there, but only that in the time between the writing of the Gospels and the epistles a more specialized terminology had developed. Both Paul and John convey the idea of conversion through the imagery of faith. Paul speaks of conversion as "being in Christ," as the "dying and rising with Christ," as the "new creation," or as "putting on the new man." John represents the new life in Christ as "new birth," as passing from death to life and from darkness to light, as the victory of truth over falsehood and of love over hate.

that we are on the wrong path, moving away from God. The Bible refers to our self-determined course as walking in sin, darkness, blindness, dullness, sleep, and hardness of heart. To convert is to make an about-face and take a new path.[3]

Correct intellectual belief was a major concern of the Greeks. The early Christians, in contrast, were more concerned with transformation. The first evangelists did not simply ask people what they believed about Jesus; they called upon their listeners to forsake all and to follow him. To embrace his kingdom meant a radical change not only in outlook but in posture, not only in mind but in heart, not only in worldview but in behavior, not only in thoughts but in actions. Conversion for them was more than a changed intellectual position. It was a whole new beginning.

Thus conversion is far more than an emotional release and much more than an intellectual adherence to correct doctrine. It is a basic change in life direction. If the key to conversion in the biblical stories is a turning from and a turning to, it is always appropriate to ask what is being turned from and what is being turned to in the account of any conversion.

Conversion begins with repentance, the New Testament word for which is *metanoia*. Our word *repentance* conjures up feelings of being sorry or guilty for something. The biblical meaning is far deeper and richer. In the New Testament usage, repentance is the essential first step to conversion. In the larger rhythm of turning from and turning to, repentance is the turning away from. Repentance turns us from sin, selfishness, darkness, idols, habits, bondages, and demons, both private and public.[4] We turn from all that binds and oppresses us and others, from all the violence and evil in which we are so complicit, from all the false worship that has controlled and corrupted us. Ultimately, repentance is turning from the powers of death. These ominous forces no longer hold us in their grip; they no longer have the last word.

Having begun with repentance, conversion proceeds to faith. The call to repentance is the invitation to freedom and the preparation for faith. Just as John the Baptist prepared the way of Jesus, so repentance makes us ready for faith in Christ. As repentance is the turning from, faith is the turning to. Repentance is

---

3. Karl Barth describes conversion as a twofold call to "halt" and then to "proceed" out of our sleep. Once awakened, we realize we are going down the wrong road and need to have our feet set upon a new one. Our former movement is halted, and we are told to proceed in another direction. The two movements of halting and proceeding belong together, says Barth, and form the essential unity of conversion. Karl Barth, "The Awakening to Conversion," in *Church Dogmatics*, trans. G. W. Bromiley (Edinburgh: T. & T. Clark, 1958), IV/2:560–561.

4. What did Jesus mean when he said "repent"? Joachim Jeremias tries to answer this question by looking especially at the parables. See his *New Testament Theology* (New York: Scribner's, 1971), p. 153. Jeremias notes that Jesus demands repentance in its breadth and depth by presenting a whole series of new pictures. The pictures are always concrete and specific to the person's situation. Jesus "expects the publican to stop cheating (Luke 19:8), the rich man to turn away from his service of Mammon (Mark 10:17–31), the conceited man to turn away from pride (Matt. 6:1–18). If a man has dealt unjustly with another, he is to make good (Luke 19:8). From hence forward, life is to be ruled by obedience to the word of Jesus (Matt. 7:24–27), the confession of him (Matt. 10:32f.), and by discipleship that comes before all other ties (verse 37).

seeing our sin and turning from it; faith is seeing Jesus and turning toward him. Together, repentance and faith form the two movements of conversion.[5]

Faith is turning to belief, hope, and trust. As repentance dealt with our past, faith opens up our future. Faith opens us to the future by restoring our sight, softening our hearts, bringing light into our darkness. We are converted to compassion, justice, and peace as we take our stand as citizens of Christ's new order. We see, hear, and feel now as never before. We enter the process of being made sensitive to the values of the new age, the kingdom of God. The victory of Jesus Christ over the powers of death has now been appropriated to our own lives; we are enabled to live free of their bondage. Christ has vanquished the powers that once held us captive and fearful; we now stand in the radical freedom he bought for us with his own blood. "So if the Son makes you free, you will be free indeed" (John 8:36 RSV). Our freedom, like Jesus', will now become a threat to the existing order of things. It is no mere coincidence that immediately after Jesus says, "You will be free indeed," he says, "Yet you seek to kill me" (John 8:37 RSV).

Conversion in the Bible is always firmly grounded in history; it is always addressed to the actual situation in which people find themselves. In other words, biblical conversion is historically specific. People are never called to conversion in an historical vacuum. They turn to God in the midst of concrete historical events, dilemmas, and choices. That turning is always deeply personal, but it is never private. It is never an abstract or theoretical concern; conversion is always a practical issue. Any idea of conversion that is removed from the social and political realities of the day is simply not biblical.

In the biblical narratives, the "from" and "to" of conversion are usually quite clear. Conversion is from sin to salvation, from idols to God, from slavery to freedom, from injustice to justice, from guilt to forgiveness, from lies to truth, from darkness to light, from self to others, from death to life, and much more.[6]

---

5. Gabriel Fackre, *Word in Deed: Theological Themes in Evangelism* (Grand Rapids, Mich.: Eerdmans, 1975), pp. 84–94. Fackre's chapter on conversion is a well-organized summary of the meaning of conversion as it is understood in this book. Conversion is primarily a turning, which always involves a "turning from something" and a "turning toward something." Conversion is turning to Christ in repentance and faith. *Epistrephein* always includes the element of faith. Since the connotation of *metanoia* is less broad (it refers to repentance), faith is often expressly used in a complementary way with it. If there is a distinction to be made between the two New Testament words, then *metanoia* emphasizes somewhat more strongly the element of turning away from the old, and *epistrephein* emphasizes turning toward the new (see Fackre, *Word in Deed*, p. 85).

6. This is only a partial listing of the innumerable threads that are part of the whole cloth of conversion. A more exhaustive list might include: from fear to hope, from spiritual blindness to the light of Christ, from idolatry to true worship, from control to relinquishment, from despair to joy, from wealth to simplicity, from the Bomb to the Cross, from alienation to reconciliation, from domination to servanthood, from anxiety to prayer, from false security to trust, from selfishness to sacrifice, from superiority to equality, from chauvinism to mutuality, from consumption to conservation, from accumulating to giving away, from hate to love of enemies, from swords to plowshares, from mammon to the God of the poor, from violence to peace, from exploitation to justice, from hardness of heart to compassion, from oppression to liberation, from individualism to community, from America first to Jesus first.

Conversion always means to turn to God. But what it means to turn to God is both universal and particular to each historical situation. We are called to respond to God always *in the particulars of* our own personal, social, and political circumstances. But conversion is also universal: it entails a reversal of the historical givens *whatever they may be* at any place and time—first-century Palestine, sixteenth-century Europe, or the United States in the 1980s. As such, conversion will be a scandal to accepted wisdoms, status quos, and oppressive arrangements. Looking back at biblical and saintly conversions, they can appear romantic. But in the present, conversion is more than a promise of all that might be; it is also a threat to all that is. To the guardians of the social order, genuine biblical conversion will seem dangerous.

In both the Old and New Testaments conversion involved a "change of lords."[7] Conversion from idolatry is a constant biblical theme: False gods enter the household of faith; alien deities command an allegiance that rightly belongs to God alone. The people, then as now, resisted the naming of their idols and stubbornly clung to them. What were the idols that lured the people of God? Which were the false gods that demanded service and fidelity? Our contemporary idols are not so different from those of biblical times: wealth, power, pride of self, pride of nation, sex, race, military might, etc. Conversion meant a turning away from the reigning idolatries and turning back to the true worship of the living God.

There are no neutral zones or areas of life left untouched by biblical conversion. It is never solely confined to the inner self, religious consciousness, personal morality, intellectual belief, or political opinion. Conversion in Scripture was not a self-improvement course or a set of guidelines to help people progress down the same road they were already traveling. Conversion was not just added to the life they were already living. The whole of life underwent conversion in the biblical accounts. There were no exceptions, limitations, or restrictions.

If we believe the Bible, every part of our lives belongs to the God who created us and intends to redeem us. No part of us stands apart from God's boundless love; no aspect of our lives remains untouched by the conversion that is God's call and God's gift to us. Biblically, conversion means to surrender ourselves to God in every sphere of human existence: the personal and social, the spiritual and economic, the psychological and political.

Conversion is our fundamental decision in regard to God. It marks nothing less than the ending of the old and the emergence of the new. "When anyone is united to Christ, there is a new world; the old order has gone, and a new order has already begun" (2 Cor. 5:17, NEB). Heart, mind, and soul, being, thinking, and doing—all are remade in the grace of God's redeeming love. This decision to allow ourselves to be remade, this conversion, is neither a static nor

---

7. Laubach, Goetzmann, and Becker, "Conversion," *NIDNT*, 1:355. "Conversion involves a change of lords. The one who until then has been under the lordship of Satan (cf. Eph. 2:1f.) comes under the lordship of God, and comes out of darkness into light (Acts 26:18; cf. Eph. 5:8)."

a once-and-finished event. It is both a moment and a process of transformation that deepens and extends through the whole of our lives. Many think conversion is only for nonbelievers, but the Bible sees conversion as also necessary for the erring believer, the lukewarm community of faith, the people of God who have fallen into disobedience and idolatry.[8]

The people of God are those who have been converted to God and to God's purposes in history. They define their lives by their relationship to the Lord. No longer are their lives organized around their own needs or the dictates of the ruling powers. They belong to the Lord and serve God alone. They have identified themselves with the kingdom of God in the world, and the measure of their existence is in doing God's will. Transformed by God's love, the converted experience a change in all their relationships: to God, to their neighbor, to the world, to their possessions, to the poor and dispossessed, to the violence around them, to the idols of their culture, to the false gods of the state, to their friends, and to their enemies. The early church was known for these things. In other words, the early Christians were known for the things their conversion wrought. Their conversion happened in history; and, in history, the fruits of their conversion were made evident.

Biblical conversion is never an ahistorical, metaphysical transaction affecting only God and the particular sinner involved. Conversion happens in individuals in history; it affects history and is affected by history. The biblical accounts of conversion demonstrate that conversion occurs *within* history; it is not something that occurs in a private realm apart from the world and is then *applied* to history.[9]

---

8. See Walter E. Conn, ed., *Conversion: Perspectives on Personal and Social Transformation* (Staten Island, N.Y.: Alba House, 1978). The overall thrust of this book is that conversion is a progressive, integrative process that has consequences in society—not merely in the spiritual life of the individual. Conversion is not a single event, but an ongoing process in which the totality of a person's life is transformed. Also see Orlando E. Costas, "Conversion as a Complex Experience: A Personal Case Study," in *Down to Earth: Studies in Christianity and Culture,* ed. John R. W. Stott and Robert Coote (Grand Rapids, Mich.: Eerdmans, 1980). In addition to showing that conversion is a continuous process, Costas emphasizes the "challenge of conversion inside the church. . . . In order to call others to conversion, it must be converted itself." Conversion is most often used for the turning of unbelievers for the first time to God (Acts 3:19; 26:20), but sometimes it is linked to erring believers (James 5:19f.) who are brought back into a right relation with God (see G. Bertram, "Epistrepho," *TDNT,* 7:727). Repentance (*metanoia*) can likewise be used of believers, and is found in reference to the problem of apostasy inside the church (Rev. 2:5, 16, 21, 22; 3:3, 19).

9. See Lesslie Newbigin, *The Finality of Christ* (Richmond: John Knox Press, 1969), pp. 93–94. Newbigin describes the historical characteristic of the call to conversion as found in the prophets and in John:

It is a call to concrete obedience here and now in the context of the actual issues of the day. . . . Conversion is [not] some sort of purely inward and spiritual experience which is later followed by a distinct and different decision to act in certain ways. The idea that one is first converted, and then looks round to see what one should do as a consequence, finds no basis in Scripture. And yet this idea (perhaps not usually expressed so crudely) is very common. . . . A careful study of the biblical use of the language of conversion, of returning to the Lord, will show that, on the contrary, it is always in the context of concrete decisions at the given historical moment.

The goal of biblical conversion is not to save souls apart from history but to bring the kingdom of God into the world with explosive force; it begins with individuals but is for the sake of the world. The more strongly present that goal is, the more genuinely biblical a conversion is. Churches today are tragically split between those who stress conversion but have forgotten its goal, and those who emphasize Christian social action but have forgotten the necessity for conversion. Today's converts need their eyes opened to history as much as today's activists need their spirit opened to conversion. But first, both need to recover the original meaning of conversion to Jesus Christ and to his kingdom. Only then can our painful division be healed and the integrity of the church's proclamation be restored. Only then can we be enabled to move beyond the impasse that has crippled and impoverished the churches for so long.

Conversion in the New Testament can only be understood from the perspective of the kingdom of God. The salvation of individuals and the fulfillment of the kingdom are intimately connected and are linked in the preaching of Jesus and the apostles. The powerful and compelling call to conversion in the Gospels arose directly out of the fact of an inbreaking new order. To be converted to Christ meant to give one's allegiance to the kingdom, to enter into God's purposes for the world expressed in the language of the kingdom. The disciples couldn't have given themselves to Jesus and then ignored the meaning of his kingdom for their lives and the world. Their conversion, like ours, can only be understood from the vantage point of the new age inaugurated in Jesus Christ. They joined him, followed him, transferred their allegiance to him, and, in so doing, became people of the new order. His gospel was the good news of the kingdom of God. There is no other gospel in the New Testament. The arrival of Jesus was the arrival of the kingdom.

Our conversion, then, cannot be an end in itself; it is the first step of entry into the kingdom. Conversion marks the birth of the movement out of a merely private existence into a public consciousness. Conversion is the beginning of active solidarity with the purposes of the kingdom of God in the world. No longer preoccupied with our private lives, we are engaged in a vocation for the world. Our prayer becomes, "Thy kingdom come, thy will be done, on earth as it is in heaven." If we restrict our salvation to only inner concerns, we have yet to enter into its fullness. Turning from ourselves to Jesus identifies us with him in the world. Conversion, then, is to public responsibility—but public responsibility as defined by the kingdom, not by the state. Our own salvation, which began with a personal decision about Jesus Christ, becomes intimately linked with the fulfillment of the kingdom of God. The connection between conversion and the kingdom cannot be emphasized enough.[10]

---

10. According to Newbigin, one of the "very practical and indeed painful" questions that conversion brings to a focus is the relation of Christ to our secular history:

> Conversion has always an ethical content; it involves not only joining a new community but also accepting a new pattern of conduct. Conversion implies that the convert accepts

But what if our particular conversion is misshaped by an inadequate preaching of the gospel or the church's lack of faith? What if our particular conversion event knows little of the intimate connection between conversion and the kingdom? We must submit our conversion to the standard of Scripture. Having stressed the importance of the kingdom, we will now turn to Jesus' own description of it.

The preaching of John the Baptist set the stage for Jesus. His radical call to repentance was clearly in the prophetic tradition, which always called the people of God to return. Jesus' preaching followed directly upon John's call to the people to repent and believe the good news of the kingdom which he came to announce. Both called for the fundamental turning that is always the substance of conversion. After the announcement of the kingdom, Jesus called his disciples and quickly moved on to set forth the meaning of his kingdom. His description of the new order is found in the Sermon on the Mount (Matt. 5–7; Luke 6). The Sermon explains what the kingdom is all about. Its message is clear and compelling. The Sermon is a practical vision of how to live in the new order and of what it will mean to follow Jesus. It is not a new law, but it is a vivid description of the kind of behavior involved in accepting the good news of the kingdom.

In fact, the Sermon on the Mount is the declaration of the kingdom of God, the charter of the new order. It describes the character, priorities, values, and norms of the new age Jesus came to inaugurate. The early church took it to be a basic teaching on the meaning of the kingdom; the Sermon as used to instruct new converts in the faith.

Examining the content of the Sermon, we quickly realize that this new order is not as theoretical and abstract as we might have hoped. It has to do with very concrete things. Jesus speaks to the basic stuff of human existence. He concerns himself with money, possessions, power, violence, anxiety, sexuality, faith and the law, security, true and false religion, the way we treat our neighbor, and the way we treat our enemies. At stake are not just religious issues. These are the basic questions that every man and woman must come to terms with and make choices about. The way we respond to these issues will determine our allegiance to the kingdom of God.

Yet, the sermon begins not with a list of obligations but with with a series of blessings. The beatitudes, as they are called, reveal the heart of Jesus and the core values of the kingdom. Jesus' blessings are for the poor, both in spirit and in substance. They know their need of God. He promises comfort to those who have learned how to weep for the world. Those with a meek and gentle spirit will have the earth for their possession. He blesses both those who are hungry for justice and those who show mercy; they will receive satisfaction and obtain

this new pattern of conduct as that which is relevant for the doing of God's will and the fulfillment of his reign at this particular juncture of world history. Every conversion is a particular event shaped by the experience of the convert and by the life of the Church as it is at that place and time (Newbigin, *The Finality of Christ*, p. 91).

mercy. It is the pure in heart, he says, who will see God. Jesus blesses the peace-makers and says they will be called God's own children. Finally, he blesses all those who suffer unjustly for the cause of right; the kingdom of heaven will be theirs. This is the personality of the kingdom. It is straightforward. It is both gentle and strong.

Jesus goes on to counsel his disciples to live simply and without hypocrisy. He tells them to trust God for their care and security rather than relying on the accumulation of possessions. In Luke's account of the beatitudes, Jesus pronounces a series of "woes" upon the rich and warns of the judgment that awaits them. He tells his followers to turn the other cheek when attacked and to go the extra mile when prevailed upon. Jesus instructs his disciples to love their enemies and not to return evil for evil. If they live this way, they will be like salt and light to the world. If they seek the kingdom of God first and value it above all else, everything they ever need will be theirs as well.

Jesus concludes by saying that his disciples, like good and bad trees, will be known by the fruit they bear. Not everyone who calls him Lord will enter the kingdom, but only those who obey his words. They will be like the wise person who builds a house solidly, on a good foundation; when the rains come, that person will be prepared. Those who don't listen to Jesus' words will be washed away because their houses are built on sand.

Blessing and cursing in the Bible are matters of life and death. Blessing is life and the power of God poured into our lives. Cursing is, inevitably, to die. Clear in the sermon is the fact that the specific things that Jesus blesses are the very things we most try to avoid. On the other hand, the things that are so opposite to the description of the kingdom are the things we seek most eagerly. We can only conclude that the values of the kingdom of God are utterly incompatible with our own values and the way of the world. Our culture rejects those who live in the way Jesus calls blessed. Only those who are willing to be despised by the world are ready to enter the kingdom of God. The sermon reveals that God's will for us is completely different from our own inclinations and social training.

The kingdom indeed represents a radical reversal for us. Aggrandizement, ambition, and aggression are normal to us and to our society. Money is the measure of respect, and power is the way to success. Competition is the character of most of our relationships, and violence is regularly sanctioned by our culture as the final means to solve our deepest conflicts. The scriptural advice "Be anxious for nothing" challenges the heart of our narcissistic culture, which, in fact, is anxious over everything. To put it mildly, the Sermon on the Mount offers a way of life contrary to what we are accustomed. It overturns our assumptions of what is normal, reasonable, and responsible. To put it more bluntly, the Sermon stands our values on their heads.

Not everyone responded to this upside-down value system the way the fishermen did. The chief priests and scribes were critical and unbelieving from the beginning. These leaders of society, the holders of wealth and power, plotted against Jesus, mocked him, and sought to destroy him. They wielded religious and political authority. Jesus showed no respect or deference toward any of them. Some of his harshest words were reserved for them. He called them "hyp-ocrites" and "vipers"; he referred to his political ruler as a "fox." Jesus' teach-ing and behavior created conflict with the ruling authorities wherever he went. The kingdom he proclaimed undermined their whole system. His confrontation with the religious and economic powers in the temple was the incident that led to his crucifixion.[11]

To receive his kingdom, Jesus said we had to become as open as children (Mark 10:13–15). Wealth would be a great obstacle (Mark 10:21–25). Pride, self-satisfaction, and complacency would be enemies of his kingdom. Jesus said he came not to save those who already considered themselves righteous, but to call sinners to repentance (Mark 2:17). Humility would be necessary for conver-sion (Luke 18:10–14).

The Gospels and the book of Acts record examples of many conversions. The theme is constant. The good news of salvation created a changed heart and life in those who heard and received. Whether in Paul's language of being justified by faith instead of works, or in John's picture of passing from darkness to light, the movement is one from death to life.

The early Christians were referred to as the people of "the Way."[12] There is a lot in a name.

First, it is highly significant that they were called the people of *the Way*. Chris-tians at the beginning were associated with a particular pattern of life. Their faith produced a discernible lifestyle, a way of life, a process of growth visible to all. This different style of living and relating both grew out of their faith and gave testimony to that faith. To all who saw, Christian belief became identified with a certain kind of behavior. Unlike our modern experience, there was an unmis-takable Christian lifestyle recognized by believers and nonbelievers alike. That style of life followed the main lines of Jesus' Sermon on the Mount and his other teaching. To believe meant to follow Jesus. There was little doubt in anyone's mind: Christian discipleship revolved around the hub of the kingdom. The faith of these first Christians had clear social results. They became well known as a

---

11. See Richard J. Cassidy, *Jesus, Politics and Society: A Study of Luke's Gospel* (Maryknoll, N.Y.: Orbis Books, 1980). A good summary of relevant material about Jesus' relationship to the authorities can be found in chapter 4, "Jesus and His Political Rulers" (pp. 50–62). Several appendices provide helpful historical background about the Romans and the religious rulers of Jesus' day.

12. See Acts 9:2; 19:9, 23; 22:4; 24:14, 22. While the word *way* is used both literally and figuratively more than one hundred times in the New Testament, its use in an unconditional and absolute sense as a name for the Christian movement is unique to these six passages in Acts. English translations usually capitalize it as "the Way," which becomes a designation for the Christian community and its preaching. G. Ebel, "Way," *NIDNT*, 3:933–947; Wilhelm Michaelis, "Hodos," *TDNT*, 5:42–114.

While the origin of the self-designation has not yet been fully explained, most scholars would agree that the Christian's unique lifestyle contributed to the name. The dictionaries mentioned above emphasize this term as a "designation for Christians and their proclamation of Jesus Christ, which includes the fact that this proclamation also comprises a particular walk or life or way," and refer to "the mode of life which comes to expression in the Christian fellowship."

caring, sharing, and open community that was especially sensitive to the poor and the outcast. Their love for God, for one another, and for the oppressed was central to their reputation. Their refusal to kill, to recognize racial distinctions, or to bow down before the imperial deities was a matter of public knowledge.

Aristides described the Christians to the Roman emperor Hadrian in this way:

> They love one another. They never fail to help widows; they save orphans from those who would hurt them. If they have something they give freely to the man who has nothing; if they see a stranger, they take him home, and are happy, as though he were a real brother. They don't consider themselves brothers in the usual sense, but brothers instead through the Spirit, in God.[13]

The early Christians were known for the way they lived, not only for what they believed. For them, the two were completely intertwined.[14] The earliest title given to them reflected the importance of their kingdom lifestyle. They were not called the people of "the experience" or the people of "right doctrine" or even the people of "the church." Rather, they were the people of "the Way."

Second, it is equally significant that the Christians were known as *the people of the Way*.[15] More than just individuals who had been converted, they were now a people, a new community of faith, which had embarked together on a new way of life. The first thing Jesus did after announcing the kingdom was to gather a community. To follow Jesus meant to share Jesus' life and to share it with others. From the beginning, the kingdom would be made manifest through

---

13. From Aristides, Apology 15, in *The Ante-Nicene Fathers*, ed. Allan Menzies, 5th edition (New York: Charles Scribner's Sons, 1926), 9:263–279.

14. The pagan religions of the day stood in stark contrast to Christian faith both in their separation of belief from behavior and in their refusal to require exclusive loyalty to any one god. As we have seen, biblical conversion demanded a total change of life direction: it forged the vital connection between faith and discipleship, and it called for absolute allegiance to the true and living God. The claim made on the lives of Christian converts was total, unlike the partial and syncretistic observances of the pagan deities. In an atmosphere of lukewarm religious pluralism, the single-minded commitment of Christian conversion "stood out like a sore thumb," says Michael Green. There is a good study of this contrast in the "conversion" chapter (chapter 6) of Green's *Evangelism in the Early Church* (Grand Rapids, Mich.: Eerdmans, 1970): "Helenistic man did not regard ethics as part of religion. . . . This separation of belief from behavior was one of the fundamental differences between the best of pagan philosophical religion and Christian religion. . . . Conversion, then, in our sense of an exclusive change of faith, of ethic, of cult was indeed utterly foreign to the mentality of the Graeco-Roman world" (p. 146).

A. D. Nock's classic study, *Conversion* (London: Oxford University Press, 1933), comes to the same conclusion. Christian conversion "demanded a new life in a new people" and was a radical change in behavior as well as belief (p. 7f). This all-encompassing quality of conversion is stressed by Nock's contrast between Christian conversion and what he calls general religious "adhesion." Adhesion is the label-changing kind of conversion that was characteristic of other religious cults.

15. One recent study concludes that the amazing spread of early Christianity was due to "a single, over-riding *internal* factor . . . the radical sense of Christian community—open to all, insistent on absolute and exclusive loyalty, and concerned for every aspect of the believer's life. From the very beginning, the one distinctive gift of Christianity was this sense of community." J. C. Gager, *Kingdom and Community: The Social World of Early Christianity* (Englewood Cliffs, N.J.: Prentice Hall, 1975), p. 140.

a people who shared a common life. Their visible fellowship would be the sign and the first fruits of God's new order begun in Jesus Christ. Those who had left everything to follow Jesus were given the gift of community with one another. Henceforth they would belong to Jesus and be inextricably bound together as brothers and sisters in the family of God. The call of Jesus was not only to a new commitment; it was also to a new companionship, a new community established by conversion.

The quality of life shared in the Christian community was a vital part of the evangelistic message of the early church. Christian fellowship became the companion of the Christian gospel; demonstration was vitally linked to proclamation. The oneness of word and deed, dramatically evident in their life together, lent power and force to the witness of the early Christians. In a classic study of evangelism in the early church, Michael Green concludes: "They made the grace of God credible by a society of love and mutual care which astonished the pagans and was recognized as something entirely new. It lent persuasiveness to their claim that the New Age had dawned in Christ."[16] The word was not only announced but seen in the community of those who were giving it flesh.

The message of the kingdom became more than an idea. A new human society had sprung up, and it looked very much like the new order to which the evangelists pointed. Here love was given daily expression; reconciliation was actually occurring. People were no longer divided into Jew and Gentile, slave and free, male and female. In this community the weak were protected, the stranger welcomed. People were healed, and the poor and dispossessed were cared for and found justice. Everything was shared, joy abounded, and ordinary lives were filled with praise. Something was happening among these Christians that no one could deny. It was very exciting. According to Tertullian, people looked at the early Christians and exclaimed, "See how they love one another!"[17] The fervent character of Christian love not only bound them to one another; it also spilled over the boundaries of their own communities and extended to all in need. The economic sharing practiced by the early Christians, together with their generosity toward the poor, was one of the most evangelistic characteristics of their life. Radical, practical love became the key to their public reputation.

The basic movement of conversion is a change of allegiance to the kingdom of God, the good news which Jesus brings. To convert means to commit our lives unreservedly to Jesus Christ, to join his new order, and to enter into the fellowship of the new community. Our sins are forgiven, we are reconciled to God and to our neighbor, and our destiny becomes inextricably bound to the purposes of Christ in the world.

16. Michael Green, *Evangelism in the Early Church,* p. 120.
17. This is quoted from Tertullian's *Apology 39* in William J. Walsh and John P. Langan, "Patristic Social Consciousness: The Church and the Poor," *The Faith That Does Justice: Examining the Christian Sources for Social Change,* ed. John C. Haughey (New York: Paulist Press, 1977), p. 138.

Evangelism is to this end. The purpose of evangelism is to call for conversion and to call for it in its wholeness. The most controversial question at stake in the world, and even in the church, is whether we will follow Jesus and live under the banner of his kingdom. The evangelist asks that question and aims it right at the heart of each individual and at the heartbeat of our society. Evangelism confronts each person with the decisive choice about Jesus and the kingdom, and it challenges the oppression of the old order with the freeing power of a new one. The gospel of the kingdom sparks a fundamental change in every life and is an intrusion into any social order, be it first-century culture or our twentieth-century world. Evangelism that is faithful to the New Testament will never separate the salvation of the individual from visible witness to God's kingdom on earth. Rather, biblical evangelists will show people how to "cast off the works of darkness" and how to live "as in the day" (Rom. 13:12, 13 RSV), in the light of the kingdom that is coming and has already begun in Christ Jesus.

In every renewal movement since the time of the early church, the true nature of conversion has been freed from the narrow limitations and restrictions imposed by the world, and the wholeness of conversion recovered. The power of evangelism is restored and the gospel again becomes a message that turns things upside down. The task of the evangelist is not to make the gospel easy but to make it clear. Instead of merely passing on knowledge or imparting an experience, evangelism should call for (and expect) a radical change in behavior and lifestyle.

The unequivocal assertion of the evangelist is that we are saved only through Jesus Christ. Evangelism refutes every ideological prescription for the salvation of the world, defying the suggestion that we can, after all, save ourselves.

The recovery of the fullness and centrality of conversion is essential to genuine renewal. The monastic movements of the Middle Ages, the radical reformation of the sixteenth century, and the evangelical revivals in eighteenth-century England and nineteenth-century America were each marked by a primary emphasis on conversion. That emphasis continues today in the revolutionary consciousness of Third World Christians. Gustavo Gutierrez calls conversion "the touchstone of all spirituality."[18]

Our need, in the rich countries of the northern hemisphere, is for a fresh consciousness of conversion. In the midst of social conditions so oppressive to others and to ourselves, we must again turn to Jesus. Then will authentic evangelism flower and genuine revival break forth in this land once more. But first we must examine and honestly face up to the ways our evangelism has been corrupted and our conversion distorted.

18. Gustavo Gutierrez, *A Theology of Liberation*, trans. and ed. by Sr. Caridad Inda and John Eagleson (Maryknoll, N.Y.: Orbis Books, 1973), p. 205.

Chapter 7

"Love Is Stronger than Hate" and "The Reconciled Community"

1982

John Perkins

That was the night God gave me a real compassion for whites—the night those Mississippi police officers beat me almost to death.

It was Saturday, February 7, 1970, about 6:30 p.m. The sun was just going down. Two vans driven by Louise Fox and Doug Huemmer were returning students to Tougaloo College near Jackson from Mendenhall where they had joined us in a civil rights march. In Plain, Mississippi, a few miles after the vans rolled over the line separating Simpson County from Rankins County, the highway patrol car that had trailed them from Mendenhall flashed on its blue lights and cut in between the two vans signaling for Doug to pull over.

A few minutes later our phone was ringing. It was Louise. "The people in Doug's van have been taken to the Brandon jail."

Reverend Curry Brown, Joe Paul Buckley and I set out for the Rankin County Jail in Brandon to set bail for Doug and his group.

During the 45-minute drive up highway 49 my mind churned. Why had the policeman let Louise go? To call me? Was it a trap? Was another ambush waiting for us on highway 49?

We got to the county courthouse and jail and a highway patrolman showed us where to park. We had met no ambush on the highway. We got out of the car and told the patrolman, "We'd like to see the sheriff."

"Okay," he said. "You stay here and I'll go tell him you're here." Moments later out of the building came not Sheriff Edwards but a dozen highway patrolmen. They searched us, arrested us and even before they got us to the building started beating us. It was an ambush after all!

Inside the jail house the nightmare only got worse. At least five deputy sheriffs and seven to twelve highway patrolmen went to work on us. Sheriff Edwards joined in.

Here's how I described that scene later in the court trial: "When I got to the jail and saw the people in jail, of course I was horrified as to why we were arrested and when I got in the jail Sheriff Jonathan Edwards came over to me right away and said, 'This is the smart nigger, and this is a new ballgame. You're not in Simpson County now; you are in Brandon.' . . . He began to beat me, and from that time on they continued beating me. I was just beat to the floor and just punched and really beaten."[1]

Manorris Odom, one of the Tougaloo students there, testified that Sheriff Edwards beat me so hard that his "shirt tail came out."[2] During the beatings I tried to cover my head with my arms, but they beat me anyway till I was lying on the floor. Even then they just kept on beating and stomping me, kicking me in the head, in the ribs, in the groin. I rolled up into a ball to protect myself as best I could. And the beatings just went on and on.

It got worse as the night wore on. One officer brought a fork over to me and said, "Do you see this?" And he jammed it up my nose. Then he crammed it down my throat. Then they beat me to the ground again and stomped on me.

Because I was unconscious a lot of the time I don't remember a whole lot about the others. I do know that Doug and some of the students were beaten, and that Curry probably suffered the most of any of us.

And I remember their faces—so twisted with hate. It was like looking at white-faced demons. For the first time I saw what hate had done to those people. These policemen were poor. They saw themselves as failures. The only way they knew how to find a sense of worth was by beating us. Their racism made them feel like "somebody."

When I saw that, I just couldn't hate back. I could only pity them. I said to God that night, "God, if you will let me get out of this jail alive"—and I really didn't think I would, maybe I was trying to bargain with Him—"I really want to preach a gospel that will heal these people, too."

1. Perkins vs. State of Mississippi, p.18
2. Perkins vs. State of Mississippi, p. 9, 19.

Well, although the students who watched over me through the night in that jail cell were sure for a while that I was dead or about to die, I came out alive—and with a new call. My call to preach the gospel now extended to whites.

That night in the Brandon jail I had for the first time seen how the white man was a victim of his own racism. For the first time I wanted to bring him a gospel that could set him free. But that was only a start. I still harbored in my heart a deep-seated bitterness against whites for all they had done to me and my family. It went back to that night when Clyde was shot. Back beyond that to my mother's death. As my case went through the Mississippi courts and the majority of judges proved to be just as racist as the policemen who had almost killed me, my bitterness grew. There was no justice for a black man!

My beating and the frustration and bitterness that followed took their toll. In July of 1970 I had a heart attack. I was hospitalized in Mound Bayou, a small black community where I had helped organize some co-ops. After a partial recovery I found myself back in the same hospital with ulcers. Dr. Harvey Sanders, a black doctor, had to take out two-thirds of my stomach.

Lying in that hospital bed I had a lot of time to think. I thought about blacks and whites. About how, in a country that claimed to stand for "liberty and justice for all," a black man in Mississippi could get no justice. I thought about how in Mississippi, "Christians" were the most racist whites of all. How white preachers were in on most of the murders of civil rights leaders. How Sunday School teachers were leading members of the Klan. I thought of how the white "Christian" businessmen supported the whole economic system which exploited blacks. And I began to think that maybe there was only one way to go—to give up on whites and white Christians and just work for me and mine.

I could start a little gospel radio station right there in Mound Bayou that would broadcast to the blacks all through the delta area. I could feature Bible preaching and good gospel music, and Vera Mae and I could live here in Mound Bayou where there were no more than half a dozen whites. We could just leave all that struggle behind us.

But when I was most tempted to give up, about to decide that the gospel couldn't reconcile—at least not in Mendenhall, two doctors administered healing to my spirit even as they cared for my body. Dr. Joanne Roberts, one of the few white persons in the center, and Dr. Sanders, a black, were themselves images of hope—living examples of reconciliation.

Hope began to flicker again.

I thought of the white people in Mendenhall who had not bowed their knees to Baal. There was Mr. Neely, the head of the savings and loan who had gotten blacks to save there, and blacks had benefited from it. When many people involved in the civil rights movement had trouble getting credit, Mr. Neely never turned his back on us.

There was Mr. Boyles who carried our insurance. While other churches lost their insurance because they were involved in civil rights, we didn't lose insurance on anything—our church building, our car, or any of our facilities—because Mr. Boyles stuck with us.

And then there was Mr. Barnett, a blacksmith and piano tuner. Growing up in the black community of Hawlpond, he had sung gospel music in black churches. Probably because of the friendships he formed growing up, he never turned his back on blacks. He helped us put our old school bus body on a new chassis, tuned up our piano, and supported us every way he could.

So a few white people in Mendenhall stood out as glimmers of hope. And even when things looked darkest, when I most wanted to run, I couldn't get away from my new call—God had called me to take the gospel to whites, too.

The Spirit of God worked on me as I lay in that bed. An image formed in my mind—the image of a cross, of Christ on the cross. This Jesus knew what I had suffered. He understood. He cared. Because He had gone through it all Himself.

He too was arrested and falsely accused. He too had an unjust trial. He too was beaten. Then He was nailed to a cross and killed like a common criminal. But when He looked at the mob who had crucified Him, He didn't hate them; He loved them! And He prayed, "Father forgive them; for they do not know what they are doing" (Luke 23:34).

His enemies hated, but He forgave. God wouldn't let me escape that. He showed me that however unjustly I had been treated, in my bitterness and hatred I was just as sinful as those who had beaten me. And I needed forgiveness for my bitterness.

I read Matthew 6:14, 15 again and again in that bed: "For if you forgive men for their transgressions, your heavenly Father will also forgive you. But if you do not forgive men, then your Father will not forgive your transgressions." To receive God's forgiveness, I was going to have to forgive those who had hurt me. As I prayed, the faces of those policemen passed before me one by one, and I forgave each one. Faces of other white people from the past came before me, and I forgave them. I could sense that God was working a deep inner healing in me that went far back beyond February 7, 1970. It went clear back to my earliest memories of childhood. God was healing all those wounds that had kept me from loving whites. How sweet God's forgiveness and healing was!

As soon as that happened I saw how these unhealed memories had limited God's will. I recalled a scene from 12 or 13 years before. I was still in California. God had just started talking to me about coming back to Mississippi. It was on one of those days that I went with the Christian businessmen to share my testimony in a prison camp. As the car climbed that Southern California mountain road I turned to Ed Anthony beside me. "Ed, God is calling me to preach the gospel to black people."

"John," he responded, "God may be calling you to preach the gospel to everybody—not just blacks." When Ed said that, I don't think I fully understood how much he was saying.

I came to Mississippi convinced that because of the historical oppression of my people, God was calling me to preach the gospel especially to blacks. My whole drive for those first 10 years was to lift blacks from their oppression. I heard the voices calling for black self-determination and black liberation, and accepted that. What I really wanted in the sixties was for the white man to leave us alone, to let us be. Because of the hostility, I had very little contact with the white Mississippi community.

Even as I felt this way, I knew in my mind that the gospel was supposed to reconcile people across economic, racial, and social barriers. But that all just seemed theoretical until Brandon. At Brandon God showed me how racism had psychologically damaged whites just as much as it had blacks. Through those sick men, God showed me the need to take a gospel of love to whites filled with hate.

I was beginning to understand what Ed Anthony meant. The same gospel that frees blacks also frees whites. You can't free one without the other. I was beginning to see what Martin Luther King saw long before: our destiny was tied to their destiny. What liberated me liberated them; what liberated them liberated me.

Demanding our rights had not softened the white community as we hoped it would. Instead, it had stiffened their opposition. Lying there on my bed I was able to see that confronting white people with hostility was only going to create war. If there was going to be any healing it would have to take place in an atmosphere of love. I had been trying to demand justice. Now God was opening my eyes to a new and better strategy—seeking reconciliation. I could not bring justice for other people. As a Christian, my responsibility was to seek to be reconciled. Then out of that reconciliation, justice would flow.

Affirmative action, integration, and so on, might be useful, but they alone were not justice. Real justice would never be achieved by passing laws or going to court. "Many seek the ruler's favor, but justice for man comes from the Lord" (Prov. 29:26 NASB). True justice could come only as people's hearts were made right with God and God's love motivated them to be reconciled to each other.

Now that God had enabled me to forgive the many whites who had wronged me, I found myself able to truly love them. I wanted to return good for evil. In my own life God had cleansed away bitterness and hatred and replaced it with love. If He could do that in my life, He could do it in other people too—whether black or white.

A hope began to take root. God could heal the bitterness of blacks and replace it with forgiveness. God could forgive whites. He could move them beyond guilt-motivated patronization to responsible partnership with blacks in working for justice. How that could be achieved I didn't know. But God called me. He gave me the dream. He would make it happen. . . .

To carve out of the heart of Jackson, Mississippi a community of believers reconciled to God and to each other—that was our dream. To bring together a fellowship of blacks and whites, rich and poor, who would live together, worship together and reach out together as the people of God. We believed that if we would faithfully be the people of God in our neighborhood we could make a positive difference in the lives of people enslaved by poverty and racism.

Others might have thought our dream absurd or impossible. Yet H. and I, our families, and the sending fellowship at Mendenhall dared to believe it was possible for one reason: God said so. His Word made it clear that racial reconciliation was not only possible, but mandatory for the Body of Christ. God, that night in the Brandon jail, called me to take the gospel to whites as well as blacks. And now it seemed clear to me and Vera Mae, to H. and Terry, and to the Mendenhall fellowship, that Jackson was to be our next mission field.

We wanted our church to be much more than a worshiping congregation; we wanted it to be the family of God, the Body of Christ within our community. To really function as Christ's Body we would each have to recognize the unique spiritual gifts which each person brought to the fellowship. We would have to recognize that we could not truly operate as a Body unless we used our spiritual gifts to minister to each other, to sharpen each other. And then we would have to blend our gifts together in reaching out into the neighborhood in a way that would meet the needs of people and bring glory to Christ . . .

Though Mississippi might not have offered any historical precedents for a reconciled fellowship, the book of Acts did. We drew inspiration particularly from the Antioch fellowship—a church which demonstrated both the possibility and the necessity of reconciliation within the Body of Christ.

"Now there were at Antioch, in the church that was there, prophets and teachers: Barnabas, and Simeon who was called Niger, and Lucius of Cyrene, and Manaen who had been brought up with Herod the tetrarch, and Saul" (Acts 13:1). This one verse reveals a lot about the church at Antioch. The leadership team included black—Simon called Niger, and white—Gentile Lucius of Cyrene, and Jew—aristocrat Manaen, and the common man. The fellowship of Antioch transcended racial, cultural, and social barriers. Not only were these groups represented in the congregation, they were its leaders. Evidently there weren't any Jews saying, "Now you black folk come from a bad background, and what you've got to do is study and work your way up, and when you get it all together you can be a teacher." Rather, it seems the Holy Spirit spontaneously gifted those He chose and brought them together into a unified team.

Now that doesn't mean that the Antioch church was without its tensions. When the Jewish Christians first went there they preached the gospel only to Jews. It was not until Christians from Cyprus and Cyrene—evidently converted at Pentecost—came to Antioch that the gospel was preached to the Greeks (see Acts 11:19, 20).

Then Peter touched off a tense situation. While he was visiting in Antioch, Jews from the circumcision party arrived. Fearing their criticism Peter quit eating with the Gentiles. Then the rest of the Jews from that local fellowship followed Peter's lead. Even Barnabas gave in to the pressure.

Paul minced no words about the seriousness of Peter's sin. He said that Peter "stood condemned" (Gal. 2:11 RSV), that his act was "hypocrisy" (v. 13) and that the Jews were not being "straightforward about the truth of the gospel" (v. 14 RSV). So severe was Peter's offense that Paul publicly rebuked him before the whole church. For the Jews to hold themselves separate from the Gentiles when God had declared them one was to violate the very truth of the gospel.

And so it is today. When blacks and whites who have worked and shopped and studied and eaten side by side all week go to segregated churches on Sunday morning at 11:00 A.M., the gospel itself is betrayed. Where I come from in Mississippi, I don't know what we assume the gospel is supposed to do. If the gospel doesn't bring you into relationship with God, then bring you into relationship with your fellowman, then make you want to bring other people into that relationship, I can't imagine what the gospel is for.

The only purpose of the gospel is to reconcile people to God and to each other. But in America it seems as if we don't believe that. We don't really believe that the proof of our discipleship is that we love one another (see John 13:35). No, we think the proof is in numbers—church attendance, decision cards. Even if our "converts" continue to hate each other, even if they will not worship with their brothers and sisters in Christ, we point to their "conversion" as evidence of the gospel's success. We have substituted a gospel of church growth for a gospel of reconciliation.

And how convenient it is that our "church growth experts" tell us that homogenous churches grow fastest! That welcome news seems to relieve us of the responsibility to overcome racial barriers in our churches. It seems to justify not bothering with breaking down racial barriers, since that would only distract us from "church growth." And so the most segregated racist institution in America, the evangelical church, racks up the numbers, declaring itself "successful," oblivious to the fact that the dismemberment of the Body of Christ broadcasts to the world every day a hypocrisy as blatant as Peter's at Antioch—a living denial of the truth of the gospel.

Black separatism and white exclusiveness often grow out of a fear of what interracial relationships might bring. Our exclusiveness is our attempt to avoid suffering and conflict. Whenever two different groups of any kind come together, there is conflict. For that conflict to be resolved, somebody has to take the heat. The work of reconciliation calls for a leader who can draw out that hostility, who can accept that hostility himself, and who can bring together the conflicting people or groups.

Jesus, the Great Reconciler, suffered the agony of all our sins—an agony far beyond our comprehension. Yet without that suffering there would have been no reconciliation. We would still be God's enemies. If we are going to share in Christ's mission we must also share in His suffering. "For to you it has been granted for Christ's sake, not only to believe in Him, but also to suffer for His sake" (Phil. 1:29 NASB). We cannot follow Christ without taking up our crosses (see Matt. 10:38).

James says, "Consider it all joy, my brethren, when you encounter various trials; knowing that the testing of your faith produces endurance. And let endurance have its perfect result, that you may be perfect and complete, lacking in nothing" (Jas. 1:2–4 NASB). I think James needed to think of a word other than "joy" because it's not going to be joyful. But it is going to be good and it's going to be healthy. We must not try to avoid the suffering and short-circuit this process. Even when we ask for physical healing our primary motive should not be to end the suffering, but rather to be able to throw our whole bodies back into God's work again.

H. and I were under no illusion that the work in Jackson would be easy. Most blacks didn't want whites in their churches, and most whites didn't want blacks in their churches. What we were coming to establish, most people didn't want. To be reconcilers in a racist city we would have to suffer the hostility of both blacks and whites.

The duty to "bear one another's burdens" (Gal. 6:2 NASB) takes on added meaning in an interracial fellowship. When a white brother comes to the community he's bringing all his superiority and all his guilt which society has put on him. I must be able and willing to absorb that if we are to be reconciled.

And my white brother in the community must also recognize that I bring my history of being treated inferior, of being told I am a nobody, a nigger. He must understand that I am trying to claim my worth as a person created in God's image. So he must bear the burden of all my bitterness and anger that grows out of my past.

To be reconciled to each other, then, we must bear the burdens created by each other's pasts. And to be reconcilers in the world, to bring others together, we must bear the burdens of both the parties we seek to reconcile.

Since we wanted our ministry to be to both blacks and whites, we chose a target neighborhood which was about 80 percent white, and turning black. At the rate it was changing over, it would be all black in four or five years. In establishing our community there, one of our goals was to transform the neighborhood into one where blacks and whites would live together in harmony.

We bought a big house in our target area which we called the Four C Center—the Center for Continuous Christian Community. H. and Terry moved into it. The Four C Center was seven blocks from the Jackson State University campus, a black university where we wanted to establish a ministry.

From the beginning we were convinced that the ministry had to be based in Christian community. We had to be based in community because only that kind of intense interdependence—an actual sharing of our lives—could mold us into the kind of ministry team that could make a strong positive impact on our neighborhood. And we needed to be a Christian community because community would provide just the right kind of laboratory for working out the tough nitty-gritty of reconciliation.

Chapter 8

"Biblical Faith and the Reality of Social Evil"

1982

Stephen Charles Mott

In the time of Jesus, violence and oppression led people to see underlying the lawless deeds of humanity a structure of evil, personified by fallen angels. Some Israelite visionaries believed that events of the days of Noah explained their own. The bloody warriors then raging over their Mediterranean world were like the giants in Noah's day, the offspring of the rebellious chief angel, Shemihazah, and other "sons of God" who followed him. The treacherous technology of the making and using of metal and weapons had been taught to humankind by Asael, another chief of angels. In response to the pleas of humanity, God had provided (and would again provide) deliverance. God sent the mighty angels Michael and Gabriel to "bind Asael" and "to bind Shemihazah and his companions," so that the evil on the face of the earth might be destroyed and a new age of justice and truth brought in (1 Enoch 6–11).[1]

---

1. For this interpretation of 1 Enoch 6–11, see George W. E. Nickelsburg, "Apocalyptic and Myth in 1 Enoch 6–11," *Journal of Biblical Literature* 96 (1977): 383–405; Nickelsburg, *1 Enoch 1: A Commentary on the Book of 1 Enoch, Chapters 1–36*; 81–108, Hermeneia (Minneapolis, Minn.: Fortress, 2001), 137–232. The Shemihazah material is basic to the passage and tentatively goes back to the wars of the Diadochi at the end of the fourth century B.C. The Asael material was added later.

The explanation of the injustices of history through reference to angels may seem unrelated to the economic and political problems of our communities. But as we shall see this overshadowing community of evil described by New Testament writers as "the powers" is cited frequently in recent efforts to provide a biblical account of the contemporary social situation.[2] Such personages as Shemihazah and Asael, along with the New Testament concept of *the world (cosmos),* may help us to see that injustice and other evils not only depend upon the decisions of individuals but also are rooted in manifestations of culture and social order. This recognition affects our understanding of the spiritual struggle and victory in which we participate, for God has "disarmed the powers and the authorities and made a public mockery of them, leading them as captives in Christ" (Col. 2.15). These biblical concepts relate to phenomena that can be sociologically described, and they extend rather than nullify personal responsibility in society.

THE WORLD AS THE EVIL SOCIAL ORDER

A basic way of describing evil in the New Testament uses the term *cosmos,* "the world." This word refers to the order of society and indicates that evil has a social and political character beyond the isolated actions of individuals.

It is unfortunate that *cosmos* has been translated in English Bibles as *world,* which primarily refers to a physical place. The Greek term, *cosmos,* however, essentially means *order, that which is assembled together well.* In this sense it is used in a variety of ways. Adornments that make a woman beautiful are thought to "make her orderly." So I Peter 3.3 admonishes wives not to let their "external adornment [or *order (cosmos)*] be with braided hair, gold ornaments, or dressing in robes." From such usage comes our term *cosmetics.*

The term naturally came to be attached to the most important ordering of earthly life, the social order. It referred to the structures of civilized life and specifically the civic order represented by the city-state, which among other things secured the bonds of friendship in the face of the threat of social chaos (Plato, *Prot.* 322c).[3] As *cosmos,* the universe itself is a city-state. Plato wrote, "Heaven and earth and gods and people are held together by sharing and friendship and

---

2. See, among others, Walter Wink, *The Powers,* 3 vols. (Minneapolis, Minn.: Fortress, 1984–1993); John Howard Yoder, *The Politics of Jesus* (Grand Rapids, Mich.: Eerdmans, 1994), 139–161 [1972, 140-162]); Jim Wallis, *Agenda for Biblical People* (New York: Harper, 1976), 63–77; Richard J. Mouw, *Politics and the Biblical Drama* (Grand Rapids, Mich.: Eerdmans, 1976), 85–116; and C. Peter Wagner, *Confronting the Powers: How the New Testament Church Experienced the Power of Strategic Level Spiritual Warfare* (Venture, Calif.; Regal, 1996). The work most influential upon the early phase of the current discussion was Hendrikus Berkhof, *Christ and the Powers* (Scottdale, Pa.: Herald, 1962). The purpose of this chapter is to clarify and validate the thrust of these writers.

3. See Hermann Sasse, "Kosmos," *TDNT* (1965), 3.868; Tebtunis Papyri 45.20; 47.12 (113 B.C.); George W. Redding, "KOSMOS from Homer to St. John," *Asbury Seminarian* 4 (1949): 63.

self-control and justice; therefore the universe [*to holon*] is called *cosmos*, not disorder [*acosmia*] or licentiousness" (*Gorg.* 508a).

The New Testament uses cosmos in a variety of ways. Among these, it can mean all people (John 3.16), the inhabitants of the universal social order. But most striking and most important theologically is a usage that picks up the meaning of social order that I have discussed, but with a difference. For classical Greece, *cosmos* protected values and life, but in the apocalyptic thought patterns of first-century Judaism, and particularly of the New Testament,[4] *cosmos* represents the twisted values that threatened genuine human life. For Plato the order stood guard against licentiousness; now the order is the intruder bearing immorality. Paul writes that to avoid the immoral persons of the social order (*cosmos*) one would have to leave human society *(cosmos)* altogether (I Cor. 5.10). Ephesians 2.1–2 provides another example. The author refers to the individual "trespasses and sins" of the Gentile readers of the letter and then describes the greater order of evil after which their individual acts were patterned: "You were dead through the trespasses and sins in which you once lived, following the course of this world [*cosmos*], following the ruler of the power of the air, the spirit that is now at work among those who are disobedient" (NRSV).

There is no radical distinction between the actions of the person as an individual and as a social being. Evil exists in the society outside the individual and exerts an influence upon him or her (cf. Rom. 12.2 with *aiōn* for *society*).

The basic fiber of society is comprehended in the New Testament use of *cosmos*. It includes the system of property and wealth: I John 3.17 speaks of "whoever has the world's means of livelihood [*bios tou cosmou*]."[5] It thus includes necessary economic relationships; Paul admonishes his readers to "make use of the world" (meaning the essential functions from which one cannot get away) but not to "overuse" it (I Cor. 7.31). The world also has a stratification of class and status. Reference is made to the poor, foolish, weak, and lowly of the world (James 2.5; I Cor. 1.27–28). Paul associates the world with status distinctions based on religion (Gal. 6.14–15 [circumcision]; cf. Gal. 3.28 [slavery and sexual status]).[6] The world has its "wisdom" (I Cor. 1.20), its system of learning. The political rule of societies also belongs to this order (Matt. 4.8). In Revelation 11.15 heavenly voices shout, "The kingdom of the world has become the kingdom of our Lord." *Cosmos* here is grammatically parallel to "our Lord." Both terms indicate the sovereign force (subjective genitives): "the kingdom ruled by the world has become the kingdom ruled by our Lord." The government had been controlled by the evil social order but was now to be subject to Christ. Finally, the most characteristic social aspect of *cosmos* in the New Testament is a

---

4. Sasse, "Kosmos," 891.

5. Bios in 1 John 2.16 and 3.17 signifies means of subsistence, property, wealth (see Bauer, *Lexicon*, 177; Rudolf Schnackenburg, *The Johannine Epistles* (New York: Crossroad, 1992 (1984), 122.

6. For a discussion of *cosmos* and the powers as structuring the hostile divisions of humankind, see Paul S. Minear, *To Die and to Live* (New York; Seabury, 1977), 66–106; see Amos N. Wilder, *Kerygma, Eschatology, and Social Ethics,* Facet Books, Social Ethics 12 (Philadelphia: Fortress, 1966), 28.

system of values that are in opposition to God: "Love neither the world nor the things of the world. If one loves the world, the love of the Father is not in that person. Because everything that is in the world—the desire of the flesh and the desire of the eyes and the boasting of wealth—is not of the Father but is of the world" (I John 2.15–16).

C. H. Dodd writes that the cosmos is "human society in so far as it is organized on wrong principles." It is characterized by the sensuality, superficiality, pretentiousness, materialism, and egoism that are the marks of the old order.[7]

In this usage, *cosmos* is not a place. It is a collectivity that in many Johannine references is personified: it loves, hates, listens, knows, and gives.[8] This does not mean that *cosmos* is simply the sum total of human beings. We are told to hate it, and to hate all people would contradict God's example of loving the world in the sense of *humanity* (John 3.16). The *cosmos* we are to hate is human values and conduct insofar as they are organized in opposition to God. Evil is in the very fabric of our social existence . . .

SOCIAL REALITY

The biblical concepts of cosmos and the supernatural powers constitute an objective social reality that can function for good or for evil. Careful observation of institutional life suggests ways in which the powers and the cosmos protect or threaten human life in the spheres attributed to them in the biblical world. A mystery of evil appears in our social life. The existence of an evil order ruled by supernatural beings must be either accepted or rejected on faith, but such reality would not be dissonant with our social experience. Our concern here is not to settle the cosmological question of whether angels and demons should be demythologized but rather to come to terms with the social material to which their biblical existence points. The cosmos, a more pervasive theme in the New Testament than the powers, represents the social structuring of evil without necessitating recourse to the symbolism of supernatural personages.

An examination of the objective characteristics of social reality can help us understand how there can be an intermediary locus of evil. One obvious characteristic of social life is that *its formal elements are much older than the individuals who constitute it*. Even in our very mobile society the continuity outweighs the changes by far. The symbol system, the customs, the traditions, the basic laws, the technology, the techniques for getting things done and distributing power were here long before we came and will be here long after we are gone. The

---

7. C. H. Dodd, *The Johannine Epistles*, Moffatt New Testament Commentaries (New York: Harper, 1946), 42–44.

8. Sasse, "Kosmos," 894. See Paul in 1 Cor. 1.18–21, Hans Conzelmann, *A Commentary on the First Epistle to the Corinthians*, Hermeneia (Philadelphia: Fortress, 1975), 43.

invisible agreement upon which society depends regarding politics and morals contains evil that is part of the bondage that is the price of society.[9]

Gentrification is the process of home buying in which a more wealthy class of home owners takes over a community by their ability to pay a higher price for housing. The community may be attractive because of its proximity to downtown jobs and the original style of the buildings. The previous working-class and low-income inhabitants can no longer afford the rising rents, and they are forced out. The community loses its previous character. The buyers, nevertheless, had no intention of harming the previous residents. Mel King, an African American leader, commented on the gentrification of the South End of Boston: "People come in, they push people out, they're nice people, they're not evil or anything, but they assume because they got money and money is might that they have the right and we have a system that operates on that."[10] They are operating within a long-standing economic structure and value system that is assumed rather than chosen.

People go into business and enter a kind of enterprise that existed long before they started and may continue long after they retire. It will go on with little regard to their personal morality, for "business is business." We die, but society goes on.

This social longevity is beneficial. We could not invent the wheel or discover metallurgy anew in each generation. The stability of society requires that we build on the solutions of previous generations.[11] As a consequence, however, the evils of those earlier generations continue as well. Another characteristic of social life, therefore, is that it not only goes on but does so with relatively *little dependence on conscious individual decision making or responsibility.*

Robert Lifton commented to a survivor of the slaughter of the Jews at Auschwitz about the ordinariness of most of the Nazi doctors who carried it out, that they were not demonic figures. The friend replied, "But it is *demonic* that they were not *demonic.*"[12]

A former president of the Midas Muffler Corporation described business corporations as "a circumstance of large, impersonal forces over which no one seems to have much control." Even heads of corporations, he said, are like a muffler. They are "fungible": "One part can be replaced with another, a replacement part . . . So indeed are corporate chairmen and presidents—and they know it." They are not that important. The corporation itself goes on with or without them.[13]

9. Patrick Devlin, *The Enforcement of Morals* (London: Oxford University Press, 1965), 9–10, 17.

10. "Interview: Mel King," *South End News* 9.

11. Patrick Kerans, *Sinful Social Structures* (New York: Paulist, 1974), 74–75. Pages 55–82 have an excellent discussion of the meaning of social structures in the context of individual responsibility.

12. Robert Lifton, *The Nazi Doctors* (New York: Basic, 1986), 4–5.

13. Gordon Sherman, "The Business of Business Is to Make a Profit," *Unauthorized Version* (Divinity School, Harvard University, 13 March 1972), 10; see Mary Douglas, *Natural Symbols: Exploration in Cosmology* (New York: Vintage, 1973), 90-91, 135.

The process is driven by the pursuit of power and often even more by system maintenance. The result is the drive to grow and the fear of any decline in sales or innovation.[14] An individual director may have regret regarding the impact that his or her company's pursuit of profits has on the poor in developing countries but feels that there is no use in resisting the process. If one is not willing to do it, he or she will be replaced by someone who is; and if the company stopped the practice, other companies would continue so that first company would face disaster in a few years in terms of profits and stockholders. They are caught up in a web of obligations and a competitive structure that knows no mercy.

Who is responsible for the evil in such a bureaucracy? We become more conscious of evil as what people suffer than evil as what people do.[15] Social life includes objective realities that evolve according to their own laws.[16]

Some of our greatest evils are characterized by this absence of conscious individual decisions on the critical issues. One thinks of the horrible evil of American slavery. Even those who appeared to be the better and more considerate people of the society not only acquiesced in it but supported it. The moral choices took place on minor issues—whether to take 150 slaves rather than 200 on a particular ship. The major issue of the evil of the institution of slavery itself was seldom faced or considered.

Our churches are not exempt from this moral myopia. The members of an all Euro-American church in a racially mixed neighborhood may assert that they are aware of no thoughts or acts of discrimination on their part. They may need to see not merely that their outreach really extends only to Euro-Americans but also that, in a society that tells African Americans in countless ways that they are not accepted in equality or association with Euro-Americans, they must take the initiative if they are to be any different from other Euro-American institutions in this respect.

We are socialized into the acceptance or the avoidance of major ethical issues. Our socialization reflects the moral conscience of others who share our position in society, and our ethical reasoning is shaped before we actually come to reflect upon life or make conscious moral decisions. David Wells states, "Worldliness is when sin seems familiar."[17] In Reinhold Niebuhr's terms, virtue is being defeated at a lower level.[18] In short, social life consists of group ways of thinking and acting in which every individual participant's decisions are but a small portion of the development of the whole.

---

14. Bob Goudzwaard, *Capitalism and Progress: A Diagnoses of Western* Society (Grand Rapids, Mich.: Eerdmans, 1979), 94.

15. Kerans, *Sinful Social Structures,* 59.

16. Roger Mehl, "The Basis of Christian Social Ethics," in *Christian Social Ethics in a Changing World,* ed. J. Bennett (New York: Association, 1966), 45.

17. David F. Wells, sermon, 18 April 1989, Gordon-Conwell Theological Seminary, South Hamilton, Massachusetts.

18. Reinhold Niebuhr, *Moral Man and Immoral Society* (New York: Scribners, 1932), 40.

Finally, social life often consists of complex problems for which there seem to be no solutions. Every attempt at solution only creates serious problems at another point. Jürgen Moltmann calls these patterns "vicious circles" and speaks of the "hopeless economic, social and political pattern formations which drive life toward death." He appropriately suggests that in them we sense the presence of the demonic in our lives.[19]

Examples of these vicious circles abound. There is the cycle of deprived children who become depriving parents, of welfare payments that are necessary to sustain life but do not produce a free life, of armed actions against terror that in effect multiply the motivation and action of terror, of the standoff in world trade between workers in industrial countries and workers in others hurt by trade policies designed to protect the former. We can also think of our drive to solve our material problems through technology and growth while in the process depleting our resources and threatening the ecological balance. Certainly, rational analyses of the problems are needed and can help, but beyond what we can analyze there is the mystery of evil, which defies our understanding and thwarts our efforts to improve people's lives. This evil is real and powerful and more than the sum of its individual parts.[20]

Various systems work together, compounding the difficulty of solution. A Christian leader of development in India, Jayakumar Christian, describes the various systems that bind the poor in that country. There is the local social system that validates the superior position of the nonpoor, for example, the landlord choosing the names of children or deciding who will marry whom. As a result the poor believe that they were meant to be inferior and without value. Another system is the religious worldview of the culture. The idea of karma tells the poor that their current condition is in response to their former life and must be accepted. Another system that impacts them is the international trade system by which land formerly devoted to domestic food consumption is transferred to export crops. The new production is less labor-intensive. The result is increased hunger and poverty. The Christian sees all these levels as existing in a cosmic system in which the principalities and powers work out their rebellion against God's intentions for human life in creation.[21]

In describing social reality and social evil our intention is by no means to argue against individual responsibility for our social life, blaming everything on the Devil. The powers are able to rule because individuals follow their influence

---

19. Jürgen Moltmann, *The Crucified God: The Cross of Christ as the Foundation and Criticism of Christian Theology* (New York: Harper, 1974), 293, 329. Using the example of the federal bureaucracy, Hugh Heclo shows that we are unwilling to eliminate the components that create the dilemma. To protect democracy, we keep the tenure short at the top levels of government; to avoid patronage, we remove the bureaucracy from political control (*Government of Strangers: Executive Politics in Washington* [Washington, D.C.: Brookings Institute, 1977], 109; see 112).

20. N. T. Wright, *Evil and the Justice of God* (Downers Grove, Ill.: InterVarsity, 2006), 76; see 38.

21. Bryant Myers, "Poverty as a Disempowering System," *MARC Newsletter* 98, no. 3 (September 1998): 3–4.

and conform themselves to the world order in actions that are system serving rather than system critical. The objective social situation and individual choice exert influence on each other. Social entities came into being through individual decisions; they result from the conscious decisions of individuals over the years. But they also are powerful influences upon our choices. Jesus recognized the interrelatedness of the social source of evil and individual responsibility. "Woe to the world because of temptations to sin! For the coming of temptations is necessary; nevertheless woe to the person through whom the temptation comes" (Matt. 18.7). We must admit to unknowables in this matter of responsibility. One of the most challenging problems in ethics is to assign responsibility for the exploitation that goes on around us, which we participate in or fail to correct, yet fail to acknowledge. "How many times can a man turn his head, pretending he just doesn't see?" One way to increase individual responsibility is to increase awareness of social evil: this is our concern.

Our social systems are not eternal or absolute but reflect the ambiguous nature of humankind and of the angelic guardians of culture. Our institutions are not just a constraint on sin (a conservative attitude toward institutions); they themselves are full of sin. The structures of social life contain both good and bad. Because of the hold of self-interest we will tend to see only the good in those social forms that favor our interests unless we have a strong theology of sin. Our social life is fallen with us, and no social system is beyond the need of reform or perhaps even of reconstitution.

A qualification must be made at this point. One cannot evolve a total theology of culture from the concept of the fallen order of society and of the fallen powers of the world. These concepts must not be understood to mean that society, government, or other institutions are evil or demonic in themselves. We cannot do without institutions. They are integral to human life. This point is not always made clear in discussions of the powers. The New Testament passages that we have examined deal with a battle for the *control* of creation, of which the social life of humanity is a part. In this battle God has the advantage— the opponents are God's own creatures and appointees. They cannot create; they can only thwart. They must start with the materials, powers, and designs made by God. As indicated in the prologue to John, even in the darkness exists the divine creation.[22] "The light shines in the darkness, and yet the darkness did not overcome it" (John 1.5).

Earthly authorities are appointed by God and serve God (Rom. 13.1, 4), but government is marred by the disobedience and opposition of the angelic lieutenants, a disobedience that is more in evidence at some times than others and will culminate in the demonic capture of the state at the end time (Rev. 13). But even then that rule is under God's permission (Rev. 13.5). The claim of the Devil in the wilderness that the authority and glory of the kingdoms have been

22. Günther Baumbach, "Gemeinde und Welt im Johannes-Evangelium," *Kairos* 14 (1972): 125.

entrusted to him (Luke 4.6) should be treated for what it is, a claim of the Devil. The fallen angels have authority only to the degree that they are serving God. It is a characteristic of the demonic powers to deny their divine source and claim to be on their own.[23] The world order and the evil presence of the powers are never *synonymous* with the concrete forms of social and institutional life. Institutions function both to enslave and to liberate human existence. The powers are always present along with enslavement and death in small or large degree; but their real existence is behind the scenes in a system of hostile values vying for control of the life of the world.

IMPLICATIONS OF EVIL RESIDING IN SOCIETY

In its teaching about the world the New Testament provides direct witness for a conclusion that should be inferred from our theology of sin. If sin is as pervasive as we say that it is, if it violates a divine intent that is not removed from history, if it is not tolerable to life but a force that is viciously destructive of person and society, if it is not only against the will of God but against nature,[24] then it will affect not only our personal motivations, decisions, and acts but also our social life. It will powerfully influence our customs, traditions, thinking, and institutions. It will pervert our *cosmos*.

The consequences of acknowledging the presence of evil in institutions are considerable. Our attitude to society will be changed. Our struggle with evil must correspond to the geography of evil. In combating evil in the heart through evangelism and Christian nurture we deal with a crucial aspect of evil, but only one aspect. Dealing with the evil of the social order and the worldly powers involves social action, action in the world. Christian social reform has been effective when there has been a sense of a stronghold of evil in society that must be resisted. Evangelical reform in the nineteenth century was characterized by this perspective, particularly in the struggle against slavery. William Knibb, a British missionary who was a hero in the struggle for abolition in Jamaica, wrote upon his arrival on that island, "I have now reached the land of sin, disease, and death, where Satan reigns with awful power, and carries multitudes captive at his will."[25] His mission board, like many Christian bodies before and since, failed to discern the intrusion of evil into the prevailing practices of social life. Aware of the anger of the powerful planters at amelioration proposals, they wrote to Knibb: "You must ever bear in mind that, as a resident of Jamaica, you have nothing to do with its civil or political affairs; with these you must never

---

23. Heinrich Schlier, *Principalities and Powers in the New Testament,* Quaestiones Disputatae (New York: Harper, 1964), 37.

24. Ernst Troeltsch, *The Social Teachings of the Christian Churches* (New York: Harper, 1960), 344, draws such a distinction.

25. John Hinton, *Memoirs of William Knibb,* 45, as quoted by Philip Wright, *Knibb "The Notorious": Slaves' Missionary 1803–1845* (London: Sidgwick, 1973), 24.

interfere." "The Gospel of Christ, as you well know, so far from producing or countenancing a spirit of rebellion or insubordination, has a directly opposite tendency."[26]

The discovery that evil resides in the social order as well as in our personal life confounds the common inventory of besetting sins. Sins that are emphasized often relate to direct personal relationships and have a connection to sexuality and reproduction, such as the important matters of pornography and abortion. An otherwise excellent sermon that I heard recently is typical of such omission. In order to illustrate how we need God's power, not just our own willpower, the preacher talked about how we must use that power of God to take a public stand on matters in the areas of the unborn, sexuality and marriage, and euthanasia. That was all, however. The biblical sins of economic exploitation or oppression or hoarding of wealth from the poor have vanished. But the prophets spoke out not only against sinful personal relationships but also against breakdowns of complex social relationships between groups with unequal shares of power. Thus they attacked broad economic patterns, such as the consolidation of the holdings of peasants into vast estates of the rich (Isa. 5.7–8). In Scripture, sin includes participation in social injustices or failure to correct them. Yet insensitivity to social evil often dulls comprehension when this dimension is encountered in the reading of Scripture. Isaiah 1.18 (KJV) is familiar: "Come now, and let us reason together, saith the Lord: though your sins be as scarlet, they shall be as white as snow; though they be red like crimson, they shall be as wool."

Some familiar hymns use the striking wording of this verse: "Whiter than snow, whiter than snow, wash me and I shall be whiter than snow." But do we recognize that the sins spoken of are a failure to address particular social needs and unjust practices? The preceding two verses state: "Wash yourselves; make yourselves clean; remove the evil of your doings from before my eyes; cease to do evil, learn to do good; seek justice, rescue the oppressed, defend the orphan, plead for the widow" (NRSV; cf. v. 23 also, which involves governmental neglect and injustice).

"The heart is deceitful above all things and beyond cure" (Jer. 17.9, NIV) is a familiar verse. Less well known is the fact that the first example of this condition that Jeremiah gives is the one who "gains riches by unjust means" (v. 11). The biblical witness provides the key to the identification of the characteristics of the fallen social order and the marks of the social holdings of the powers.

The Christian should become sensitive to sin arising from social conditioning. Social evil lies close to home. The powers that rule through the *cosmos* speak with a familiar voice. As mentioned earlier, the sociology of knowledge has shown us the degree to which, through socialization, our class position affects the way we think. According to John Bennett, the interests of class distort the day-to-day decisions of the ordinary citizen more than do his or her individual

---

26. S. C. Lord's report from the Select Committee on Slave Laws in the West Indies, as quoted by Wright, *Knibb*, 31–32.

interests.[27] But we are also conditioned in our outlook by considerations of race, sex, and national loyalty. We should examine our inner selves to discover these biases.

The recognition of the habitation of evil in social life will affect our activity in the world. It will change the mode of Christian citizenship from passive obedience to active responsibility. We can no longer discharge our responsibility by passively accepting the status quo (the order which is) as the will of God. John Calvin spoke of "public error," in which vice was protected by customs and laws; "one must either completely despair of human affairs or grapple with these great evils—or rather, forcibly quell them. And this remedy is rejected for no other reason save that we have long been accustomed to such evils" *(Institutes, Prefatory Address, 5)*. It is in this context of the corruption of the system that the Christian is enjoined to be the salt of the earth (Matt. 5.13), resisting corruption just as light resists and combats darkness: "You are the light of the world" (v. 14; cf. John 9.4–5).

We serve a different order, the Reign of Christ, which he sets up in contrast to the prevailing way of life in the social order as supported by the fallen powers. To the old order there must be enmity; according to James 4.4, to be a friend of the fallen order is to be an enemy of God.[28] We are to follow the Lordship of Christ who judges the world and conquers it. Christ's victory over the powers is sure; he has disarmed them (Col. 2.15). The hostilities still continue, however, for it is only at his return that "every power and every authority and power" will be brought to an end (1 Cor. 15.24).[29] By faith we live in Christ's victory, yet we must continue to struggle.

This struggle against the hold of the forces of evil is expounded in the Letter to the Ephesians. We are to fight the demonic powers that rule the world by arming ourselves with truth, justice, peace, and the Word of God (6.10–18). We are to "expose" "the unfruitful works of darkness," taking the offensive against sin (5.11). The many-sided wisdom of God will be made known to the "rulers and authorities in heavenly places" through the church (3.10). In his interpretation of these passages, Heinrich Schlier sees the church opposed to the principalities, as the church provides a haven of justice and truth. Human history is seen as a great struggle between the principalities and the church, ending in

---

27. John C. Bennett, *Christian Ethics and Social Policy* (New York: Scribner's, 1946), 67.

28. In John 3.23 Jesus asserts that he "is not of this world-order," which means that he does not share its values. Yet he came "to take away the sin of the world" (John 1.29). The order is judged in Christ; the "ruler of the world will be thrown out" (John 12.31). Thus, according to John 17, although the Christians cannot be taken out of the social order, opting for ascetic retreat, they are not to belong to it; their existence and values cannot have that source (vv. 14, 15, 18). Christ has come to "destroy the works of the Devil," and his followers are not to participate in them (1 John 3.8).

29. Wilder, *Kerygma, Eschatology, and Social Ethics*, 24–25; Alan Richardson, *An Introduction to the Theology of the New Testament* (New York: Harper, 1958), 214. Against the background of the apocalyptic materials, in which the defeat of the fallen angels is a victory for justice and truth (see Nickelsburg. "Apocalyptic and Myth," 391–393), Christ's victory over the powers is seen as a divine act achieving justice and liberation from oppression.

the down-fall of the demonic spirits.[30] The church is to be engaged in a battle against evils within the social structure because they mark the points of these powers' penetration into our history.

Mobilization for social change follows more clearly, however, from the mandates and models associated with God's activity in the world than from this theology of the cosmos. The direction of our efforts is suggested by such themes as the scope of Christian love, the implications of divine grace, the mandate to justice, and the dimensions of the Reign of God. We turn to these themes in the next chapters.

THE ACTIVIST WHO TAKES SIN SERIOUSLY

A conviction of the existence of evil in the social system can lead to one of two responses according to a typology worked out by Max Weber.[31] Weber called both patterns "asceticism." Asceticism is a mode of religious response in the face of a larger society given over with little restraint to self-seeking. The goal of ascetics is to achieve mastery over fallen nature. To achieve this control, they structure the whole of life in an effort to be conformed to the will of God. Asceticism produces a systematic, methodical character and an avoidance of what is purposeless and ostentatious.

Weber identified two very different forms of asceticism. One he called "other-worldly asceticism," the other "inner-worldly asceticism." Of the two, inner-worldly asceticism was the most likely to provide leverage for evolutionary social change. Inner-worldly ascetics, best represented in certain types of Puritanism, apply their concern about sin and spiritual discipline to a mastery of life around themselves, rather than to defeating sin within. Other-worldly ascetics flee the world. Inner-worldly ascetics face the world, extending the quest for the mastery of evil to all aspects of the human condition.

Because inner-worldly ascetics reject the existing world order, the world is their place of mission. The theocentric viewpoint on which their criticism of the world is based is also the source of a calling to glorify God in the world. The energies committed to the struggle with evil within are channeled into vigorous support of this outward mission. For the Calvinists, for example, in addition to a specific calling in daily work, there was also a general vocation in the world to work for the establishment of a society of justice and mercy.[32] Calvinism

---

30. Schlier, *Principalities and Powers,* 50–52.

31. For Weber's discussion of inner-worldly asceticism, see Max Weber, "Religious Rejections of the World and Their Directions," in *From Max Weber,* ed. H. Gerth and C. W. Mills (New York: Oxford University Press, 1946), 323–359; and Weber, *The Protestant Ethic and the Spirit of Capitalism* (New York: Scribners, 1958), chap. 4.

32. James Luther Adams, "The Protestant Ethic' with Fewer Tears," in *The Name of Life,* E. Fromm Festschrift, ed. B. Landis and E. Tauber (New York: Holt, 1971), 178, 185 (most recently reprinted in Adams, *Voluntary Associations* [Chicago: Exploration, 1986], 107, 114).

everywhere formed voluntary associations for deeds of neighborly love and was engaged in a systematic endeavor to mold society as a whole.[33]

Evangelical Christianity has borne several marks of the inner-worldly ascetic pattern. Although in modern times the drive for social righteousness has frequently been lacking, the unmatched commitment to worldwide missions is a form of activism expressing that religious energy and discipline in financial sacrifice, physical suffering, vocational choice, and prayer. The plethora of supportive organizations is also characteristic. Even separatist patterns in church polity and personal ethics can be seen in part as a methodical discipline to support the mission. Accordingly, zealous activity has been directed not to saving one's own soul but to setting one's redeemed soul to the saving of the world. In ancient Israel one also sees a separated people with a mission to the nations. In the Bible, the notion of the separation of a people from the evils of the world around them is but the corollary of the revelation of the Lord to a people who will become a missionary to all humanity and a demonstration of the life that God requires of the nations (Exod. 19.5–6).[34]

Biblically informed concern about sin thus provides a piety capable of energizing effective social action. Vigorous and systematic social involvement requires not that Christians weaken the structure of their piety but rather that they carry it through to its natural social consequences.

Finally, there is a danger that an awareness of evil may lead to nothing more than dogmatic condemnation of the surrounding society. But social evil also means the fear, the humiliation, the suffering, and the loss when people hurt people. God knows that hurt and cries out against it. We do not know what sin is until we weep with the weeping of the earth. We are in touch with the substance of justice when the hunger for righteousness within us is one with our anguish at human suffering. Then we know more fully what it means that Christ was "made sin" for us.

33. Troeltsch, *Social Teachings*, 604.

34. R. Tamisier, "La séparation du monde dans l'Ancien et le Nouveau Testament," in *La séparation du monde*, Problèmes de la religieuse d'aujourd'hui (Paris: Cerf, 1961), 29, and Christopher J. H. Wright, *An Eye for an Eye: The Place of Old Testament Ethics Today* (Downers Grove, Ill., InterVarsity, 1983), 40–43, 61.

Chapter 9

"World-Formative Christianity"

1983

Nicholas Wolterstorff

The entrance of the Christian gospel into history worked like a leaven through the Roman world, causing profound changes in the social order. But after some three or four centuries the leaven was no longer the source of much ferment except on the periphery. From then on through the high Middle Ages, the Christian church, with few exceptions, taught its members to acquiesce in the social world in which they found themselves, instructing them in how to regard the delights it yielded and how to endure the sufferings it caused as they worked within the roles offered them. Then in the sixteenth century a profoundly different vision and practice came forth from the "reformed" church in Switzerland and the upper Rhine valley. The structure of the social world was held up to judgment, was pronounced guilty, and was sentenced to be reformed. *World-formative Christianity*, as I propose to call it, came out from the wings of history onto center stage.

It has been there ever since—sometimes prominent, sometimes inconspicuous; sometimes acting with repressive triumphalism, sometimes with liberating modesty; sometimes breathing fire and fomenting revolution, sometimes only smoldering. Of that new way of inserting oneself into the social order that came into the lights there in central Europe three and a half centuries ago all of us in the modern world are inheritors.

In his book *The Revolution of the Saints,* political theorist Michael Walzer says of the late sixteenth- and early seventeenth-century English Puritans that "the saints were responsible for their world—as medieval men were not—and responsible above all for its continual reformation. Their enthusiastic and purposive activity were part of their religious life, not something distinct and separate."[1] Walzer does not use the phrase "world-formative Christianity," but I know of no more succinct characterization of this form of religion than his words here. The saints are responsible for the structure of the social world in which they find themselves. That structure is not simply part of the order of nature; to the contrary, it is the result of human decision, and by concerted effort it can be altered. Indeed, it *should* be altered, for it is a fallen structure, in need of reform. The responsibility of the saints to struggle for the reform of the social order in which they find themselves is one facet of the discipleship to which their Lord Jesus Christ has called them. It is not an addition to their religion; it is there among the very motions of Christian spirituality.

My project . . . is to ask how Christians should insert themselves into the modern social order. The pattern of thought and action that I have described as world-formative Christianity is the over-arching perspective of what I shall urge, and I propose to begin our discussion by looking at this pattern in its first appearance. I do not suggest that the program of those early Calvinists was in all respects admirable, and certainly I do not contend that we should try to implement it in our own century: not only is much of it simply irrelevant to our present-day world; much of it was misguided even in its own day. Neither do I hold that the ideology behind the early Calvinist version of world-formative Christianity ought to be recaptured: that too was not without fault. In short, I shall not be conducting an apology for the early Calvinist *version* of world-formative Christianity. Yet this form of life as such, apart from the peculiarities of the early Calvinist version thereof, constitutes one of the enduring patterns for the Christian's insertion into the social world. It is a pattern which is both biblically faithful and relevant to our modern world. And I think that there is no better way to grasp the essence of this enduring pattern—the issues it poses and the choices it makes—than to place it in the historical context within which it arose.

In his magisterial book *The Social Teaching of the Christian Churches,* Ernst Troeltsch remarks that original Calvinism was led

> everywhere to . . . a systematic endeavor to mould the life of Society as a whole, to a kind of "Christian Socialism" . . . it lays down the principle that the Church ought to be interested in all sides of life, and it neither isolates

---

1. Walzer, *The Revolution of the Saints: A Study in the Origins of Radical Politics* (Cambridge: Harvard University Press, 1965), p.12.

the religious element over against the other elements, like Lutheranism, nor does it permit this sense of collective responsibility to express itself merely in particular institutions and occasional interventions in affairs, as in Catholicism.[2] . . .

We can do no better, as we now turn to investigate in more detail the contours of [this] Christian vision, than begin with Calvin himself. . . . In doing so my intent will be to describe the general vision of the early Calvinists concerning our relation to the social order, rather than to outline their specific practices or ideas on social formation, or the influence of those practices and ideas on "modernization."[3]

Calvin opens his *Institutes* in the great medieval tradition of theological treatises with a discussion of the knowledge of God as the true end of man. But no one who reads what he says will miss the fact that beneath this commonality of language a profound alteration of perspective has taken place. Knowledge of God is no longer understood as contemplation of God's essence: it consists in the appropriate *response* to his *works*. Knowledge of God consists in *ac*knowledgment of God. And *ac*knowledgment of God occurs in life as a whole, comprising such things as trust, reverence, gratitude, service. This all comes out nicely in a small section of the *Geneva Catechism* (1541) on the end of man:

MASTER: What is the chief end of human life?
SCHOLAR: To know God by whom men were created.

MASTER: What is the highest good of man?
SCHOLAR: The very same thing.

MASTER: What is the true and right knowledge of God?
SCHOLAR: When he is so known that due honor is paid to him.

MASTER: What is the method of honoring him truly?
SCHOLAR: To place our whole confidence in him; to study to serve him during our whole life by obeying his will; to call upon him in all our necessities, seeking salvation and every good thing that can be desired in him; lastly, to acknowledge him both with heart and lips, as the sole Author of all blessings.

The scholar here cites various things as belonging to that knowledge of God which is the true end of human life: placing one's whole confidence in God, serving him in one's whole life by obeying his will, calling upon him in need, seeking every good thing from him, acknowledging him with heart and lips as

2. Troeltsch, *The Social Teaching of the Christian Churches*, trans. Olive Wyon (New York: Macmillan, 1931), 2:602.

3. The ideas and practices of the early Calvinists and their relation to "modernization" have of course been much discussed, but for an especially judicious treatment, see David Little's *Religion, Order, and Law: A Study in Pre-Revolutionary England* (New York: Harper & Row, 1969).

the sole author of all blessings. There can be no doubt that of all these it will often be obedience that becomes most prominent in later Calvinism. Correlatively, God will come to be apprehended predominantly as lawgiver. But we fail to grasp the structure of *original* Calvinist thought and piety if we think that obedience and law-giving are the most basic to it. Fundamental in the structure of Calvin's thought about God is the idea that he dispenses good gifts to us his children. To this our appropriate response is gratitude. What makes gratitude appropriate is not first of all that it is commanded (although, of course, it is), but simply that it is right and proper. Obedient action in society enters the picture as one of the manifestations of gratitude; as such, it is to God's glory. Thus, deeper in Calvin's thought than the image of God as lawgiver is the image of God as the "Author of all blessings," as the scholar in the *Catechism* puts it. God's law is itself one of his blessings. One has not caught the peculiar flavor of early Calvinist piety, nor indeed of much of later Calvinist piety, until one sees it as commitment to obedience out of gratitude for blessings received.[4]

At this very point Max Weber makes a fundamental mistake in his famous discussion of Calvinism in *The Protestant Ethic and the Spirit of Capitalism* when he argues that the peculiar activism of the Calvinist was energized by the desire to establish that one is among the elect. Certainly that is a caricature. The Calvinists' action was energized by their gratitude to God for his blessings, blessings that included the blessing of election, with its promise of eternal life.

It is obvious that Calvin's formulation of the true goal of human existence as the acknowledgment of God in one's life constitutes a profound turn toward this world and a repudiation of avertive religion. But we saw earlier that the preference for formative over avertive Christianity need not necessarily take the shape of *world*-formative Christianity; one's endeavors at reform may be confined, for example, to one's inwardness. Our next step will be to see why in this case it did take the world-formative path.

The terrain to be described here can be approached from many different directions. I shall approach it by speaking first of the Calvinist understanding of the relation between our actions of obedient gratitude and our social roles, and then speaking of the Calvinist notion of the holy commonwealth.

It is important to keep in mind that our social roles include more than what have customarily been labeled our "callings," that is, our occupations. On this Calvin himself was very clear. Although he speaks a good deal about how we ought to act in society, he speaks relatively little about callings. In the *Institutes* he devotes only two paragraphs to the subject (III, x, 6), and they are curiously unemphatic, as is clear from the opening: "Finally, this point is to be noted: the

4. It has often been said that Calvinism was instrumental in the rise of our modern secularized society, and it is of course true that the Calvinists turned their religious endeavors toward this world, this *seculum*, and that they passionately resisted the worship of anything in this world as well as the granting of an authority to anyone who might compete with God's authority; but at the same time, they profoundly sacralized the world by recognizing within it the actions of God and by attempting to stamp it with the patterns of obedience. The Calvinist world is thoroughly secularized—and at the same time suffused with the sacral.

Lord bids each one of us in all life's actions to look to his calling." After a brief discussion he remarks, "But I will not delay to list examples. It is enough if we know that the Lord's calling is in everything the beginning and foundation of well-doing. And if there is anyone who will not direct himself to it, he will never hold to the straight path in his duties." The truth is that what the Calvinists wish to say about our callings is merely one aspect of what they wish to say about our social roles in general. Nonetheless, it has to be admitted that their teaching about callings is a paradigm of their teaching about social roles in general. I shall so treat it. Gratitude, obedience, and vocation—these are at the center of Calvinist social piety: obedience motivated by gratitude and expressed in vocation.

In the medieval church ordinary occupational roles would have been among the last things to be described as vocations, as callings. A vocation was some special religious occupation to which one was usually officially appointed by the church. Most Catholics today, at least in the United States, still talk the same way. They would find it strange to speak of the shopkeeper's occupation, for example, as a "vocation"; it is the person who is called by the church to do mission work in Venezuela who is said to have a vocation.

The change occurred in Lutheranism. There the ordinary occupations of the social world were spoken of as callings. The idea was that God calls us to them. However, though one is indeed called by God *to* some occupation, and though it would be disobedient to evade that call by going into some other occupation or trying to make do without an occupation, nonetheless what one does *in* one's occupation is thought of not so much as a matter of obedience as it is a matter of social necessity. Correspondingly, Luther still tended to think of the whole occupational structure of society as God-ordained rather than as something created by us to be rearranged if that seems desirable. Troeltsch sheds some valuable light on this distinction:

> Luther's view of vocation agreed with that of Paul, the Early Church, and the Middle Ages. To him the "calling" was simply the sphere of activity in which one was set, and in which it was a duty to remain. . . . Although at the same time Luther pointed out that it is precisely through the ordered work of one's calling, and the intricate network of mutual service that the preservation of the whole community is effected, and with that peace, order, and prosperity, he attributes it all to the wise ordering and the kindly guidance of Providence, and not to deliberate human initiative. The vocational system was not consciously designed and developed for the purposes of the holy community and of Christian Society, but it was accepted as a Divine arrangement. The individual, moreover, regarded his work, not as a suitable way of contributing to the uplift of Society as a whole, but as his appointed destiny, which he received from the hands of God. That is why it was possible for the Lutheran to regard the work of his vocation in an entirely traditional and reactionary way—as the duty of remaining within the traditional way of earning a living which belongs to one's position in Society. This point of view coincides with the traditional Catholic view. Christian morality was exercised *in vocatione* but not *per vocationem.*[5]

5. Troeltsch, *Social Teaching of the Christian Churches,* 2:610.

The core of what was different in the Calvinist concept of calling is alluded to in the concluding sentence of this passage: the Calvinist saw his occupation as something *through which* to exercise his obedience. *Remaining in that role* is not the thing which is to be done out of obedient gratitude; rather, *the actions performed in that role* are what is to be done out of obedient gratitude. However (and here I go beyond Troeltsch's point), each occupational role must either *be made* to serve the common good, or if in some case that cannot be done, then that role must be discarded. It's not true that if everyone works devotedly in the occupation to which God called him or her, the common good will automatically be served; one has to see to it that one's occupation serves the common good rather than simply assuming that it does, for—and here we come to perhaps the most profound of all breaches between the Calvinist and the medieval vision—we live in a fallen, corrupted society: the structures of our social world are structures which in good measure do not serve the common good.

What naturally follows among those who hold this perspective is the social activism that Weber found so striking. What also follows is that one will begin to think of the whole array of occupations as man-made. Once one is convinced that each occupational role ought to serve the common good, but that as a matter of fact many are corrupted so that they do not, then it will be impossible to think of the social order as given by God. One will inevitably think of it as made by human beings and capable of alteration. One will think of us as responsible for its structure.[6]

Yet another inference will follow naturally from the conviction that our obedience is to be rendered *per vocationem* and not merely *in vocatione* when it is coupled with the conviction that the structure of the social order is a fallen one: it will be increasingly difficult to tolerate the idea that a person is *born* into an occupation. If each of us is to reshape his or her occupation into a channel of obedience, then presumably each of us must also search for that occupation which will best serve as a channel of obedience. Thus in the Calvinist concept of the calling there is a powerful pressure toward the diminution of what sociologists call "ascriptivism," a phenomenon of which I shall speak in the next

---

6. Once again Troeltsch's insights are germane: Calvinism, he says, "coordinated the activity of the individual and of the community into a conscious and systematic form. And since the Church as a whole could not be fully constituted without the help of the political and economic service of the secular community, it was urged that all callings ought to he ordered, purified, and enkindled as means for attaining the ends of the Holy Community. Thus the ideal was now no longer one of surrender to a static vocational system, directed by Providence, but the free use of vocational work as the method of realizing the purpose of the Holy Community. The varied secular callings do not simply constitute the existing framework within which brotherly love is exercised and faith is preserved, but they are means to be handled with freedom, through whose thoughtful and wise use love alone becomes possible and faith a real thing. From this there results a freer conception of the system of callings, a far-reaching consideration for that which is practically possible and suitable, a deliberate increasing of the intensity of labour" (*Social Teaching of the Christian Churches,* 2:610–11).

chapter. Calvin already remarked that "it would be asking for too much, if a tailor were not permitted to learn another trade, or a merchant to change to farming."[7]

One more thing must be added to have the full Calvinist concept of the calling before us—the fact that all those different modes of obedience rendered to God in the diversity of society-serving occupations are fundamentally equal in God's sight. Some may be more crucial than others for the welfare of society, but all are equal: "If the chambermaid and the manservant go about their domestic tasks offering themselves in their work as a sacrifice to God, then what they do is accepted by God as a holy and pure sacrifice pleasing in His sight."[8] What the Calvinists especially had their eye on with this radical levelling of occupations was of course the monasteries. For a thousand years, Christian Europe had said that the life of the monastery is the noblest form of life, inasmuch as it is dedicated to the contemplation of God. When the Calvinists levelled the occupations, they were saying that a career turned toward this world with God behind one's back is not inferior to a career turned toward God. It is no farther from the true end of man. Indeed, many Calvinists said it was closer—closer to that knowledge of God which is the true *ac*knowledgment of him in life.[9] A friend of mine told me how annoyed he was, upon visiting the St. Bavo Kerk in Haarlem, to see how the Calvinists had put representations of good solid Dutch burghers in the windows where the medievals would have had saints—until he realized that these *were* the Calvinist saints.

We have been considering what it was in the thought of the early Calvinists that made their turn toward the world take the shape of world-formative Christianity. I have argued for the importance of two convictions on their part: first, the conviction that the obedient gratitude that constitutes the basis of this turn ought to be exercised within our occupations; and second, the conviction that the occupational structures as presented to us are corrupted and would not serve that goal. Put these elements together and, with a few other assumptions that I shall mention shortly, one has a powerful argument for social reform and, in extreme cases, even for revolution.

But first, why were the Calvinists so persuaded that the social structures as presented to us are fallen? And where did they get their guidelines for reform? What was the root of their radical social critique? The answer is clear: it is the Word of God, presented to us in the Bible, that shows up for us the corruption

---

7. Calvin, *Calvin's Commentaries: The First Epistle of Paul the Apostle to the Corinthians*, trans. John W. Fraser, ed. David W. Torrance and Thomas F. Torrance (Grand Rapids, Mich.: Eerdmans, 1960), p. 153 (1 Cor. 7:20).

8. Paraphrase of a point made by Calvin in his sermon on 1 Cor. 10:31–11:1, by Ronald S. Wallace, *Calvin's Doctrine of the Christian Life* (London: Oliver and Boyd, 1959), p. 155.

9. Consider Calvin's caustic comments on the elitism of the monks in the *Institutes*, IV, xiii, 11. In this connection we should also be reminded of Calvin's break with the elitism characteristic of the humanists, in which the liberal arts were praised more highly than the manual arts (*Institutes*, II, ii, 14).

of our social order. And it is that same Word of God that provides us with our fundamental pattern for reform. The reformation of society according to the Word of God: this was the Calvinist goal.

The Calvinists did not deny—indeed, they insisted—that the capacity for apprehending the will of God for our lives belongs to all human beings simply by virtue of our created nature. And no matter what the extent of a given person's perversity, that capacity is never entirely lost; indeed, the *workings* of that capacity are never fully *suppressed:* God's will is communicated in natural law. But our apprehension of that law is at best wavering and fallible. The Bible comes then to make clear to us the content of that law. Accordingly, it would be folly to try to extract the grounds for our critique of the social order from our faltering apprehension of God's natural law, and it would be worse than folly to try to extract it from the voice of reason within us, or from our inward desires for happiness or freedom, or from tradition. To that end, we have a word *from outside*—a word from God.[10]

To complete our attempt to grasp the contours of this original version of world-formative Christianity, I must now at one point broaden what has been said, and at another, deepen it. The broadening consists in recalling that though our discussion has been formulated in terms of the Calvinist doctrine of occupational callings, it in fact applies to the Calvinist teaching concerning social roles in general, and particularly to our roles in church and state, the great ordering institutions of human life. The deepening consists in bringing to light two assumptions in the line of thought as I have presented it.

For one thing, it is assumed that Christians, as they struggle to find or shape an occupation in which to exercise their obedience, will not stray far from those occupations characteristically found in our ordinary social world. We heard Calvin speaking of tailors, merchants, and farmers; such occupations are of course thoroughly familiar to us. But why would Christians not exercise their obedience in a special set of occupations? Why in this range of relatively ordinary occupations? Why not all, say, become evangelists and medical workers?

The answer to this question lies in the Calvinist's understanding of the goal of God's redemptive activity. If we had lived as God meant us to live, we would all be members of an ordered community bound together by love for each other and gratitude to God, using the earth for our benefit and delight. In fact we do not live thus. A fall has occurred. God's response to this fall of mankind was to choose from all humanity a people destined for eternal life. They in obedient gratitude are now to work for the renewal of human life so that it may become

10. If the Bible were to be a comprehensive guide for our social activities, it was essential that the Calvinist take the Old Testament seriously. Appeals to the Old Testament in Calvinism have a function similar to appeals to *nature* in Thomist Catholicism (and in Lutheranism). It is fascinating to observe, in his *Letters and Papers from Prison,* that as Bonhoeffer moves toward world-formative Christianity and away from a formative version of Christianity based on inwardness and religious practices, he also begins to emphasize the importance of the Old Testament. He saw, as did the Calvinists, that the New Testament in isolation gives insufficient guidance for the new praxis.

what God meant it to be. They are to struggle to establish a holy commonwealth here on earth. Of course it is the mandate of all humanity to struggle toward such a community; what makes Christians different in their action is that they have in fact committed themselves to struggling toward this goal, that they recognize it as God's mandate, and that they struggle toward it not just in obedience to God the creator but in imitation of Christ. It is because Christians are committed in obedient gratitude to work for the renewal of the earthly community that they will render their obedience in such ordinary earthly occupations as tailor, merchant, and farmer.

The other assumption can be brought to light by asking this question: Suppose we grant that the holy commonwealth will be a truly earthly commonwealth with tailors and merchants and farmers; why, then, would it not be a *separated* community? Why would not the Christian pull out of general society and set up the holy commonwealth in a separated area? In short, why not follow the Anabaptist experiment?

Against the Anabaptists the Calvinists threw up a great flurry of arguments, far more than I can here review. But even if we had the time and space to review them, my guess is that in doing so we would not touch the real issues. The multiplicity of the Calvinist arguments against the Anabaptists, when viewed in conjunction with the violence of their rhetoric, leads one to surmise that their ideological defenses were not strong. The truth, I think, is that, on this issue especially, social realities shaped the thinking of the Calvinists. They assumed that the Constantinianism which Europe had known for more than a millennium was basically correct. They resisted questioning seriously the hoary assumption that the membership of the institutional church and the membership of civil society were identical. And though they never identified the elect with the membership of the institutional church, they resisted the idea of the "believers' church" on the ground that we had no way of making the separation between the elect believers and others. Accordingly, rather than calling for the church of believers to withdraw from mixed society and set up its own holy commonwealth, they went in the opposite direction and insisted that all the members of the institutional church—and thus all the members of civil society—were to be subjected to ecclesiastical admonition and discipline.[11] We all know of the repressiveness that this system entailed; on this point, social and psychic dynamics, if not theological arguments, made the system of original Calvinism intolerable almost everywhere within a century. One may well wonder whether the comparable social disciplines imposed by those secular saints of revolutionary regimes in our own century will ultimately fare any better!

As the Calvinists in their turn toward the world struggled to reshape society and institute the holy commonwealth on earth, they encountered resistance. It became their experience that humanity in general was not eagerly awaiting their

11. Cf. Troeltsch, *Social Teaching of the Christian Churches,* 2:591.

program of social reform. They interpreted the Bible as telling them that this is what they should expect: the fallenness of the social order is not a result of mere blundering; behind it is a body of humanity committed to resisting the work of God. "You have great works to do," remarked the Puritan preacher Stephen Marshall in 1641, "the planting of a new heaven and a new earth among us, and great works have great enemies . . . "[12] Beneath the social order the Calvinist discerned conflict, the Augustinian conflict between the City of God and the City of the World, the war of the Lamb with the Beast.[13] This conflict was not incidental to the social order. It was explanatory of its fundamental dynamics. Later this idea would be developed by Abraham Kuyper and his followers into the theory of *antithesis,* in which the concept of idolatry is used as a basic category of social analysis.[14] The Augustinian/Calvinist conviction that a fundamental conflict underlies the social order provides us with history's first version of conflictive social theory—a form of social theory of which we in our Marxist age have all become vividly aware.[15]

I have been speaking of the social thought of the early Calvinists, but of course what was remarkable about them was that this did not remain with them a pattern of thought, but became a component in their praxis. A new way of life came into being, its thought and practice interacting.[16] Along with it a typical psychological formation emerged—call it "the Calvinist social piety"—at the heart of which was the awareness of a tension between demand and reality. The Calvinists knew that they ought to be exercising their obedient gratitude in their occupations and in their social roles in general, but the very Word of

12. Marshall, quoted by Walzer, *Revolution of the Saints,* frontispiece.

13. Cf. Walzer, *Revolution of the Saints,* pp. 100 ff.

14. On this point one again finds a fundamental contrast between the vision characteristic of the Thomist Catholic and that of the Calvinists: the Catholic tends to see all humanity as reaching out for God, albeit often in misguided ways, whereas the Calvinist tends to see a fundamental division in humanity, between those who worship the true God and those who worship idols. This explains, of course, the tendency of Catholics to absorb a great many of the native religious practices into their liturgy, and the contrasting tendency of Calvinist Protestants to sweep away all such practices as "pagan."

15. Troeltsch gives a fine summary: "In Calvin's view the individual is not satisfied with mere repose in his own happiness, or perhaps with giving himself to others in loving personal service; further, he is not satisfied with an attitude of mere passive endurance and toleration of the world in which he lives, without entering fully into its life. He feels that, on the contrary, the whole meaning of life consists precisely in entering into these circumstances, and, while inwardly rising above them, in shaping them into an expression of the Divine Will. In conflict and in labour the individual takes up the task of the sanctification of the world, always with the certainty, however, that he will not lose himself in the life of the world; for indeed in everything the individual is only working out the meaning of election, which indeed consists in being strengthened to perform actions of this kind . . . The individual was drawn irresistibly into a whole-hearted absorption in the tasks of service to the world and to society, to a life of unceasing, penetrating, and formative labour" *(Social Teaching of the Christian Churches,* 2:588–89).

16. In later Calvinism the world-formative character of this new way of life will often diminish to the point of disappearance. All too typically what takes its place is a concern for the formation of ideas—especially theological ideas. Where the Lutheran becomes concerned with the formation of inwardness, the Calvinist becomes concerned with the formation of theology—or "philosophy."

God which told them this also showed them that the social roles presented to them were corrupted and not fit instruments for obedience. In some people this double awareness produced a restless impulse toward reformism along with the self-discipline that Weber so strongly emphasized. In others it produced a feeling of guilt. These are the people who found themselves in the aching situation of being persuaded in their hearts that they ought to be working for reform but stymied by a will too weak to bring themselves to do so. One does not apprehend the contours of the characteristic Calvinist social piety until one discerns the pervasive presence of this form of guilt. Some will say that it is not guilt at all, but a peculiar form of hypocrisy: people saying that they ought to work at reform but not believing it and happily filling their social roles in the ordinary way. Perhaps in some cases this acquiescence is the result of hypocrisy, but my own experience suggests that it is more often otherwise.

There is nothing in the Calvinist system to assuage this form of guilt—nothing other than the general word of pardon for our human failings. By contrast there is a special word of consolation for the persons who have done their best to secure reform but failed: to them the Calvinist says that in this fallen world of conflicting demands there is nonetheless (often) a *best* thing to do, and that this best thing is the *right* thing to do. Those who do the best thing can live with an easy conscience. This stands in contrast to the typical Lutheran formulation that the best of one's options is often nothing more than the lesser of two evils, and that one must accordingly pray to be forgiven for doing the unavoidable evil. The Calvinist does not demand that a politics appropriate to heaven be practiced here already on this fallen earth.

Restless disciplined reformism, or guilt for not being restlessly reformist: these are the characteristic components of the Calvinist social piety. When these are missing, one can reliably surmise that one is confronted with a person who has some other understanding of his or her social role than that characteristic of early Calvinism—with one exception: sometimes one is instead confronted with that most insufferable of all human beings, the triumphalist Calvinist, the one who believes that the revolution instituting the holy commonwealth has already occurred and that his or her task is now simply to keep it in place. Of these triumphalist Calvinists the United States and Holland have both had their share. South Africa today provides them in their purest form.

Original Calvinism represented, then, a passionate desire to reshape the social world so that it would no longer be alienated from God. Thereby it would also no longer be alienated from mankind, for the will of God is that society be an ordered "brotherhood" serving the common good. Once this passion to reshape the social world entered Western civilization, it remained. Later it would be energized by the desire to make the world expressive of one's "self"—to overcome the alienation between the desires of the self and the world. Originally it was energized by the passion to place on the world the stamp of holy obedience.

Is not that passion as relevant and imperative today as it was then? Admittedly, when we hear this word "obedience" we think immediately of the repressiveness of early Calvinism. Though the Calvinists spoke of justice, they failed to think through how they could live together in a just society with those with whom they disagreed. That was their great and tragic failing—though a failing scarcely unique to them. And a second failing, closely related, was their recurrent triumphalism. But is our need today for a society of justice and of peace not just as desperate as it was then? And when we struggle for such a society, do we not stand in continuity with the prophetic tradition of the Old Testament—and with Jesus Christ, who in the inaugural address of his ministry said that in him the words of the prophet Isaiah were fulfilled?

> The Spirit of the Lord is upon me,
> because he has anointed me to preach good news to the poor.
> He has sent me to proclaim release to the captives
> and recovering of sight to the blind,
> to set at liberty those who are oppressed,
> to proclaim the acceptable year of the Lord.

There are those in this world for whom the bonds of oppression are so tight that they cannot themselves work for a better society. Their lot falls on the shoulders of you and me. For I write mainly to those like myself who live in societies where the space of freedom is wide. To us I say: the Word of the Lord and the cries of the people join in calling us to do more than count our blessings, more than shape our inwardness, more than reform our thoughts. They call us to struggle for a new society in the hope and expectation that the goal of our struggle will ultimately be granted us.

Chapter 10

"Toward an Hispanic American Pentecostal Social Ethic"

1993

Eldin Villafañe

Not by might, nor by power, but by my
Spirit, says the Lord Almighty.
  —Zechariah 4:6 NIV

So far, I have understood that the most fruitful approach to developing the theological foundations for a social ethic for Hispanic Pentecostalism rest in the development of a social spirituality. This spirituality must emerge and thus cohere with Hispanic Pentecostal experience—particularly as it relates to the ministry of the Spirit. I have presented those needed elements for a social spirituality, the missing dimension in Hispanic Pentecostal experience. Our pneumatological paradigm coheres with Hispanic Pentecostal experience and seeks to extend its self-understanding as the community of the Spirit *in* the world and *for* the world, but not *of* the world.

In this [essay] I will first present under "Ethics as Pneumatology" the implications of our pneumatological paradigm for an Hispanic Pentecostal social ethic. Then I will need to address two significant areas in the development of an Hispanic Pentecostal social ethic, the role of Scripture and the "two pillars" of ethics—Love and Justice. I will conclude . . . with the implications for the life and mission of the church.

ETHICS AS PNEUMATOLOGY

If we live in the Spirit, let us also walk in the Spirit. (Gal. 5:25 KJV)

Ethics in Hispanic Pentecostalism emerges from its experience of the Spirit. The love of God in Jesus Christ poured out by the Spirit begins the spiritual pilgrimage (Rom. 5:5). This love becomes the source, motive and power of the living in the Spirit. It is this transforming experience of love that challenges the believer to seek "in obedience to God to follow Jesus in the power of the Spirit." This is both a spirituality and an ethic of the Spirit. Paul in his letter to the Galatians reminds us that both our theological self-understanding and our ethical self-understanding is grounded in the Spirit (Gal. 5:25).

> If we live in the Spirit [theological self-understanding], let us also walk in the Spirit [ethical self-understanding]. (Gal. 5:25 KJV)

It is important to note that the New Testament word for "walk" used by Paul in this verse is *stoichomen* (present active subject of *stoicheo)*. As such, it has a military sense in its etymology and has been paraphrased by some as "to follow the marching orders of the Spirit."[1] The New International Version of the New Testament translates the word "walk" as "let us keep in step with." The rich nuances of our "walk" in the Spirit suggest that our ethical conduct, whether personal or social, is a following of the leading of the Spirit[2] . . .

Consider the ethical implications of three major categories or themes . . . from my pneumatological paradigm. These can be schematically presented as follows:

If we live in the Spirit, [Theological Self-understanding]	*let us also walk in the Spirit.* [Ethical Self-understanding]
1. The Spirit's historical project	– The challenge to participate in the Reign of God.

---

1. See Gerhard Delling, *Stoicheo - Stoicheion, TDNT,* Vol. Vii, pp. 666–687; it is very suggestive Veiling's notation that, "The military use strictly differentiates *stoichos* for those arranged behind one another from *zugon* for those beside one another," *Ibid.,* p. 666; see also, Fritz Rienecker "Galatians 5:25", *A Linguistic Key to the Greek New Testament,* p. 518.

2. We may even say a *dancing* after the Spirit—our ethical pilgrimage should be performed in celebration. Ridderbos reminds us that "the word [*stoicheo*] was used for movement in a definite line, as in military formation or in *dancing."* Herman Ridderbos, *The Epistle of Paul to the Church of Galatians: The New International Commentary on the New Testament* (Grand Rapids, Michigan: Eerdmans, 1970), quoted in Fritz Rienecker, *A Linguistic Key to the Greek New Testament,* p. 518, my italics; for a current and insightful presentation that highlights Paul's use of the metaphor of *walking* to describe the moral life of the believer, see, J. Paul Sampley, *Walking Between the Times: Paul's Moral Reasoning* (Minneapolis: Augsbury Fortress Press, 1991).

2. The Spirit's power encounters   – The challenge to confront
                                           structural sin and evil.

3. The Spirit's "charismatic"   – The challenge to fulfill the
   empowerment   prophetic and empowerment
                                           vocational role of the "baptism
                                           in the Spirit"

THE CHALLENGE TO PARTICIPATE IN THE REIGN OF GOD

C. René Padilla reminds us that "el imperativo de la ética cristiana se deriva directamente del indicativo del Evangelio. Lo que *hacemos* es solo la respuesta a lo que *Dios ha hecho*."[3] It can be equally stated that the imperative of Christian ethics—particularly social ethics—is derived directly from the indicative of the Spirit's historical project—the Reign of God. Not only is the framework of New Testament theology eschatological, but equally is its social ethics. The Gospel of Jesus Christ is the Gospel of the Reign of God. In Jesus Christ the Reign was particularized and made efficacious through the Cross. The eternal redemption (Hebrew 9:12) wrought in Calvary was made through the eternal Spirit (Hebrew 9:14). In the Spirit, through whom the risen Christ is mediated to us, the Reign has been universalized.

A proper understanding of the *present reality and scope* of the Reign of God is critically needed by Hispanic Pentecostals. The present *charismata*—glossolalia, divine healing, other manifestations of the Spirit—in Hispanic Pentecostalism can only be biblically and theologically understood if the Reign of God is a present reality. While there may be certain understanding of the relation of the Reign and the Spirit's *charismata* in the Hispanic Pentecostal church, it is the social and political implications that are lacking.

The Spirit of God, by whom Christ "went about doing good and healing all that were oppressed of the devil" (Acts 10:38 KJV) and through whom Christ "offered himself . . . to God" (Hebrews 9:14 KJV), is *still* carrying out the Reign task. To participate in the Reign of God is to participate in the power of the age to come that are present and available to the church by the Spirit. The church must follow the Spirit as Christ. It too must be an "anointed one," the body of Christ thrust in the world to do good and heal all those oppressed of the devil, wherever and however that is manifested. It also must, like Christ, offer itself to God: as a true incarnation in the affairs of the world and as a true cross bearer in social "redemption."[4]

---

3. "the imperative of Christian ethics is derived directly from the indicative of the Gospel. What *we do* is only the response to what *God has done*," in C. René Padilla, "El Evangelio y la Responsabilidad Social," in C. René Padilla, *El Evangelio Hoy* (Buenos Aires, Argentina: Ediciones Certeza, 1975), p. 79, (Padilla's italics).

4. In the words of Leonardo Boff, "The church has always understood itself as the continuation of Christ and his mission," Leonardo Boff, *Church: Charism and Power* (New York: Crossroad Publishing Company, 1986), p. 144.

To participate in the Reign of God means to participate in God's rule. It is to take seriously God's call as a church to be a community of the Spirit *in* the world and a community of the Spirit *for* the world. This participation implies that there is no area of life where the rule of God cannot be exercised. While God rules in the Church through the pneumatic (risen) Christ, the church must not see itself as the only *locus* of the Reign of God. Boff reminds us that "the church must . . . define itself as an instrument for the full realization of the Kingdom and as a sign of a true yet still imperfect realization of this Kingdom in the world."[5] The church is thus challenged not to see itself as an *end* but as a means towards the building of God's Reign.

To participate in the Reign of God is to participate in the political process. Christian participation in the political process is predicated in the understanding that Christ is Lord of the Kingdom of this world, too. Although, the rule of Christ has not been fully manifested—awaiting the *eschaton*—his claim and dominion are to impact all human relations, meaning, the political process. James W. Jones, in speaking about participating in the political process, makes clear the significance of participating in the Spirit's historical project:

> The people of God are still bidden to seek the peace of the city in which they dwell (cf. Jer. 29:7) and to witness to the Lordship of Jesus Christ over the whole of life. Therefore, a total separation from the political Kingdom of this world is probably neither possible nor desirable. The political process can serve the relative peace of the world. . . . The Christian knows that political activity will not bring in the Kingdom of God nor undercut the eschatological tension of the Kingdom of God, which, because it has not yet come, stands over and against the human state of affairs. Therefore, politics is not his ultimate concern. His primary concern must be submission to the plan of God to fill all things with himself through his Spirit. But political activity can serve to fulfill the biblical injunction to seek for peace and to proclaim the Lordship of Christ over all.[6]

The challenge to participate in the Reign of God implies that the Hispanic Pentecostal church must discern the signs of God's reign in the world. While it may be a difficult and often a treacherous task, given the experience of Hispanics being exploited and oppressed in the world-outside-the-church, the need to discern the Spirit's action in the world and unite with the Spirit in the struggle is part of the calling of the church as it witnesses to the full liberation of the Reign. Justo L. González, commenting on the need for Hispanics to develop a political spirituality, notes the importance of discerning the signs of God's reign.

> . . . porque la humanidad no tiene otro futuro sino el Reino, los cristianos debemos saber que no tenemos un monopolio sobre toda señal del Reino. Porque Dios es el Rey, su voluntad se hará con nosotros, en nosotros, y

---

5. *Ibid.*, p.146.
6. James W. Jones, *The Spirit and the World*, pp. 73–74.

hasta a pesar de nosotros . . . doquiera se alimenta al hambriento, se viste al desnudo o se visita al cautivo, Dios está presente, y hay señales de su Reino. La espiritualidad que tenemos que desarrollar consiste precisamente en aprender a ver esas señales, aún cuando no vengan de nosotros ni de la iglesia, y a unirnos a Dios en su acción en el mundo, en anticipo de su Reino.[7]

To Hispanic Pentecostals the challenge to participate in the Reign of God also implies reading anew the signs of the Reign present in their own Hispanic culture, religious traditions, and social reality. One finds in these rich resources for ethical reflection that affirm, point to and express genuine signs of the Reign in their midst. The Hispanic Pentecostal church must learn to see and affirm those signs of the Reign in its midst in the "barrios" if it is to discern those signs outside. A proper self-understanding (identity) is critical for vocation—for carrying out any missional endeavor.[8] Among the many signs/themes that can be noted we will list five that the Hispanic Pentecostal church needs to acknowledge, reappropriate and share with others—witness to in the greater society.

1. "Mestizaje"

Hispanics as the *Raza Cósmica*. The Hispanic Pentecostal church reflects this "mixed" constituency—Spanish (white), African (black) and Amerindian stock. It embodies and witnesses to the shalom of the races—signs of the Reign.

2. "La Morenita"

The significance of the "brown lady" in evangelization in Catholicism, . . . although not part of its religious symbols, Hispanic Pentecostals, nevertheless, should be able to affirm with the dominant Hispanic Catholic culture the positive image of womanhood of "La Morenita" in the liberating process.

3. "Migración"

Since 1848 the migration experience has defined most Hispanics. In a real historical sense they are a pilgrim people. This migration experience has made Hispanics a

7. " . . . because humanity has no other future but the Kingdom, Christians should know that we do not have a monopoly over all signs of the Kingdom. Because God is the King, his will shall be done with us, in us, and even in spite of us . . . wherever the hungry are fed, the naked clothed or prisoners visited, God is present, and these are signs of his Kingdom. The spirituality that we must develop consist precisely in learning to see these signs, even when they do not come from us nor the church, and to join God in his action in the world, in anticipation of his Kingdom," Justo L. González, "Espiritualidad Política", in *Apuntes*, Vol. 3, No. 1 (Primavera 1983), pp. 8–9; see also Juno L. González's "Spirituality and the Spirit of Mañana" in his *Mañana: Christian Theology from a Hispanic Perspective* (Nashville: Abingdon Press, 1990) pp. 157–163.

8. This is a truth I have learned in matters of race and ethnic relations. It requires an authentic recovery, reappropriation and appreciation of one's history and culture (e.g. identity) before one can properly participate in genuine dialogue with other persons of different culture or race.

3. "Migración" (*cont.*)   "pueblo puente" or "pueblo fronterizo." The Hispanic Pentecostal church is challenged to live not only between the "times" (the *now* and *not yet* of the Reign), but also, "must look at 'our' mission as Christian Hispanics in the U.S. Being *a border people,* no matter where we live, we must serve as a means of communication between the rich, over-affluent and misdeveloped world of the North, and the poor, exploited and also misdeveloped world of the South. This, and the mission to other Hispanics, requires that we continue to be a bilingual and bicultural church."

4. "Menesterosos" (the indigent, poor and the oppressed)   The Pentecostal church is indeed the "haven of the poor and the masses"—the poor and the working class. While not "ghettorizing" or locking-out the Hispanics from up-grading their economic conditions, nevertheless the Hispanic Pentecostal church must affirm and see itself as a *locus* where the poor and oppressed can find liberation; where solidarity with the poor and the oppressed can be found in the struggle for a full liberation in the world.

5. "Modelos Sociales" (the significant role models by the Hispanic Church)   The Hispanic Pentecostal church as it fulfills these roles in the "barrios" it embodies and witnesses to the Reign of God.
  (a) Survival—A Place of Cultural Survival
  (b) Signpost—A Signpost of Protest and Resistance
  (c) Salvation—A liberated and liberating community
  (d) Shalom—An Agent of Reconciliation
  (e) Secret of the Reign—Hermeneutical Advantage of the Poor
  (f) Seedbed for Community Leaders—Emerging leadership nurtured
  (g) Social Service Provider—Natural Support Systems—Source of Strength

Ultimately, the challenge to participate in the Reign is to understand that the signs of the Reign of God are the Spirit's work in the world to *both* "restrain" evil and "help" establish the conditions for a more just and peaceful moral order in all human affairs. They point to the New Age—the new order that has broken into History. It is a work of grace—God's love reaching out by the Spirit to keep and to make human life human.[9] As Paul Lehmann states,

> Let it be noted that the signs which point to and point up what God is doing in the world are *ethical* signs. What is *indicated* is that the politics of God does make a discernible difference in the world, and the ongoing life of the *Koinonia* is the context within which to come in sight of this difference. The *Koinonia* is the bearer in the world of the mystery (secret) and the transforming power of the divine activity, on the one hand, and on the other, of the secret (mystery) and the 'stuff' of human maturity.[10]

Culture and social institutions and structures must be seen as legitimate arenas where God's grace is manifested to make and keep human life human—thus, the task of the church (the *Koinonia)* is to discern God's presence, and "to follow the marching orders of the Spirit," who goes before us in the struggle. While the church knows that its actions in the world does not bring in the Reign, as a "community of exiles and pilgrims,"[11] it faithfully joins the Spirit in witnessing to its historical task.

THE CHALLENGE TO CONFRONT
STRUCTURAL SIN AND EVIL

The Spirit's power encounter defines the cosmic struggle being waged for God's creation . . . The Spirit as "the restrainer" *(to Katechon)* and as "the Helper" *(Parakletos)* sets the framework for this struggle.[12] In the person and work of Jesus, the "charismatic Christ," this power encounter identified the Reign of God as present (Matthew 12:28). This spiritual power encounter reached its zenith in Jesus' death on the cross—an apparent victory for sin and evil. Of course, this was followed by the Empty tomb—the Resurrection—thus, the Victory. The Cross, seen both as death and resurrection, signals the triumph over the "powers" (Colossians 2:15 KJV). Sin and evil have been conquered. Whether manifested in individual-personal life or in social existence (in structures and institutions) the "powers" have been "disarmed," their idolatrous-demonic claims have been shattered.

---

9. For a provocative and insightful view, see Paul Lehmann's chapter, "What God Is Doing in the World" in Paul Lehmann, *Ethics in a Christian Context* (New York, N.Y.: Harper and Row, Publishers, 1963), pp. 74–101.

10. *Ibid.*, p.112, italics are Lehmann's.

11. See George W. Webber, *Today's Church: A Community of Exiles and Pilgrims* (Nashville, Tennessee: Abingdon, 1979).

12. Also it is important to note Otto Maduro's conflict analysis as setting the socio-cultural framework for confrontation, creative-conflict.

Yet, the church is still engaged in a bitter struggle—spiritual power encounters. In the words of John Wimber:

> the final and full establishment of the Kingdom of God, with Christ as its head, was assured at the resurrection, but we have yet to realize its fullness in these days in which we live . . . there is a war yet to be fought . . . we must equip ourselves by allowing the power of the Spirit to come into our lives and work through us to defeat the enemy.[13]

The tendency of many, including Wimber, is to see this struggle too individualistically and not see that spiritual warfare must correspond with the geography of evil—the sinful and evil structures of society. The Hispanic Pentecostal church must see itself not only as a *locus* for personal liberation, but also as a *locus* for social liberation. They must see that the texture of social living makes no easy distinctions between the personal and the social. That beyond the security— often more an illusion than a fact—of the "culto," beyond individual-personal struggles and outreach, where there are structures and institutions that must be confronted in the power of the Spirit. The church's mission includes engaging in power encounters with sinful and evil structures.

Our confrontation responds to the nature of the structures themselves. On the one hand, we are aware of their creatureness—they are institutions and structures *by* and *for* humans, although their reality *sui generis*. On the other hand, we are aware of their possible demonic nature—the "powers." On one level of the struggle, it means that the church must bring to bear, through our witness and labors, the power of the Spirit to break the chains of hate, hostility, and injustice embedded in them by introducing the values of the Reign of God (i.e., love, justice, fair play) and setting in place a "chain of change"[14] that immediately (thus, radical change—revolution), or gradually (thus, multiple and cumulative amelioration—reformation) humanizes these structures and institutions. On the other level of the struggle, the church must witness to the demonic powers that lie behind the scene, by reminding them of their defeat in Christ and the coming New Age. This witness must be in the power of the Spirit, armed with the "full armor of God" (Ephesians 6:10–18 NIV). Jim Wallis states it well.

> The church demonstrates Christ's victory over the powers by reminding them of their created role as servants, rebuking them in their idolatrous role as rulers, and resisting them in their totalitarian claims and purposes . . . We are not asked to defeat the powers. That is the work of Christ, which he has already done and will continue to do. Our task is to be witnesses and signs of Christ's victory by simply standing firmly in our faith and belief against the seduction and slavery of the powers.[15]

13. John Wimber, *Power Evangelism*, p.21.
14. See Mel King, *Chain of Change: Struggles for Black Community Development* (Boston, Mass.: South End Press, 1981).
15. Jim Wallis, *Agenda for Biblical People*, pp. 48–49.

THE CHALLENGE TO FULFILL THE PROPHETIC
AND VOCATIONAL ROLE OF THE BAPTISM IN THE SPIRIT

The Spirit's "charismatic" empowerment has been a singular and distinguishing emphasis in Pentecostalism. Hispanic Pentecostals, as other Pentecostals, have tended to interpret this experience narrowly. While it is true that Pentecostalism has been recognized as a powerful force in evangelism, world missions, church growth and spirituality, it is equally true that their services and prophetic voices against sinful social structures and on behalf of social justice have been missing.

For Pentecostals five episodes in the book of Acts set the biblical precedent of Spirit baptism, thus, building "their distinctive theology regarding the gift of the Spirit."[16] The scope of this study does not permit us to enter the dialogue on the methodological issue of the "normativeness" for theology of Luke's historical record. Be that as it may, it is important to note that Roger Stronstad's *The Charismatic Theology of St. Luke* presents a formidable *apologia* contra Frederick Dale Bruner and James D.G. Dunn, two highly influential works on the baptism of the Spirit.[17] Stronstad, in my opinion, not only makes an excellent case for the theological character of Lukan historiography and its theological independence (from Pauline interpretation), but through a careful study of the Old Testament, Intertestamental Period, life and work of Christ (whom he calls the Charismatic Christ), and the primitive church (the charismatic community) he traces the purpose of the baptism in the Spirit distinctively as empowerment for witness and service. He states:

> For Luke, the gift of the Spirit has a vocational purpose and equips the disciples for service. Thus, it is devoid of any soteriological connotations and, contra Dunn, it does not mean that 'it is God's giving of the Spirit which makes a man a Christian.'[18]

Stronstad further underlines the universal potential and objective of the baptism in the Spirit:

> In Old Testament times, and even in the Gospel era, the activity of the Spirit is restricted to chosen leaders. From Pentecost onwards, however, the vocational gift of the Spirit is potentially universal. . . . At His baptism, Jesus becomes the unique bearer of the Spirit, and at Pentecost He becomes the giver of the Spirit . . . with the qualification that the vocational activity

16. Roger Stronstad, *The Charismatic Theology of St. Luke*, p. 5; the Scripture references are: (1) Acts 2:1–13; (2) Acts 8:14–19; (3) Acts 9:17–18; (4) Acts 10:44–46; and (5) Acts 19:1–7.
17. Frederick Dale Bruner, *A Theology of the Holy Spirit: The Pentecostal Experience and the New Testament Witness* (Grand Rapids, Michigan: Wm. B. Eerdmans, 1970); James D.G. Dunn, *Baptism in the Holy Spirit: A Re-examination of the New Testament Teaching of the Gift of the Spirit in Relation to Pentecostalism Today* (London: SCM Press Ltd., 1970); for an excellent exposition contra Dunn see also, Howard M. Ervin, *Conversion-Initiation and the Baptism in the Holy Spirit* (Peabody. Mass.: Hendrickson Publishers, Inc., 1984).
18. Roget Stronstad, *The Charismatic Theology of St. Luke*, p. 64.

of the Spirit is now potentially universal and *its new object is the ongoing mission of the Messiah,* the gift of the Spirit is in continuity with the way in which God has always poured out His Spirit upon His servants.[19]

What is of critical importance and the *crux interpretum* relative to the baptism of the Spirit is its prophetic and vocational purpose, its universal-egalitarian scope and its missional focus.

The social ethical implications for Hispanic Pentecostalism are significant. While the universal-egalitarian scope of the baptism of the Spirit is present in the "culto," its greater purpose and missional focus in the service of the Spirit's historical project is not present. The baptism of the Spirit in Hispanic Pentecostalism is rightfully seen as empowerment for service, impacting the believer deeply—giving him/her tremendous boldness, a heightened sense of personal holiness, a new sense of self worth and personal power.[20] Yet, the narrow individualistic focus and purpose implies the dissipation in the "culto," if not elsewhere, of so much energy—spiritual power—that can and should be "tapped" for the broader missional objective of the church. The Hispanic Pentecostal church has the spiritual resources to face the spiritual power encounters of our social struggles. If the "new object [of the baptism of the Spirit] is the ongoing mission of the Messiah,"[21] and that cannot be narrowed to Matthew 28:18–21, nor Mark 16:15–18, nor Acts 1:8, then it must, above all, include the Messiah's own missional self-understanding—Luke 4:18–19:

> The Spirit of the Lord is on me; therefore he has anointed me to preach good news to the poor. He has sent me to proclaim freedom for the prisoners and recovery of sight for the blind, to release the oppressed, to proclaim the year of the Lord's favor.

Hispanic Pentecostalism, as most branches of Pentecostalism, must see the bigger picture in the Spirit's economy. The Spirit's "charismatic" empowerment are valid "signs and wonders" of the presence of the Reign. It remains then for the faithful fulfillment of the prophetic and vocational role of the baptism in the Spirit.

> If we live in the Spirit,
> Let us also walk in the Spirit.
>   (Galatians 5:25 KJV)

---

19. Ibid., p.79 (my italics). It is important to note that neither glossolalia as "initial evidence'" of the baptism of the Spirit, nor as a gift for the church is at issue, rather the baptism of the Spirit's purpose then, and now.

20. Elements critically needed by all, but especially by the poor and the oppressed in our "barrios"; see, "Gerlach and Hine's Functional-Structural Analysis," Chapter III, "Socio-Theological Interpretation of the Hispanic Urban Pentecostal Reality."

21. Roger Stronstad, *The Charismatic Theology of St. Luke*, p. 79.

Chapter 11

"A Continuing Theocratic Tradition"

2002

Allen Verhey

The early church had a lively sense of being "a people." They were "a chosen race, a royal priesthood, a holy nation, God's own people" (1 Pet. 2:9). Indeed, even their opponents called them the "third people."[1] Christians themselves, however, did not simply set themselves in contrast to the Jews and the Romans; they were a "new humanity in place of the two" (Eph. 2:15). The old ways of distinguishing and dividing people had been cancelled, and not only national but social and sexual distinctions had been transcended (Gal. 3:28; Col. 3:11). They were "a new creation" (Gal. 6:15).

THE CONTINUING CHURCH

The continuing church did not cross some Jordan to take possession of a piece of real estate. They were, as Tertullian insisted, "a people of the whole world," and

---

1. Tertullian, *ad Nationes*, I.viii. See further, Adolf Harnack, "Christians as a Third Race," in *The Mission and Expansion of Christianity in the First Three Centuries*, trans. James Moffatt (New York: Harper Torchbooks, 1961; the German original was published in 1908), pp. 266–78.

national boundaries were insignificant to them.[2] Nevertheless, they still faced those theocratic questions Moses had raised for the people of God ready to enter that land. Now that we have been made a people and given "an inheritance" (1 Pet. 1:4) that surpasses the imagination, how shall we live? How shall we live a common life, a politics, which displays the lordship of Christ? And since they were not a nation but the light of the nations, they faced a second question as well. How shall we live with the politics of Rome?

The conviction that they were in fact "a people" was not just an abstraction for the early church. It entailed also a lively sense of political independence. They were not simply a part of some other people; they were not first of all or fundamentally answerable to some other nation or empire or its ruler. They were ruled by Christ, the ascended Lord. They were under his authority, and, under his authority, they were authorized to rule themselves. Their citizenship was in heaven (Phil. 3:20). They were, as their Thessalonian opponents had claimed, ruled by "another king named Jesus" (Acts 17:7). They had—or were called to have—a common life, a politics, "worthy of the gospel of Christ" (Phil. 1:27).

As the *Epistle to Diognetus* said, it is not that Christians live in cities of their own or speak a language of their own or dress differently or eat differently, but they nevertheless display that "their citizenship is in heaven."[3]

> They marry like all other men and they beget children; but they do not cast away their offspring. They have their meals in common, but not their wives. They find themselves in the flesh, and yet they live not after the flesh. Their existence is on earth, but their citizenship is in heaven. They obey the established laws, and they surpass the laws in their own lives. They love all men. . . . They are reviled, and they bless; they are insulted, and they respect.[4]

The early church displayed its citizenship and said among the nations, "God is king," by caring for the sick, by living sexual lives of chastity and fidelity, by feeding the hungry, and by helping the poor. The early church displayed its citizenship and said among the nations, "Jesus is Lord," in a politics of mutual instruction and discernment, of reconciliation and forgiveness, and of peaceable difference. This was not a politics of force or of lording it over a neighbor; it was a politics of "persuasion, not force: for force is no attribute of God."[5] The

---

2. Tertullian, *Apology*, 37. Consider also the fatuous line in *Apology*, 38: "[N]othing is more foreign to us than the state. One state we know, of which all are citizens—the universe"; in Tertullian, *Apology and De Spectaculis*, trans. T. R. Glover, Loeb Classical Library (Cambridge, Mass.: Harvard University Press, 1931).

3. *Epistle to Diognetus*, 5, in *The Apostolic Fathers*, ed. J. B. Lightfoot and J. R. Harmer (Grand Rapids: Baker, 1984), p. 506.

4. *Epistle to Diognetus*, 5, p. 506.

5. *Epistle to Diognetus*, 7, p. 507. See also *Epistle to Diognetus*, 10, p. 509:

For happiness consisteth not in lordship over one's neighbours, nor in desiring to have more than weaker men, nor in possessing wealth and using force to inferiors . . . But whosoever

apologists never tired of pointing out the way of life of these communities or of comparing it to the politics of the empire.

How, then, those in the early church wondered, should they relate to the politics of the empire? Their sense of political independence provided the freedom to disobey the authorities when obedience to Christ and to the cause of God required it. They told and lived the story of the martyrs, after all. But it also provided the freedom to honor the Roman authorities. And in ordinary circumstances their political responsibility as citizens of heaven included such honor and submission. As "servants of God" they were to live "as free people," but that freedom was not anarchy; "as free people" they were to "accept the authority of every human institution" and to "honor the emperor" (1 Pet. 2:13–17 NIV). The early church joined suspicion of political authorities to the honor due them in ways that were familiar to the theocratic tradition.

The earliest political writings of the continuing church were from the apologists, who undertook the task of defending the early church against the charges brought against it, including the charge of being a subversive movement. Understandably, this genre emphasized the honor and submission that Christians gave to the emperor. This genre of apologetic literature developed into anti-pagan polemic, of which Augustine's *City of God* is the crowning achievement, and within which the theocratic dialectic between suspicion and honor finds clearer expression. The writings against heresy within the church were a quite different genre, of course, but no less important politically. Gnosticism, Marcionism, and Manichaeism all threatened the church's link with the Jewish tradition and the identification of the God and Father of Jesus with the God of creation and covenant in the Hebrew Scriptures. Against the heretics it was necessary to defend the theocratic political tradition of Israel and of Jesus, a tradition "wrung from experience on the underside of world politics,"[6] a tradition of God's judgment against the bestial politics of empire but, at the same time, a tradition of God's blessing upon the nations.

The sense of political independence required that the church confront the empire "as a foreign power."[7] It did not require, however, the denial of whatever was good and true and just within that "foreign power." They were the people of God, but God, after all, was the creator of all and (whether recognized or not) Lord of all. The emperor could do some good; the pagan philosopher could speak the truth; local customs were not to be summarily dismissed; and "the

---

taketh upon himself the burden of his neighbour, whosoever desireth to benefit one that is worse off in that in which he himself is superior, . . . he is an imitator of God.

6. Oliver O'Donovan and Joan Lockwood O'Donovan, eds., *From Irenaeus to Grotius: A Sourcebook in Christian Political Thought, 100–1625* (Grand Rapids: Eerdmans, 1999), p. 5. This whole paragraph is indebted to the analysis there of the genres within which early Christian political thought appeared, and the whole book is a splendid resource for Christian political thought.

7. O'Donovan and O'Donovan, eds., *Irenaeus to Grotius*, p. 6. The O'Donovans add parenthetically, "even when the emperor was a Christian." They also observe that this inference from the meaning of the church's *politeia* was less clear in the East than in the West.

Samaritan" could still put "the righteous" to shame. "Whatever is true, whatever is honorable, whatever is just, whatever is pure, whatever is pleasing, whatever is commendable" (Phil. 4:8) is not to be denied but credited to God and counted as God's gifts to humanity. To many of the apologists—and surely to Clement of Alexandria and Origen—Christ was the powerful and creative Word of God, present in the creation and in history, the *logos* who has always generated the good and the true. The audacious claim of these apologists was that whatever goodness and truth and justice existed was the work of Christ. The wisdom of other peoples could and did enter the deliberations—and the political deliberations—of Christians. The final test, however, for reasons given and heard in the church remained the story of Jesus. Discernment—and political discernment—was still to be exercised in memory of the Christ, who is Lord of all.

THE CONSTANTINIAN CHURCH

The dialectic of suspicion and honor was not easy to preserve, and it did not get easier with the conversion of Constantine, his victory over Maxentius, and the Edict of Milan in 313. Eusebius surely spoke for many other Christians in his celebration of these events and in praise of Constantine. One can understand the enthusiasm. Only a decade before, in 303, the emperor Diocletian had issued a series of edicts requiring that Christian churches be destroyed, that their Scriptures be burned, and finally that all Christians should be put to death. Hard on the heels of Diocletian's persecution came this remarkable reversal. Suddenly, the emperor was a Christian!

One can understand the enthusiasm. For nearly three centuries they had been saying that Christ was Lord, that he had ascended to the right hand of God, and that he would return to judge and to save. In their mission to all nations they had been saying, "The LORD is king!" They had envisioned a future emptied of tyranny, filled with peace. Many had heard them gladly, but the more the people responded, the more the rulers had opposed them. Now, suddenly, the ruler was on their side. It was the victory of Christ!

The Inordinate Praise of Constantine

That was, of course, the explanation Eusebius gave in his praise of Constantine. One can understand Eusebius's enthusiasm, but his praise was still inordinate. He claimed too much when he claimed to see in Constantine's accession an end to the "despotic violence" of emperors.[8] He claimed too much when he claimed

---

8. Eusebius, "From a Speech for the Thirtieth Anniversary of Constantine's Accession," in *Irenaeus to Grotius*, ed. O'Donovan and O'Donovan, pp. 60–65, p. 62.

to see in Constantine's victories the fulfillment of the ancient oracles of peace.[9] He claimed too much when he claimed to see in Constantine "a transcript of the divine sovereignty" and "the semblance of heavenly sovereignty."[10] It was almost as if the accession of Constantine were the *parousia*. The reign of God was identified too uncritically with the reign of Constantine. Honor was due Constantine as emperor, and what Christian would not be glad at his conversion, but Eusebius undercut the suspicion of conventional politics that had been part of the theocratic tradition since the amphictyony. (Constantine himself claimed too much when he claimed to be a bishop, if only over external matters in the church. In the *politeia* of the church he should have been regarded as another member.) Against the enthusiasm of Eusebius the church would need to struggle to recover its sense that this, too, was not yet God's good future, to retrieve its capacity to confront the empire as "a foreign power" (even when the emperor was a Christian), and to articulate the boundaries between the church as a new humanity and the empire as the old order.[11]

The Inordinate Criticism of "Constantinianism"

Eusebius went too far in his celebration of Constantine. Critics of "Constantinianism," notably John Howard Yoder and Stanley Hauerwas, sometimes go too far, too.[12] One can understand their concerns. I share many of those concerns, and I am deeply indebted to them both, especially for their emphasis on the politics appropriate to the common life of the Christian community; but they go too far in their criticisms of "Constantinianism," construing it, it seems, as "the fall of the church." Consider, for example, the litany of complaints in Yoder's "The Constantinian Sources of Western Social Ethics."[13]

One can understand his concern that the church after Constantine included many who were only nominally Christians, since it was no longer dangerous to be named a Christian.[14] But he claimed too much when he said, "After Constantine, the church was everybody," and when he took the persecution of pagans and heretics to be a necessary result of Constantine's conversion and rule.[15] The Edict of Milan (313) did not make Christianity the official religion

9. Including Psalm 72:7–8 and Isaiah 2:4. Eusebius, "From a Speech on the Dedication of the Holy Sepulchre Church," in *Irenaeus to Grotius*, ed. O'Donovan and O'Donovan, pp. 58–59, p. 59.

10. Eusebius, "From a Speech for the Thirtieth Anniversary of Constantine's Accession:' in *Irenaeus to Grotius*, ed. O'Donovan and O'Donovan, pp. 60–65, p. 60. Even so, it ought to be noted that Eusebius began his praise of Constantine with praise of God, the "Great Sovereign."

11. It is a long—and continuing—story. It is told with great insight in Oliver O'Donovan, *The Desire of the Nations* (Cambridge: Cambridge University Press, 1996), pp. 199–242.

12. See John Howard Yoder, "The Constantinian Sources of Western Social Ethics," in *The Priestly Kingdom: Social Ethics as Gospel* (Notre Dame: University of Notre Dame Press, 1984), pp. 135–47; and Stanley Hauerwas, *After Christendom?* (Nashville: Abingdon, 1991). They regard Constantinianism as "the fall of the church."

13. Yoder, *The Priestly Kingdom*, pp. 135–47.

14. Yoder, *The Priestly Kingdom*, pp. 135–36.

15. Yoder, *The Priestly Kingdom*, pp. 135–36.

of the empire; indeed, it did not even give Christianity a preferred position; it recognized religious pluralism. It was not until Theodosius I that the assemblies of heretics and the rituals of pagans were prohibited, and not until the Theodosian Code of 438 that Theodosius II ordered the death penalty for heretics and decreed that pagans could not serve in the army. A Theodosius was not a necessary successor of Constantine. A Christian emperor could have and should have protected religious freedom—not because religion is a private matter, not because religion should be publicly regarded as irrelevant, or at best as secondary, to the public loyalties of citizens, and not because religious freedom signals that one's primary loyalty belongs to the state. A Christian emperor could have and should have protected religious freedom precisely because loyalty to God is more fundamental than loyalty to the state. The emperor could have and should have acknowledged the limitations on his own sovereignty, the limits on that secondary loyalty of citizens that he could claim for the empire. There are good theocratic reasons to protect religious freedom.[16]

The celebration of Constantine had confused Constantine's conversion with the final victory of God and confused the empire with the kingdom of God and the emperor's authority with the reign of God. Those are important concerns, named by Yoder as concerns about "the new eschatology" and "the new 'servant of the Lord,'"[17] but they are more appropriate to Eusebius's inordinate celebration than to Constantine's conversion and accession. Yoder claimed too much when he said, "Ethics had to change because one must aim one's behavior at strengthening the regime."[18] That was not the aim of most Christians, as happy as they might have been about Constantine's conversion. And if they expected the emperor to be a (rather than *the*) "Servant of the Lord," there were resources for such an expectation not only in the political reflections of the Yahwist and the royal psalms but also in the political reflections of Paul and others long before Constantine's conversion.

Yoder claimed too much when he complained that "after Constantine" moral deliberation was reduced to "universalizability" and "effectiveness."[19] It was almost as if the Enlightenment, with its Kantian and utilitarian theories of ethics, was the direct descendent of Constantine. It may be admitted that "Constantinians" were interested in identifying moral agreements where they could be found, but the apologists of earlier centuries, as we have observed, had already celebrated moral truth and goodness wherever they found it. Such moral truth was still regarded as the work of the *logos* in creation and history, the very *logos* revealed finally and decisively in the Christ whose story is told in Scripture.

16. See Allen Verhey, *Remembering Jesus: Christian Community, Scripture, and the Moral Life* (Grand Rapids: Eerdmans, 2002), ch. 16, pp. 342–43.
17. Yoder, *The Priestly Kingdom*, pp. 136–39.
18. Yoder, *The Priestly Kingdom*, p. 137. See also Hauerwas, *After Christendom?* p. 39, and the charge that the church took up "Rome's project."
19. Yoder, *The Priestly Kingdom*, pp. 139–40.

And the memory of Jesus could remain the test for appeals to such moral commonplaces in the deliberation of apologists (and "Constantinians").

It may also be admitted that "Constantinians" were interested in effectiveness. This is a charge that Yoder repeated often. "The prevailing assumption, from the time of Constantine until yesterday, [was] that the fundamental responsibility of the church for society is to manage it."[20] Yoder was surely right to claim that the "fundamental" responsibility is not management but mission, but he goes too far in the claim that Christians should have no interest in the consequences of their acts and nothing to do with "managing the world." A theocrat will have to disagree.[21] To be sure, there are limits to our efforts to predict and calculate the consequences of our actions, but the moral life requires some such effort. Could we drive a car morally without making such an effort? And if God gave human beings "dominion" in the world (Gen. 1:26, 28), it is not self-evident that the refusal to "manage" the world is appropriate. Of course, one should not use that power to oppress and enslave. (That story of creation was written against the tyranny of the Babylonians, as we have seen.) But Joseph and Daniel and Nehemiah served in Egyptian, Babylonian, and Persian governments. The judges and kings and prophets and lawmakers of Israel used their capacities to consider and predict the outcomes of their actions and policies. If these managed and calculated, then it does not seem that Christians should always refuse to participate in managing a society or to consider the effects of actions and policies.

Against "Constantinianism" Yoder set the story of Jesus, and particularly the story of his obedient "powerlessness" on the cross.[22] Yoder did ethics "by way of reminder," too. He is right to set the stories of our lives alongside the story of Jesus so that our lives may be judged and made new by the memory of Jesus. And he is right about this: our common life is still possessed by demons that will not be exorcised by violence. But he goes too far. We need not repeat here what was said earlier concerning the story of Jesus—discussion about his power and "authority" in exorcism (or about the social and political significance of exorcism), about the "authority" he displayed in cleansing the temple, about the "authority" of his words (or about the saying concerning non-retaliation). Let it simply be said again that soldiers and a centurion and scribes were not called to give up their power; they were called to construe and use their power to protect and to serve those who were least. Constantine and "Constantinians" have plenty to repent of here, but they need not repent of power or authority itself. They may not be tyrants. They may not "lord it over" those who are subject to

---

20. John Howard Yoder, *The Politics of Jesus* (Grand Rapids: Eerdmans, 1972), p. 248. In "The Biblical Mandate," *Post-American* (April 1974), p. 25, Yoder made the same point with another memorable phrase, that we should "see our obedience more as praising God, and less as running the world for Him." If it were simply a matter of "less" and "more," there should be no objection to this claim, but for Yoder Christians have no business running the world.

21. Yoder sees an association of the "theocratic" and Calvinist traditions; see his *The Christian Witness to the State* (Newton, Kans.: Faith and Life Press, 1964), pp. 64–65.

22. Yoder, *The Politics of Jesus*, pp. 244–48.

them. They may not pursue policies that only serve the interests of the rich and powerful. Jesus and the theocratic tradition neither divinized nor demonized political authority in the context of a common life; they called it to account; they called it to respond to the vision of a humble king and to that king's announcement of God's good future. Neither Constantine nor any Christian politician is the Messiah, but they are all called to remember that there is one, and to exercise authority as a form of discipleship. The Christian communities of which they are a part are called to remind them of that.

Finally, Yoder claimed too much when he drew so sharp a distinction between the pacifism of pre-Constantinian Christians and the post-Constantinian Christians who "considered imperial violence to be not only morally tolerable but a positive good."[23] To be sure, there is a clear distinction, but both sides of Yoder's contrast are overstated. We know that there were Christians serving in the Roman army from the second century on.[24] Tertullian, whose pacifist credentials were as good as any, defended the church against the charge of being "useless" by telling the provincial proconsul of Carthage that "we sail with you, and fight with you, and till the ground with you."[25] Moreover, he reported with pride that the army of Marcus Aurelius was saved from drought by the prayers of the Christians within it.[26] More significant, however, is the other side of Yoder's contrast.

Not even Eusebius saw Constantine's violence as a positive good; he celebrated his victory as a victory in the war against violence, his rule as the end to the "despotic violence" of emperors.[27] In this he was naive, of course, but he hardly regarded violence as a positive good. The emergence of the Christian accounts of "just war" did not make of violence a positive good; on the contrary, they were motivated by their recognition of the evil of violence to attempt to limit it and to restrain it.

The Old Word in a New Situation

There can be no doubt that the situation of the church changed with the conversion of the emperor, but the Christian emperor should be confused neither with Christ nor with the anti-Christ. The theocratic tradition had undergone revision in the light of new circumstances before, its creativity and fidelity tested before. The tradition continued, and so did the memory of Jesus in the church.

23. Yoder, *The Priestly Kingdom*, p.135.
24. See Roland Bainton, *Christian Attitudes toward War and Peace* (Nashville: Abingdon, 1960), pp. 68–69.
25. Tertullian, *Apology*, 4, cited by Lisa Sowle Cahill, *Love Your Enemies* (Minneapolis: Fortress, 1994), p. 47.
26. Tertullian, *Apology*, 5, cited by Cahill, *Love Your Enemies*, p. 47. Origen, *Contra Celsum*, 8.73, also insisted that Christians had helped the emperor in battle by praying on behalf of his armies.
27. Eusebius, "From a Speech for the Thirtieth Anniversary of Constantine's Accession," in *Irenaeus to Grotius*, ed. O'Donovan and O'Donovan, pp. 60–65, p. 62.

Consider Lactantius. He lived through the persecution of Diocletian, and he ended up serving as a scholar in the court of Constantine. Early in his life he had written *Divine Institutes*. It was a pearl of the apologetic tradition. He saw the church as a new humanity, as citizens of heaven, responding to the Christ of blessed memory and glorious hope and bringing a new civilization to the world.

Lactantius was the first Christian thinker to work through the notion of "justice," but he did it *before* the conversion of the emperor.[28] His Christian account of "justice" is shaped by the memory of Jesus, especially by Jesus' double love commandment and his announcement of the reign of a God who humbles the exalted and exalts the humble. Like the apologist he was, Lactantius set this justice, a justice displayed (if imperfectly) in the common life of the Christian community, at once polemically over-against the civilization of the Greeks and Romans and apologetically as the very fulfillment of their (and all) human hope for justice.

Justice was, he said, constituted by piety and equality. Here he echoes the commandment to love God and the neighbor. Piety is the worship of God, and it is the "originating impulse" of justice. Anticipating Augustine, Lactantius insisted that without piety there can be no genuine knowledge of justice. "The second constituent part" and the "energy and method" of justice is equality, "treating others as one's equals."

> With him [God] there is no slave or master. Since we all have the same father, so we are all alike his freeborn children. No one is poor in his eyes, except for want of justice; . . . no one has the title "Excellency" without accomplishing all the stages of moral growth. And that is why neither the Romans nor the Greeks could sustain justice, since they had so many levels of disparity in their societies, separating poorest from richest, powerless from powerful, the obscure from the most elevated dignities of royal state. . . . But someone will say, "Don't you have poor and rich, slave and master, in your community? Aren't there distinctions between one member and another?" Not at all! That is precisely the reason that we address one another as "Brother," since we believe we are one another's equals. . . . [S]laves are not slaves to us, but we treat them and address them as brothers in the spirit, fellow slaves in devotion to God. Wealth, too, is no ground of distinction, except insofar as it provides the opportunity for preeminence in good works. To be rich is not a matter of *having* but of *using* riches for the sake of justice. . . . What security is there in rank, wealth, or power, when God can bring even kings lower than the low? And so among the commands which God took care to give us, he included this in particular: "Whoever exalts himself will be humbled, and whoever humbles himself will be exalted" (Matt. 23:12).[29]

---

28. Stanley Hauerwas goes too far in *After Christendom?* pp. 45–68, when he suggests that "justice is a bad idea for Christians" and that a concern for it is "Constantinian."

29. Lactantius, *Divine Institutes*, bk. V, sections 14–15, in O'Donovan and O'Donovan, *Irenaeus to Grotius*, pp. 52–53.

This was written *before* Constantine's conversion. His conversion and the new freedom of Christians in the empire might be taken, of course, as an empirical correlate of that axiom of reversal. The humble were suddenly exalted. But it was not taken as the completion of that project, as if those now exalted could exalt themselves. The new situation still required the old word, lest the reign of God be forgotten. And when the popularity of *Divine Institutes* required a second edition, it was republished *after* Constantine's conversion—and with a new dedication to Constantine! The old word was republished in and for a new situation. There may be gratitude for a little vindication of the martyrs within history as well as at the end of history. But there should be no triumphalism. And the greatest danger is still forgetfulness. In memory of Jesus the church continued to serve God's cause by telling the old story and by living it, by saying among the nations, "The LORD is king!" and by reminding the emperor that the humble will be exalted, and the one who exalts himself will be humbled.

Chapter 12

"Politics: Toward a Christian Social Ethic of Salt, Light and Deeds"

2003

Glen H. Stassen and David P. Gushee

Some have offered the odd argument that Jesus—in the Sermon on the Mount, and elsewhere—was not interested in social or political matters but solely in inner attitudes or the state of the human heart . . . [but] Jesus was vitally interested in deeds that shine light in the world, not only in inner attitudes. As such, his teaching is inevitably "social" and "political." We believe that limiting our ethics, our obedience, to inner attitudes is a morally disastrous argument. In the discussion that follows, drawing on the work of theologian/ethicist H. Richard Niebuhr and others, we will unpack some of the implications of the salt, light and deeds triad for the church's mission in the world, including its social and political witness. We contend that the church has a threefold mission, corresponding not only with salt, light and deeds, but with the Trinitarian nature of God . . . While this is not by any means intended as a complete presentation of a Christian political ethic, we hope it helps to point the way to some of its key elements . . .

SALT: THE CHURCH AS PIONEERING MODEL
FOR HUMAN COMMUNITY . . .

[I]n Matthew 5:13[,] Jesus was calling his disciples to a morally rigorous way of life, clearly distinct from that of the corrupt world. The church must be a repentant community, ever on its knees in acknowledgment of ways in which it has conformed to the world rather than to Christ. That is always the first step if we are to function as salt in society.

In reflecting on the implications of this we are reminded of Niebuhr's very helpful image of the church as a *pioneering community*, which takes a new path different from the world, goes out ahead of the world and provides leadership to the whole human family through its own faithful following of God's will:

> The Church is that part of the human community which responds first to God-in-Christ and Christ-in-God. . . . It is that group which hears the Word of God, which sees God's judgments, which has the vision of the resurrection. In its relations with God it is the pioneer part of society that responds to God on behalf of the whole society, somewhat . . . as science is the pioneer in responding to pattern or rationality in experience and as artists are the pioneers in responding to beauty. (Niebuhr, "Responsibility of the Church for Society," 130)

To respond to God is always to pioneer because God's will is always ahead of where society is. God's rule cannot be reduced to the way things are; it includes judgment and change. This is especially clear when we remember that God is not just an idea or a doctrine, or the possession of any church or institution, but God is living, dynamic Holy Spirit (Jn 4:24), who brings us to judgment and calls to repentance and change. Disciples are those who pioneer in saying yes to God and in being changed by the power of the Holy Spirit. They contrast sharply with those who reject divine judgment and cling defensively to ways of life contrary to God's will.

We know that the contemporary church is an inconsistent pioneer-model of faithfulness. In the wake of many scandals that have rocked the churches, and in the light of the ideological captivity of much church teaching, the church can hardly be a pioneer without leading in the act of repentance. But that has always been part of what it means to be "salt."

The mission of Christ and the church as representative of society parallels what the German theologian-martyr Dietrich Bonhoeffer wrote of both Christ and the church as representative or deputy (Bonhoeffer, *Ethics*, 224). It was Bonhoeffer who confessed his own sin powerfully during the Nazi period as a representative of German society, and thereby influenced German churches and West Germany to confess their sin publicly after the war (*Ethics*, 110ff.)—a key step in the remarkable moral reclamation of German society (Shriver, *Ethic for Enemies*). Some readers will be familiar with the heavy attention given in the mainstream American media to the pronouncements of the Southern Baptist

Convention annual meeting each June. It appears to have been the 1995 resolution on racial reconciliation that began the trend. Though far too late, it clearly and unequivocally renounced the denomination's historic acquiescence to slavery and participation in racist practices. This document served as a vivid example of the church as repentant community and as such was generally warmly received and stimulated some productive national conversation about race.

Southern Baptist Convention resolutions and statements since that time, however, have generally not followed the same pattern and have tended to be characterized by finger-pointing rather than repentance. It is no surprise that their impact has thus been more polarizing than light-spreading, tending to produce a defensive rather than reflective reaction in the society as a whole. Repentance is disarming, whereas attacks produce counterattacks. The church as pioneer is there with the rest of society, participating in the change that is sought, rather than standing aloof on the sidelines or pointing fingers from the bleachers . . .

The church as salt, pioneer or model also points toward the theme that runs throughout Mennonite ethicist John Howard Yoder's writings—the church as model and as *alternative community*. It points strongly toward the koinonia (community) nature of the church, a community of disciples obeying the particular ways of God revealed in Christ. A major way the church transforms society is by being a model, a pioneer, of what it means to live in love, justice, inclusiveness, servanthood, forgiveness—and confessing its own need for forgiveness.

Here Yoder brings a special insight that points to the character of the church as pioneer community:

> Not only are there lessons for the outside world from the inner life of the Christian church as a society; a comparable creative impulse should radiate from the church's services to the larger community. The most obvious examples would be the institutions of the school and the hospital, both of which began in Christian history as services rendered by the church . . . to the entire society. . . . The witness of the church to the state must be consistent with her own behavior. . . . A racially segregated church has nothing to say to the state about integration. . . . Only a church doing something about prisoner rehabilitation would have any moral right to speak—or have any good ideas—about prison conditions or parole regulations. (Yoder, *Christian Witness to the State*, 19–22)

The church as community also helps to correct the autonomous individualism that fragments our society, thus functioning as a critical pioneer of this important aspect of social existence. Larry Rasmussen works out the implications accurately:

> Even irrepressible dreamers know that nothing is ever real until it is embodied. . . . What counts with God and one another is not "opportunity," or even vision, but incarnation. What carries power and promise and generates conviction and courage is concrete community. . . . Very practical

> theological and technical attention must be given to what the churches do
> with their own institutional property and moneys. . . . It means attending
> to how governance happens in these ranks, the quality of our treatment of
> one another within the household of faith, the mirroring of the vision of
> inclusive, egalitarian membership in each locale. It means attending to the
> way the earth and things of the earth are cared for in this open enclave of
> creation. (Rasmussen, *Moral Fragments and Moral Community,* 152–53)

Rasmussen describes our need for community and diagnoses the causes of its
fragmentation in "calculating market logic" and interest-based association. We
associate with people and churches just like we patronize department stores—
based on calculated self-interest. The domination of market logic is seen in
"divorce, distrust, suspicion, and general alienation" (Rasmussen, *Moral Fragments and Moral Community,* 53). And because we lack community, we lack
moral formation. To resist and transform these powerful forces of fragmentation, we need pioneering community . . . So long as churches are merely associations of autonomous individuals and not pioneering communities, we will be
weak puffs of air against the winds of fragmentation.

To become such communities, churches need *shared practices* that transform
social experiences, that form and transform people morally, that provide a meaningful sense of membership and that support critical teaching of the difference
between obedience to the subtle powers and authorities of our society and obedience to the rule of God.

LIGHT: THE CHURCH AS CARING COMMUNITY
FOR THE HUMAN FAMILY.

In exegeting Matthew 5:14–16, we [can] identify several dimensions of the concept of disciples as "the light of the world." Against the backdrop of the use
of the term *light* in the Old Testament, especially Isaiah 2:2–5, we [see] the
church's vocation to be that community in which the salvation, presence, peace
and justice of the Lord of light are experienced and into which all human beings
are invited. The church is called to a role of service to the world, bearing witness
to the love of God and caring for all persons, but especially society's broken,
needy and outcast.

H. Richard Niebuhr can be helpful to us once again here. He synthesizes
several of these themes in the image of the church as *pastor.* He intends the
New Testament meaning of pastor; that is, a shepherd who is distinguished not
by authority but by caring, especially for *the lost, the outcast, the needy and the
vulnerable.* He argues that the church responds to Christ by being a shepherd, a
seeker of the lost, the friend of sinners, the lowly and the brokenhearted.

The caring or pastoral mission of the church is thus the logical implication of a key dimension of the sovereign reign of God over all things. This is
God as Creator and Ruler. All are included in God's rule and God's love, all of

society, including members of the church and outcasts, friends and enemies, the powerless and the powerful, the orphans and the powers and authorities. God sends showers of rain and sunshine on the just and unjust alike (Mt 5:45). The response to God's universal mercy is universal caring, a caring that Jesus incarnated by going first "to those excluded from human solidarity and who felt themselves excluded from God's solidarity" (Bauckham, *Bible in Politics*, 146). This was a critical part of the content of his kingdom-inaugurating ministry.

The ministry of *caring directly for the church's own members* seems so obviously essential for any church that one wonders at the need to emphasize it. But the grace dimension of the universal sovereignty of God requires special emphasis on God's caring for all diverse kinds of people within a church. Any gathering of sons and daughters of Adam and Eve is filled with people who sense that there is an inner circle from which they have been barred because of their particular faults, shortcomings, practices, vices, virtues, beliefs, inadequacies, history, class, race, gender and other unknown reasons. People try to present their acceptable frontside in the gathering and hide their backside. Membership, then, is only partial and is partially alienating.

In our culture, as we have said, we especially need community. God's grace reemphasizes the need for transforming churches to become forgiving and inclusive communities (Rom 12:1–13; 14:1–16:20). God's rule requires that we look sensitively for those whose gifts are not being called out, for groups of people not being encouraged to participate, for needs within the community still to be met . . .

As light of the world and pastor to society, *the church is also called to offer direct aid to those outside the congregation.* We must do so, of course, within the limits of our resources and wisdom. But the church can make an enormous contribution to the kingdom as it undertakes these kinds of efforts. Numerous works in recent years have chronicled such efforts by the church, both historically and today (Sider, *Cup of Water, Bread of Life*). Churches are participating in efforts that are genuinely transforming some of the most troubled neighborhoods in our nation. Churches are also leading the way in establishing relationships with those formerly dependent on welfare and mentoring them toward self-sufficiency. These and many other examples both demonstrate what is possible for the church to do on its own and the range of public and private partnerships that the church must undertake to maximize its impact.

These direct-aid mercy ministries lead almost inevitably to *broader social and political concern*, and one can imagine few better paths to such concern. Out of its pastoral concern for human beings in need, "the church has found itself forced to take an interest in political and economic measures or institutions" (H. R. Niebuhr, "Responsibility of the Church for Society," 129). Often the needy are also the powerless, and they need caring communities to intervene for their rights. Both kinds of pastoral action, direct and indirect, are needed if the church is to be faithful to God who is universal sovereign, ruling not only in the church but in all of the world.

For example, one church Glen attended invited the county Association for Retarded Persons to establish a weekday School of Hope for retarded adults in the church basement. This was direct aid, a caring service the church could help to provide. Gradually church members grew in awareness and openheartedness toward their new students' needs, their remarkable accomplishments and their joy in finally having a school.

Then an issue of city policy arose that would affect the mentally retarded. Members of the church who had never engaged in such civic action before gathered in the city hall and spoke to the mayor and city council on behalf of the powerless whom they had come to know. And they won. Then some began to ask why these adults had never had any school when they were children; why they had never received the right to a public education, when they needed an education even more than others did. Without schooling, they were helpless, could not become personally independent, care for themselves or be economically productive. With school they could. So one church member, a parent of a handicapped child, who had joined the Board of the County Association for Retarded Persons, joined with a few other parents in the state association to sue the state for the right to education for children of several varieties of handicaps, including mental retardation. Again they won. The state agreed for the first time to educate thousands of its citizens who had received no schooling before. This too was pastoral. It was action that grew out of the church's caring for people.

In recent decades the issue of Christian political engagement has exercised the attention of great sections of the church, especially in North America . . . Our reading of the Sermon on the Mount and of Jesus' entire ministry both leads us to endorse certain kinds of political engagement but also to situate such engagement within a broader approach to the public witness and social ministry of the church. It also leads us—like several other recent evangelical observers . . . —to call for a rethinking of this intense political engagement in our current American context.

Political activism carries unique dangers for the church while offering real, but limited, kingdom opportunities. The danger is to become too close to a particular political ideology and to accommodate Jesus' call to discipleship to a worldly power strategy or power center. We should not give our trust and loyalty to the political left or right. Instead, we should give practical attention to what government can do best and what churches and private groups can do best to transform the lives of the poor. The challenge for Christians is to ground political efforts in a healthy understanding of church, state, society and the reign of God . . . The plumb line for measuring policies must be the biblical narrative and the principle of justice of doing for all others what we would have others do for us (Mt 7:12).

We place social and political action and advocacy within the framework of the church's role as caring pastor to society—and within the framework of the teachings of Jesus which ground this vision. At our best, Christians vote, lobby, campaign, meet with political leaders and become such leaders themselves as a natural outflow of our pastoral concern for the social good under the sovereignty of the God who loves all persons. We are alerted to brokenness, need and injustice through ministry with people or awareness of their needs, and care for such persons then moves us, in part, toward politics. Meanwhile, we are also animated by the rich eschatological vision of the Scripture as we imagine the inbreaking of the holistic shalom that God intends—the city on a hill in which God's way is lived out. Thus we are both *pushed* into politics through hands-on ministry and *pulled* into politics through our intoxication with the biblical vision of the kingdom.

Approaching politics through caring pastoral action and compassionate and merciful pastoral moral vision also affects very deeply the way in which we conduct ourselves in the public struggle over justice for the needy and outcasts. The authentic pastor seeks not domination but service, not status but a role in helping to meet real human needs and to encourage others to do the same. This approach also shapes the tone of our engagement. As pastor, the church nudges, encourages, exhorts, sometimes chastises, but does not seek to destroy enemies or to inflame social hostilities (see Hunter, *Culture Wars;* Wuthnow, *Christianity and Civil Society*).

We believe that one good example of Christian political engagement in this style on the current scene is to be found in the American Catholic Church. Let us reflect on its public witness for a moment (cf. Wald, *Religion and Politics in the United States,* 280–303).

For centuries the Catholic Church exercised cultural and even political hegemony over Western European nations. During the medieval period Catholic leaders grew accustomed to directing the course of political events. Indeed, they became habituated to significant political power, sometimes with spiritually and morally disastrous consequences (the Crusades, the Inquisition).

As the Catholic Church lost hegemony over Europe—through the Protestant Reformation, the Enlightenment, and many other historical developments—it struggled for a long time with keeping the frustration out of its public voice. There was the same sense of being aggrieved over privileges lost that one typically hears from voices on the Christian Right in the United States. But by the late nineteenth century the Catholic Church had found a new tone. It would continue to express concern for public affairs, for the governance of nations and the international community. *But it would do so by offering thoughtful and constructive public reflection in the interests of the common human good under the sovereignty of God the Creator.* It would also do so by offering itself sacrificially/pastorally in service to those in need.

The name of one important Catholic encyclical, *Mater et Magistra* ("Mother and Teacher," 1961), illustrates these crucial points quite nicely. "Mother and Teacher" is precisely the tone taken by this document as well as by the whole body of contemporary Catholic social teaching. The Church is concerned not mainly about its own power or interests but in a motherly/pastoral way about the whole of the world and all who dwell therein. She will serve the world with all of her love and all of her energy.

This is the official Catholic approach today, and it is at times amazingly fruitful despite inevitable occasions of failure. Can Protestants learn something from it? Here is the model:

- a church that acts on behalf of the well-being of society regardless of whether the society is particularly appreciative or not—as opposed to a Christian public witness marred by a sense of aggrieved entitlement to both respect and privilege;
- a church that offers sophisticated Christian moral instruction in a respectful public language that communicates its values in a way that a wide variety of people can understand and embrace . . . —as opposed either to a withdrawn sectarianism or a hateful attack-dog politics of either left or right . . . ;
- a church that focuses its activism on the well-being of the whole society, in particular those trampled on by the current cultural and political order, rather than on its own narrow interests;
- a church that respects religious liberty and appropriate church-state boundaries in a pluralistic democracy rather than yearning for establishment or theocracy . . .
- a church that retains its independence, its saltiness, refusing to align itself with any particular politician or party, so that it might serve God and the common good, rather than being drawn inexorably either left or right under the influence of political power;
- a church that lays down its life for its society, like a mother for her children—or like a pastor—rather than fighting religious culture wars to the bitter end.

A major element in this transformation of the Catholic moral witness has been the Church's coming to terms with its role as a disestablished participant in a pluralistic liberal democracy. John Courtney Murray was a key figure in helping the American Catholic Church make the transition to seeing disestablishment as a blessing rather than a curse . . .

This insight came several centuries earlier to those in the Anabaptist tradition whose earliest experiences involved suffering at the hands of confessional states in which religious and political power were fused. Anabaptists on the Continent (such as Menno Simons), in England (Richard Overton), and America (Roger Williams, John Leland) became key advocates for religious liberty and the disestablishment of religion . . . The tradition they represent is important for us to consider here.

Anabaptist convictions on this issue were grounded not solely in harsh experience but also in biblical exegesis. Anabaptists were (and are) convinced that Jesus' Great Commission to the church (Mt 28:16–20) must be read as a call to evangelism, teaching and other means of persuasion and exhortation into the Christian faith—rather than coercion, which only creates false and hypocritical "faith." Coerced faith is not Christian faith. At least not if Christian faith follows Jesus. On the basis of Christ's command that the church be the light of the world, they argued vigorously for the church's freedom and right to spread its message via such legitimate means as preaching and teaching. They chose to die at the hands of those states that sought to stifle their Christian witness, rather than allowing themselves to be silenced. When persecuted for their convictions, Anabaptists did not fail to offer a prophetic critique to the state, just as Jesus did, in declaring such persecution an unjust misuse of government power. Anabaptists regularly declared that Christ is Lord over the government as over every institution in human life, and disciples "must obey God rather than any human authority" (Acts 5:29). . . .

Anabaptists were very clear about the need for the church as "salt" to keep its distance from government while as "light" still engaging the government. Members of this tradition are generally resistant to the blandishments and seductions of government. They embrace the legitimate work of limited government doing justice in its proper sphere, which does not include the inculcation of religious belief or the suppression of what some would view as heresy. In part influenced by Jesus' parable of the wheat and the tares (Mt 13:24–30), Anabaptists fully expect that right and wrong, truth and falsehood, virtue and vice will exist and intermingle until Christ returns, and that it is not for human governments to root out and destroy what we or they might view as displeasing to God.

In the North American context, it is easy to see how a commitment to religious liberty fits with the church's role as caring pastor for all people—but distressing to see how some Christians continue to be tempted to abandon such liberty in return for the establishment of a favored version of Christianity . . . The true pastor is concerned not just with the religious majority but with the rights of the one person who marches to the beat of a different drummer. It is unkind, uncaring, unjust and unbiblical for Christians to be unconcerned with the rights of religious minorities in our public schools, our communities, our nation or around the world. The United States was the very first nation to embrace full religious liberty in the context of religious pluralism, and Anabaptist Christians played a key role in initiating this innovation that is now appropriately recognized as part of the basic package of human rights and liberties that must be honored by any state, especially those claiming to be democratic . . .

Contemporary Reconstructionists/theonomists, "Christian America" advocates, or others who seek to establish a confessional state . . . are, we believe, fundamentally in error in terms of Scripture and both Christian and secular history, and we count it fortunate indeed that they lack the power to work their will in our society today. Their perspective reflects an enduring temptation in the history of Christianity and, as we have seen in recent years, in Islam as well. As light of the world, we invite people into a relationship with Christ and into the joyful way of life of covenant community—we invite, and never coerce, anyone who is interested to come and join our "city on a hill," in which God's shalom is beginning to be experienced.

DEEDS: THE CHURCH AS DISCIPLE-MAKING COMMUNITY OBEYING CHRIST'S COMMANDS.

We have argued . . . that the famous "salt and light" command of Jesus is actually a salt, light and deeds triad. The mission of the church is trinitarian—being faithful to God as Holy Spirit, Creator-Sustainer and Beloved Son. Christian disciples are distinguished from the world (salt) and at the same time illuminate (light) the world through their good deeds *(kala erga)* in obedience to the way of the Son, Jesus Christ. When we actually do such good deeds we cause onlookers to "give glory" to God—that is, to praise God and to recognize the divine goodness, power and plan. Thus the disciples' good deeds are part of our prayer: "thy kingdom come, thy will be done." This is true, not only in terms of the direct impact of those deeds but also through their evangelistic impact on a watching world. Being salt and light, when understood concretely, consists of a particular set of practices undertaken by the community of disciples in obedience to the teachings of Jesus Christ our Lord . . .

Chapter 13

"Racism: The Residue of Western, White Cultural Captivity"
2009

Soong-Chan Rah

It was a typical Tuesday-morning staff meeting at our church. We were taking our first coffee break when I decided to go over the week's mail. In one of the many church supply catalogs we receive, I stumbled across a full-page advertisement for Vacation Bible School curriculum from a major denomination's publishing arm. Initially I thought that the advertisement was a spoof, some sort of joke—I didn't want to believe that this was a real advertisement for actual Vacation Bible School material. The ad showed a white girl dressed in a kimono with chopsticks in her hair. She held a Chinese takeout food box. The title of this VBS material was "Rickshaw Rally: Far Out, Far East." When I typed in the website address for the curriculum, a gong appeared with (for lack of a better term) "ching-chongy" music in the background. Under the auspices of doing a VBS with a Japanese theme, the publisher caricatured and generalized all Asian cultures with various stereotypical images.[1]

Many who saw the material expressed concern ranging from the insensitive and stereotypical portrayal of Asians to the absence of input from the Asian

---

1. For more details on the offensive aspects of the Rickshaw Rally Vacation Bible School, see <www.geocities.com/reconsideringrickshawrally/>.

American community in the creation of this VBS material. I personally received a large number of e-mails from Asian American Christians expressing pain and outrage over the content of the material. When a significant number of Asian American pastors and Christians went to the publisher to protest the material, our concerns were dismissed. Rather than listen and learn from the outcry of a wide range of voices, including many from within its denomination, the publisher chose to ignore these concerns.[2] So despite the breadth of the criticism and objection, the curriculum went forward with minimal cosmetic changes—particularly when it came to many of the kitschy items available for purchase, such as the karate-kid key chain and the name tags in the shape of Chinese takeout food boxes.

What still affects me to this day is how this Christian company handled the situation. The arrogant and privileged position that would not allow for repentance and retribution by the guilty party reveals an unwillingness to deal with the sin of racism in any real way. The initial slight of creating this racially offensive material was amplified by the white leadership of this denomination and their publishing arm in their insensitive and intransigent response. The entire conflict over the Rickshaw Rally VBS curriculum taught me a lesson regarding the state of race relations in the evangelical church: we still have a very long way to go. In addition, it became evident that there is an unwillingness to deal with the issue of race. It was easier to deny the sin than to confront it and transform the system that created the commission of the sin of racism. While racial issues create an emotional tension and angst, the white captivity of the church means that we lack the tools to deal with racism in a constructive and productive way.

THE CONSTRUCT OF THE RACE MYTH

The category of race has no scientific justification. As a person of Korean ancestry, I have as much in common genetically and biologically with a Swede, a Zulu or a Lakota as I do with someone of Chinese ancestry. While different theories abound regarding the origins of the category of race, it is largely acknowledged that race is a sociologically created category, rather than a scientifically created one. "Races are not biologically differentiated groupings but rather social construction."[3] "Many scientist are now declaring that the concept of race has no basis in the biological sciences; more and more are concurring that race should be seen as a social invention."[4] It is also clear that the category of race as applied in American society does not exist in the Bible.

2. For the Southern Baptist Church and Lifeway Publication's response, see <www.floridabaptistwitness.com/1912.article>.
3. Ian Haney Lopez, *White by Law: The Legal Construction of Race,* rev. and updated (New York: New York University Press, 2006), p. xxi.
4. Audrey Smedley, *Race in North America: Origin and Evolution of a Worldview,* 3rd ed. (Boulder, Colo.: Westview, 2007), p. xi.

The Bible refers to people groups and nations, but does not distinguish people groups based upon skin color. The Bible's use of the term *people groups* does not presume race (as we use the term in the West) as a means of distinction and differentiation before YHWH. J. Daniel Hays, in *From Every People and Nation*, states "that the basic common denominator of ethnic identity, that which shows up most frequently, is that of territory and common myth of descent."[5] Race serves as a central identifier in contemporary American society, focusing on skin color and other physical characteristics. In Scripture, ethnicity based upon language, culture, social boundaries, and geographic location becomes the method of distinction.[6] Another example of Scripture's use of people groups and ethnicity rather than race as the main point of distinction can be found by looking through basic Bible dictionaries and encyclopedias. In the *International Standard Bible Encyclopedia*, the only entry for *race* reads "See Table of Nations." In the *New Bible Dictionary*, there is no entry for *race*. The biblical terminology does not include the defining of people simply by their racial characteristics.

The category of race was created by American society in an attempt to justify and regulate the social injustice of slavery. Initially, slavery in the American colonies involved both blacks and whites and did not involve hereditary slavery. "African American laborers during the first four decades after their arrival, that is, up until 1660, were not lifetime hereditary bondmen and bondwomen; rather, their status was essentially the same as that of European-American bond-laborers, namely limited-term bond-servitude."[7] The distinction of black slaves and white indentured servants needed categories of racial difference—whether by common sense, by "scientific" rationalization or by legal fiat. "In 1640 three servants, one of them a black man named John Punch, escaped from their duties in Virginia. When they were apprehended, the white servants were punished by having time added to their period of service. Punch, on the other hand, was sentenced to service for the rest of his life."[8] The creation of the category of race allowed one group of people (self-identified as white) to enslave another group of people (designated as black).

Racial distinctions based upon measurable physical distinctions were hard to justify but it became necessary to uphold the unjust system of slavery. "A 'black' was a lifelong slave, unworthy of political enfranchisement, and denied legal protection from abuse. 'Black' symbolized savagery, ignorance, lack of intelligence, and an inability to live in a civilized manner. . . . Color categories were correlated with cultural meaning. 'Whites' were viewed as civilized, intelligent,

5. J. Daniel Hays, *From Every People and Nation* (Downers Grove, Ill.: InterVarsity Press, 2003), p. 29 n. 8.

6. Ibid., pp. 28–29.

7. Theodore Allen, *The Invention of the White Race*, vol. 1, *Racial Oppression and Social Order* (New York: Verso, 1994), p. 3.

8. James Oliver Horton and Lois F. Horton, *Slavery and the Making of America* (New York: Oxford University Press, 2005), p. 29.

capable of self-government, and self restraint."[9] The codification and establishment of race became a means of social control. Ivan Hannaford, in *Race: the History of an Idea in the West,* speaks of the invention of race:

> It was not until after the French and American Revolutions and the social upheavals which followed that the idea of race was fully conceptualized and became deeply embedded in our understandings and explanations of the world. In other words, the dispositions and presuppositions of race and ethnicity were introduced— some would say "invented" or "fabricated"— in modern times.[10]

The category of race is a product of Western social history.

In early American legal history, the defining of race vacillated between using the common knowledge approach and the scientific evidence approach. "Under a common knowledge approach, courts justified the assignment of petitioners to one race or another by reference to common beliefs about race."[11] The use of the common knowledge approach signified the belief that the category of race was determined by the values and norms of society. The scientific evidence approach claimed that there were scientific reasons for racial distinctions. The use of both approaches in legal cases reflected a belief that both social norms and scientific evidence shape the definition of race. However, legal proceedings began to reject the scientific evidence approach.

> The courts deciding racial prerequisite cases initially relied on both rationales to justify their decisions. However, beginning in 1909 a schism appeared among the courts over whether common knowledge or scientific evidence was the appropriate standard. . . . The early congruence of and subsequent contradiction between common knowledge and scientific evidence set the terms of a debate about whether race is a social construction or a natural occurrence. In these terms, the Supreme Court's elevation of common knowledge as the legal meter of race convincingly demonstrates that racial categorization finds its origins in social practices.[12]

Because the category of race had no scientific justification, the determination of racial categories became dependent on legal cases that relied upon social norms for its definition. As Lopez concludes: "That common knowledge emerged as the only workable racial test shows that race is something which must be measured in terms of what people believe, that it is a socially mediated idea. The social construction of the White race is manifest in the Court's repudiation of

9. Jenell Williams Paris, "Race: Critical Thinking and Transformative Possibilities," in *This Side of Heaven: Race, Ethnicity, and Christian Faith,* ed. Robert J. Priest and Alvaro L. Nieves (New York: Oxford University Press, 2007), pp. 21–22.

10. Ivan Hannaford, *Race: The History of an Idea in the West* (Baltimore: Johns Hopkins University Press, 1996), p. 6.

11. Lopez, *White by Law*, p. 4.

12. Ibid., pp. 4, 5.

science and its installation of common knowledge as the appropriate racial meter of Whiteness."[13]

The problem of defining race is an example of a vicious circle. Racism created the categories of race (commonly-held, social perceptions of physical differences); and in turn, racial distinctions became codified legally, leading to further expressions of racism in individual, social, political and legal forms. The American creation of race as a social category ultimately had a negative social impact. If the category of race was created under the auspices of equality and affirmation of difference, the outcome may have been different. However, the creation of race as a social category had dysfunctional and sinful origins. This original sinfulness has crept into our society and culture and begins to determine how we value the "norm" in American society (and subsequently the American church). Racism, therefore, ends up creating social values and norms that become the way our culture conducts business. Racism is America's original and most deeply rooted sin.

AMERICA'S ORIGINAL SIN

As an evangelism professor, one of the expectations of my job is to teach seminary students how to lead an individual to Christ. I consider this task to be a critical part of theological education. In the process of leading a person to Christ, I do not suggest that we ask an individual to recount every single sin that he or she has ever committed. A process like that would take too long and maybe the person would lose interest after the first three days. But rather, in leading a person to Christ, I need to get to the heart of the matter by dealing with the power of original sin and the process of breaking its power with the power of the blood of Jesus.

In the same way, when we deal with the corporate sin of America, do we deal with every specific sin ever committed by American society, culture and politics, or do we address the power of America's original sin? We are quick to deal with the symptoms of sin in America, but oftentimes are unwilling to deal with the original sin of America: namely, the kidnapping of Africans to use as slave labor, and usurping of lands belonging to Native Americans and subsequent genocide of indigenous peoples. As John Dawson asserts in *Healing America's Wounds,* "We have our own unfinished business, particularly with Native Americans and Afro-Americans."[14] Dawson goes on to outline the various ways in U.S. history in which injustices were committed: the violation of treaties with Native Americans, the enslavement of Africans in the New World and the abusive handling of Chinese labor in California and the West.[15] These corporate sins have left their

13. Ibid., p. 7.
14. John Dawson, *Healing America's Wounds* (Ventura, Calif.: Regal, 1977), p. 23.
15. Ibid., pp. 80–81.

spiritual mark on America. This original sin of racism has had significant and ongoing social and corporate implications for the church in America.

All humanity is tainted with the blight of sin and the proclivity toward sinfulness. In the same way, various cultures and people groups reflect symptoms of a fallen humanity. Throughout history, this human sinfulness has manifested itself in different ways in different cultures, oftentimes as destructive behavior toward other people groups. The specific expression of corporate sinfulness in American society seems to be in the creation of racial categories in order to further exploitation and oppression of one group over another.

When we use the term *racism,* we often see this only in individual terms. As a consequence, there is often a strong, visceral and vehement denial: "I am not a racist! I have never personally owned a slave and I have never personally taken land away from a Native American, therefore, I cannot be a racist." These types of statements reduce racism purely to individual actions and behavior. If we use the language of individual sin to address sin, then no individual is guilty. We may have our prejudices, but no individual in twenty-first-century America has actually owned a slave or taken land away from a Native American. It is too easy to dismiss and disavow individual culpability for the sin of racism. But if we use the language of corporate sin, then we are all complicit. Anyone that has benefited from America's original sin is guilty of that sin and bears the corporate shame of that sin.

I was speaking at a gathering of Asian American Christian college students at a prestigious Ivy League institution. I was covering the topic of racial and economic justice with a group of extremely bright individuals who were beneficiaries of the best education that America could offer. As I spoke on the issue of a historical economic injustice perpetrated against African Americans and Native Americans, I began to sense the potential response of these Asian American college students. "This issue doesn't apply to me. Sure, horrible atrocities have been committed against African Americans and Native Americans—but that was a long time ago. Asian Americans didn't arrive in the U.S. in any significant numbers until after 1965. Surely, we are not guilty of these injustices?"

In anticipation of this response, I addressed the corporate responsibility of American society. I spoke to these Ivy League college students and reminded them they were sitting in a building on land that had once been owned by Native Americans, and they were in a school whose robust endowment could be attributed to a successful economy that had been built on slave labor. While they may not have individually committed a personal sin against these communities, they had certainly benefitted from these past atrocities.

When we claim that we are not complicit in the corporate sin of racism, we fail to grasp how being a beneficiary of an unjust system yields a culpability for those that benefit from that system. As an example, imagine that you were starting a new business. If someone were to come to you and offer a building lease for no cost and promise to provide labor at no cost, you would have to be the worst business person in human history to fail at that business. Economic success can be assumed when you have been given free land and free labor. The American economy was built upon free land stolen from the Native American community and free labor kidnapped from Africa. Our current economic success owes a large debt to an initial economic foundation built upon free land and free labor. If we live as financial beneficiaries in the twenty-first century of this system of injustice, we have a corporate culpability and responsibility, even as we claim innocence in our personal, individual lives.

John Dawson challenges us to deal with our corporate sins by stating:

> If we have broken our covenants with God and violated our relationships with one another, the path to reconciliation must begin with the act of confession. The greatest wounds in human history, the greatest injustices, have not happened through the acts of some individual perpetrator, rather through the institutions, systems, philosophies, cultures, religions and governments of mankind. Because of this, we as individuals, are tempted to absolve ourselves of all individual responsibility. Unless somebody identifies themselves with corporate entities, such as the nation of our citizenship, or the subculture of our ancestors, the act of honest confession will never take place. This leaves us in a world of injury and offense in which no corporate sin is ever acknowledged, reconciliation never begins and old hatreds deepen.[16]

Our corporate sin of racism and our corporate life as beneficiaries of a racist system require our corporate confession. This corporate confession must be led by those with a spiritual understanding and a biblical conviction—namely, the body of Christ in America.

WHITE PRIVILEGE

Acknowledging the corporate responsibility and culpability of the sin of racism can lead to the revelation of the system of white privilege, a system that oftentimes goes unrecognized in the dialogue on race. The explicit expression of the sin of racism is still evident in American society, but it has also taken a more subtle form in the expression of white privilege. "White privilege is the other side of racism."[17] White privilege is the system that places white culture in American society at the center with all other cultures on the fringes. "Research—into books, museums, the press, advertising, films, television, software—repeatedly shows that in Western representation whites are overwhelmingly and disproportionately predominant, have the central and elaborated roles, and above all are placed as the norm, the ordinary, the standard."[18]

---

16. Ibid., p. 30.
17. Paula Rothenberg, *White Privilege* (New York: Worth, 2002), p. 1.
18. Richard Dyer, "The Matter of Whiteness in White Privilege," in Rothenberg, *White Privilege,* p. 11.

While North America is becoming more and more multiethnic and we are seeing more nonwhite cultural expressions, white culture remains as the primary standard by which all other cultures are judged. An unfair advantage and privilege, therefore, is given to whites in a society that reveres and prioritizes them. "The equation of being white with being human secures a position of power. White people have power and believe that they think, feel and act like and for all people; white people, unable to see their particularity, cannot take account of other people's; white people create the dominant images of the world and don't quite see that they thus construct the world in their own image; white people set standards for humanity by which they are bound to succeed and others bound to fail."[19] Latino American theologian Virgilio Elizondo speaks of the ongoing nature of white privilege by stating: "It is the dominant society that sets the norms and projects the image of success, achievement, acceptability, normalcy, and status. It is the dominant group that sets up the educational process that passes on the traditions and values of the dominant society."[20]

Privilege, therefore, is power. Privilege, when it is unnamed, holds an even greater power. It is the invisible knapsack (as Peggy McIntosh names it)[21] that gives a position of privilege based upon racial characteristics. The power of privilege is that it can go undetected by those who are oppressed by it and even by those who have it. "It has allowed some white people to create a world in their own image and a system of values that reinforces the power and privilege of those who are white people. At the same time, because of its invisibility, it has helped foster that those who succeed do so because of their superior intelligence, their hard work or their drive, rather than, at least in part, their privilege."[22] White privilege not only deals with an economic benefit, but also speaks to a position of emotional and social power that is oftentimes reserved for white Americans . . .

THE NORM AND EVERYTHING ELSE

In the formation of Christian theology, we also see white privilege at work. Theology that prioritizes the individual and arises out of the Western, white context becomes the standard expression of orthodox theology. In our understanding of what is considered orthodoxy, we see the emphasis on the individual aspects of faith. What is considered good, sound, orthodox theology is a Western theology that emphasizes a personal relationship with Jesus, with its natural and expected antecedent of an individual sanctification and even an individualized

---

19. Ibid., p. 12.

20. Virgilio Elizondo, *Galilean Journey: The Mexican-American Promise* (Maryknoll, N.Y.: Orbis, 1983), p. 25.

21. Peggy McIntosh, "Unpacking the Invisible Knapsack," in Rothenberg, *White Privilege*, pp. 97–101; numerous online versions of the article can be found, see <www.nymbp.org/reference/WhitePrivilege.pdf>.

22. Rothenberg, *White Privilege*, p. 2.

ecclesiology. The critical issues and discussion in theology lean toward understanding issues relevant to individuals and Western sensibilities. The seemingly never-ending debate between the proponents of Calvinism and Arminianism, between predestination and free will, revolves around individual salvation.

Theologies that speak of a corporate responsibility or call for a social responsibility are given special names like: liberation theology, black theology, *minjung* theology, feminist theology, etc. In other words, Western theology with its individual locus is considered normative theology, while non-Western theology is theology on the fringes and must be explained as being a theology applicable only in a particular context and to a particular people group. Orthodoxy is determined by the Western value of individualism and an individualized soteriology rather than a broader understanding of the corporate themes that emerge out of Scripture.

Because theology emerging from a Western, white context is considered normative, it places non-Western theology in an inferior position and elevates Western theology as the standard by which all other theological frameworks and points of view are measured. This bias stifles the theological dialogue between the various cultures. "Attendant assumptions of a racial hierarchy that assumes the intellectual and moral superiority of the Caucasians, has hampered our understanding of the text by unnecessarily eliminating possible avenues of study."[23] We end up with a Western, white captivity of theology. Western theology becomes the form that is closest to God. "It is a pretentious illusion that there is something pure and objective about the way theology has been done in the Western church, as if it were handed down directly by the Almighty to the theologians of the correct methodology."[24]

This marginalization of non-Western theology is reflective of Edward Said's description of "orientalism." Said examines Western perceptions of the Orient (in Said's case, he focuses on Arabic and Middle-Eastern cultures when referring to the Orient) and reveals how the exoticizing of "oriental" culture allows Western culture to create a sense of otherness for these cultures. "Orientalism can be discussed and analyzed as the corporate institution for dealing with the Orient—dealing with it by making statements about it, authorizing views of it, describing it, by teaching it, settling it, ruling over it: in short, Orientalism is a Western style for dominating, structuring, and having authority over the Orient."[25]

Creating "the other" allowed Western culture to express its power over non-Western cultures. Inferiority is inferred when a culture or people are categorized as "the other." "European culture gained in strength and identity by setting itself off against the Orient as a sort of surrogate and even an underground

23. Peter T. Nash, *Reading Race, Reading the Bible* (Minneapolis: Fortress, 2003), p. 58.
24. Ibid., pp. 25, 26.
25. Edward Said, *Orientalism* (New York: Vintage, 1978), p. 3.

self."[26] In the same way that Western culture diminishes non-Western culture through the creation of an "otherness," Western Christianity diminishes non-Western expressions of Christian theology and ecclesiology with the creation of "otherness."

When this sense of "otherness" is created, alienation between the races is created. When "the other" is cast as an exoticized outsider, then it creates a hostile environment for the marginalized person of color. The following story from an Asian American blogger reveals the harmful aspects of the creation of "the other":

> I am sitting in a service at my home church in Missouri. During an announcement for a new outreach to international students, a non-Asian woman dressed in a kimono (traditional Japanese dress) stepped up to the mike. She was an elder's wife. She feigned an accent, in which she spoke in halting English. The congregation roared with laughter. There were two Asians in church that day. One was me. The other was my unchurched friend. He turned to me and said, "This is bullsh__." He got up, turned around (we were sitting in the front row) and walked past the crowd of 800 laughing and guffawing faces.
>
> To my knowledge, he has never stepped into a church again. When he (and I) walked out, it stirred a controversy. Some were concerned that the way we walked out was too militant and not a new testament model of reconciliation. Some were concerned that we were hurt, and needed inner healing. Some were concerned that we didn't get the joke, and did not understand that no harm was intended. Not once was the elder's wife held accountable. The problem, it seemed, was us. Thicker skin, an improved sense of humor, inner healing, less outrage, and a less serious disposition seemed to be the order of the day.[27]

In what ways do we alienate those outside of majority culture? Even as we attempt to engage in crosscultural dialogue and connection, does the system of white privilege and the dominant culture's captivity of the norms of the American church hinder genuine dialogue and true reconciliation?

For instance, what would it look like not to have white theology at the center? There would be more opportunities given to prophetic voices such as Oscar Muriu, Orlando Costas, Emmanuel Katongole, James Cone, Lamin Sanneh, K. P. Yohannan and scores of others. I am thankful for the increasing number of works that examine global theology and the rich history of contribution from non-Western theologians. Can the American evangelical church begin to prioritize works like Samuel Moffett's *Christianity in Asia*, Edwin Yamauchi's *Africa and the Bible*, *The Africa Bible Commentary* edited by Tokunboh Adeyemo, Yeo Khiokkhng's *What Has Jerusalem to Do with Beijing?* and recognize that these

26. Ibid.
27. Austin Chee, "A Public Apology to Our Asian American Brothers and Sisters," online posting (March 14, 2007) YSMARKO <www.ysmarko.com/?p=1379>.

works represent not only the next evangelicalism but a historical Christianity as well . . .

A MULTIETHNIC EVANGELICALISM

How, then, should the church respond to white privilege and white captivity? Maintaining churches that further propagate white privilege is not the answer. The popular church growth movement in the latter half of the twentieth century (see chapter 4 of Soong-Chan Rah's *The Next Evangelicalism: Freeing the Church from Western Cultural Captivity* [Downers Grove, IL: InterVarsity Press, 2009] for more on this topic) prioritized the homogenous unit principle (HUP) as a method toward numerical growth. Homogeneous churches grow faster because people prefer to attend church with those from similar racial, socio-economic, ethnic and cultural backgrounds. In an attempt to draw individuals into the church, barriers needed to be removed, and that meant that dealing with racial differences which would detract from the real work of church growth would not be considered.

I participated in a roundtable discussion reported in *Christianity Today* in 2005, where the influential pastor of Willow Creek, Bill Hybels, confessed that "Willow Creek started in the era when the church-growth people were saying, 'Don't dissipate any of your energies fighting race issues. Focus everything on evangelism.' It was the homogeneous-unit principle of church growth."[28] The homogenous unit principle allowed the white church to further propagate a system of white privilege by creating a system of de facto segregation. Segregation justified by a desire for church growth allows affluent white churches to remain separate.

As the roundtable discussion unfolded, I was thankful for Bill Hybels's willingness to acknowledge the historical misstep taken by Willow Creek in adhering to a set of principles that furthered racial segregation. There were numerous pragmatic reasons to pursue a homogenous unit principle, and acknowledging these priorities was a significant first step in addressing the racial division that resulted from a principle that segregated rather than united. To hear this type of admission from a white leader was both refreshing and encouraging.

Multiethnic churches, and the racial reconciliation and justice needed to establish multiethnic churches, do not mesh with the homogeneous unit principle. Because "racial separation in the United States is socially constructed, the church in the United States reflects a social reality rather than promoting a theological vision."[29] Multiethnic churches that focus on racial justice and reconciliation can result in theologically driven church ministry, rather than economically and pragmatically driven ministry. However, the demographic changes in American society mean that more multiethnic churches are needed

28. Bill Hybels, "Harder Than Anyone Can Imagine," *Christianity Today,* April 2005, p. 38.
29. Curtiss Paul DeYoung, Michael O. Emerson, George Yancey and Karen Chai Kim, *United by Faith* (New York: Oxford University Press, 2003), p. 131.

in an increasingly ethnically and culturally pluralistic America. "In 1960, less than 15 percent of the population of the United States was not of European origin, with the vast majority of that percentage being African American. According to the 2000 Census, people of color as a percentage of the United States population have *more than doubled* to 31 percent since 1960, and the growth of non-Europeans is expected to continue at an accelerated rate."[30] There is, therefore, an acute need for the planting and development of multiethnic churches in America. "Christian congregations, when possible, should be multiracial. . . . The twenty-first century must be *the century of multiracial congregations.*"[31]

Despite the need for more multiethnic churches, the reality of the situation is that the percentage of multiethnic churches in the United States remains relatively low. American evangelicalism still has not developed enough multiethnic churches. As DeYoung and others reveal:

> If we define a racially mixed congregation as one in which no one racial group is 80 percent or more of the congregation, just 7.5 percent of the over 300,000 religious congregations in the United States are racially mixed. For Christian congregations, which form over 90 percent of congregations in the United States, the percentage that are racially mixed drops to five and a half. Of this small percentage, approximately half of the congregations are mixed only temporarily, during the time they are in transition from one group to another.[32]

Given the rather generous criteria used by the authors, the reality that less than four percent of Christian congregations are integrated is shameful. If we were to hear of any other institution, such as a government agency or an institute of higher education, that was integrated by less than four percent, there would be justifiable outrage and protest. Yet, the American evangelical church marches along in our single-ethnic ministries focused on numerical growth over the biblical value of racial reconciliation and justice.

A major obstacle to the establishment of multiethnic churches is the system of white privilege in the American evangelical church that is a product of white captivity. When the majority culture continues to define and shape the parameters and course of the discussion on what the church will look like, those who are "the other" and who sit outside the halls of power and privilege are silenced, and the multiethnic dialogue deteriorates once again to a white monologue. When the acknowledged leadership, the noted theologians and the model pastors of American evangelicalism are white, then American evangelicalism is captive to white culture. Racial justice, therefore, must be the paradigm by which we build multiethnic churches. Rather than uplifting one race and ethnicity as

30. Ibid., p. 1.
31. Ibid., p. 2.
32. Ibid.

the ultimate image of God, we must establish churches that honor the breadth of God's image found in a range of cultural expressions.

Throughout American history, there have been numerous images to define American culture as it relates to multiethnicity. In elementary school, I remember seeing a *Schoolhouse Rock!* episode where a catchy tune was coupled with lyrics about "The Great American Melting Pot." The children's show was reflecting a common term that was used when I was in elementary school. The melting pot image claimed that the vast array of rich and diverse cultures that make up America would melt away into an unrecognizable mass of cream of mushroom. All the various flavors would blend into one bland flavor. But I don't remember the melting pot theory being taught too much after elementary school. Somebody had determined that the image doesn't work. Not everyone in America wants to have their unique cultural flavor melted away. As one Native American pastor told me, "There's something in Natives that doesn't melt very well." There was an arrogant presumption that these non-Anglo cultures could be melted away and absorbed into a larger American culture (i.e., white culture).

With the rejection of the "melting pot" image came the advent of the "salad bowl." In the salad bowl, once again, the wide range of flavors was brought together. But the salad allowed for each vegetable to retain its flavor. Unfortunately, we often took this rich array of flavors and drenched it in creamy ranch. The dressing overwhelmed and covered all of the other vibrant flavors. Even a jalapeño or *kimchi* covered in creamy ranch would come out tasting like creamy ranch. We may have all the different flavors in one place, but our style of worship, our style of preaching, and our approach to community life reflect a form of cultural dressing that covers all of the other flavors and drowns them out.

In recent years, the need for the planting and development of multiethnic churches has been recognized among many evangelicals. Among those who are pursuing multiethnic churches, two streams have emerged: the colorblind approach and the racial reconciliation approach.[33] The colorblind approach assumes that all believers have their primary identity as Christians; therefore, no concession needs to be made for cultural differences. Since we are all believers, our cultural differences should not matter. In other words, the most effective approach to multiethnicity is to cover everyone in the church with the same flavor of dressing. Usually, the use of Western, white forms of worship, teaching and community are assumed in these types of settings. After all, the "norms" of American church life are assumed; therefore, the common denominator of

---

33. See William E. Kratt, "Diversity in Evangelical Christian Higher Education" (Ph.D. diss., Claremont Graduate University, 2004), pp. 13–14. Kratt uses the term "traditional/conservative" to describe an "approach to multiculturalism [that] emphasizes one-way assimilation of fading minority identities into dominant cultural beliefs and values" versus the "moderate/liberal view" where emphasis is placed on valuing and appreciating cultural differences. I extend Kratt's perspective by stating that the "traditional/conservative" view reflects a supposed colorblindness that tends to favor majority culture and that the "moderate/liberal" view of appreciating cultural differences is not possible without racial reconciliation.

Western, white forms of ecclesiology becomes the key expression of church life in a colorblind approach.

The racial reconciliation approach asserts that significant sins have been committed related to the issue of race. These sins cannot be avoided or swept under the rug. These historical and social sins need to be dealt with when bringing the range of different races and ethnicities together as a worshiping community. The presence of the social-historical corporate sin of racism cannot be ignored. Between these two expressions of multiethnicity, the colorblind approach fails to acknowledge human fallenness. While the colorblind approach may be efficient and easier, it fails to acknowledge sin and can become a human rather than a divine effort. The racial reconciliation and justice approach moves multiethnicity out of the realm of church growth fad to a level of addressing injustice and sin.

If the American church is going to be prepared for the next phase of its development, then the white captivity of the church that assumes white privilege needs to be cast aside. If the American church is able to look toward the future with a hope and a promise, then the sin of racism must be confessed and racial justice and racial reconciliation become a theological priority over and above the priority of producing a pragmatic paradigm of church growth. To cast aside the Western, white captivity of the church means to look toward a potential of a healthy and dynamic multiethnic future for American evangelicalism.

Chapter 14

"Concrete Implications of an Ecclesial Witness Based on Repentance"
2012

Jennifer McBride

CHARACTERISTICS OF ECCLESIAL WITNESS DEMONSTRATING CHRIST'S AFFIRMATION

We have seen that God's affirmation of humanity is made manifest by God's presence in the world as the real human being in fallen flesh. God's work in Christ may be understood through the category of repentance since Jesus was intimately involved with sin through his bodily encounter with fallen existence. Christ affirms not just humanity but fallen humanity, not just the created world but the fallen world, by drawing near in solidarity with sinners, with real human beings. In his ministry, Jesus' solidarity is seen most poignantly in his first public act when he responds to John's call to repent by numbering himself with transgressors in his Jordan River baptism, and the event of Jesus' baptism introduces repentance as an activity defining God's love and righteousness and God's outworking of redemption. Repentance that participates in the affirming power of the Christ event necessitates existence with and for others, to which the fallen flesh of the incarnation and the baptismal response of the sinless Jesus testify.

The most basic feature of a public witness demonstrating Christ's affirmation of the world is, therefore, *existence with and for others* through the church-community's *incarnate presence in its own sinful flesh.* The repentant community immerses itself physically and unreservedly into a particular situation of concern, not arrogantly as if the church has answers to particular problems already sorted out but as a people committed to being engaged, listening, and learning from others. "We moved into the Southeast White House in 1996 with absolutely no preconceived notions as to how to use it. We just knew where we wanted to be, that we wanted to be used," says Sammie Morrison.[1] "We came here with no plans or programs except to listen to the needs of the neighborhood and be a presence for Jesus," echoes Scott Dimock.[2] The Southeast White House's incarnate presence . . . is a mode of repentance that witnesses to Christ's affirmation of humanity because it is based on the House's desire to exist for others and to listen and learn from them, especially those deemed the outcasts of society who are pushed to the margins of the city. Because incarnate presence in situations of social concern or injustice is vital for witnessing to Christ's affirmation of humanity, a public witness faithful to Christ cannot be based on ideology, be it political or theological. Ideologues and commentators on the sidelines cannot offer a redemptive public witness because they set themselves up as judge, the form that stands in total opposition to the shape of Christ in the world. We see Christians take the form of judge not only when their public proclamations about social and political matters are made from an armchair, but also through . . . pseudo-doing, . . . through political activism that is bodily in the sense that it may involve leg-work, mass organization, and political protest, yet nevertheless contradicts the incarnation because it is driven by moral principles and religious standards that promote the church over against the world. Christ was engaged bodily in the concerns of the world not as a moral exemplar but as one in solidarity with fallen humanity. Incarnate presence means public engagement as one numbered with transgressors.

As a community that counts itself among current transgressors, the church cannot disassociate from the sinful world. The church demonstrates Christ's affirmation of this world when it *refuses to take a defensive stance against it.* "One of the first things that Tim said to me is that we are not here to be culture warriors in the sense of fighting the surrounding society," Dave Stankiewicz says, "and I liked that the second he said it."[3] Indeed, the very impetus behind Eleuthero's incarnate presence in Portland, Maine, was to learn ecological care from the surrounding secular culture out of confidence in Christ's expansive lordship, which shines out into the world allowing non-Christians to be reflectors of Christ's truth to Christians. While a defensive stance stems from the presumption that Christians possess the truth and the knowledge of good and evil and thus protecting these from assault depends on them, the repentant community, in contrast, witnesses to Christ's affirmation of the world when it, like

1. Sammie Morrison, interview with author, August 28, 2006.
2. Scott Dimock, interview with author, October 26, 2006.
3. Dave Stankiewicz, interview with author, September 10, 2006.

Eleuthero, assumes not special favor but rather that it must listen and learn from the insights and actions of others. The repentant community recognizes that engaging culture in a positive, open, and constructive manner is faithful to Christ, who belonged wholly to this world. It also recognizes that Christians are historical, contextual beings—that this is part of the gift of being human—and that like everyone else, Christians are necessarily formed by cultural forces and societal trends, both positive and negative. This means that instead of arrogantly and blindly understanding itself in stark opposition to the surrounding culture, the repentant church in solidarity with humanity may cultivate an awareness about the ways the church has been affected by negative cultural trends . . . and may be receptive enough to alter dominant assumptions it previously held. Refusing to take a defensive stance against the world does not mean that the church sheds its distinctive identity as the body of Christ in the world. It means that its identity is not defined in opposition to the rest of humanity. Like Christ, the repentant church demonstrates in action and speech that it is for, not against, the world.

Finally, the repentant church demonstrates Christ's affirmation of this world when it displays *a love for this life* through commitment to present historical reality *driven by this-worldly hope for restoration* rather than a religious hope preoccupied with individualistic and other-worldly notions of salvation. Other-worldly preoccupation inadvertently renounces Christ's lordship over this world and risks framing matters of life and death in terms of eternal destiny to the detriment of attending to the serious effects of dehumanization and diminution in this life. This is especially dangerous when concern for eternal souls is coupled with fatalistic resignation to the inevitability of evil in a fallen world that in turn acquiesces to unjust structures. Other-worldly preoccupation misses the gift of the polyphony of life that bids the church be swept up into an earthly love that rushes headlong into the beauty and sorrow of this life because it finds Christ there. In contrast to the world-denying influences within the Christian religion, christological hope for this-worldly restoration gives the church, in the words of Eleuthero, "permission to live."[4] As Bonhoeffer writes, "It is only when one loves life and the earth so much that without them everything seems to be over that one may believe in the resurrection and the new world."[5] Love for this life will cause the repentant community to become deeply enmeshed in the places of struggle and distress out of a sense of urgency for restoration. Love for life is shown, though, not simply through hard work and toil but also through playfulness and festivity that invites others into an inclusive celebration. "They were partying," Denise Speed says of her first encounter at the Southeast White House, "and curiosity got the best of me."[6] As we saw, the Southeast White

---

4. Tim Clayton, interview with author, September 8–9, 2006.
5. Dietrich Bonhoeffer, *Letter and Papers from Prison*, trans. Reginald Fuller et al. (New York: Touchstone, 1997).
6. Denise Speed, interview with author, November 6, 2001.

House witnesses to Christ's affirmation regularly at their weekly luncheons through good food and fellowship, and the feast both manifests and cultivates this-worldly hope and love by affirming human dignity and instilling a sense of belonging.

CHARACTERISTICS OF ECCLESIAL WITNESS DEMONSTRATING DIVINE JUDGMENT

. . . Christ's affirmation of humanity includes God's judgment on humanity. The Christ event declares a simultaneous divine acceptance and protest, God's Yes and No continuously proclaimed upon the whole world, including the church. Christ's Yes includes the No, since Christ's affirmation of the world is not divine blessing on the sin and injustice that runs rampant in the world. God's judgment upon humanity is made manifest through Christ's cross, where God receives divine judgment by accepting guilt and taking responsibility for sin . . . Christ demonstrates God's judgment on the sin that destroys community and diminishes human beings by directing that judgment to himself.

The most basic way the church demonstrates God's judgment on humanity, then, is also by directing it toward itself. Conformed to the crucified Christ, the repentant church acknowledges God's rightful judgment by *accepting responsibility* for sin, suffering, and injustice *through repentant activity* in the midst of the world. Accepting responsibility for sin will lead to the incarnate presence discussed above, to the church existing for others by immersing itself in the places of struggle and distress and in the problems of social and political life while acknowledging its present complicity in the sin of society with which it is intimately interconnected. By exposing sin in itself—in its own communal life and in its relationship with other human beings and with society as a whole—the church exposes sin in the world. Because the church's exposed sin is integral to its witness, public engagement based on confession unto repentance avoids triumphalism. At the same time, making sin visible through repentant action that brings social healing witnesses to Christ's present and future lordship over the various realms of sociopolitical life. The Southeast White House's initial act of repentance—its move into the neighborhood to encounter the neglected neighbor—witnesses to Christ's lordship over the forgotten quadrant of the nation's capital, and taking responsibility for this neglect through repentant action prepares the way for Christ's concrete redemption. Likewise, Eleuthero's confession of complicity in the excesses of American culture and its repentant activity in the form of learning and applying practices of sustainability witnesses to Christ's lordship over the environment; its ecological care participates in and prepares the way for Christ's total restoration of the natural world. Thus, the church that accepts responsibility for sin not only witnesses to God's judgment on humanity but also demonstrates the nature and purpose of that judgment, namely healing transformation and concrete redemption. The notion of divine judgment has come to connote punishment, as seen through its use in the public arena by leaders of the Religious Right, who now and again gain publicity through outrageous claims identifying catastrophe with God's judgment over groups of people they deem immoral. The judgment of God is misconstrued, though, when understood as punishment, whether in political or religious spheres, since divine judgment is in the service of divine promise. The judgment of God is real and severe—it is crisis—because it holds a mirror up to the sin in us and in the structures of which we are a part and for which we are responsible. The judgment of God is severe but is severe not as punishment but as love—a love intent on bringing wholeness to humanity and this world, which can occur only when we courageously face ourselves: our dualistic mindsets, shallow theologies and easy answers, commitments and lack thereof, our fears of others and the unknown, of being responsible, of losing privilege, comfort, and a sense of control.

Thus, a repentant church receiving God's judgment on itself will be marked by *honesty* and *courage*. It will be honest as it searches out the truth about itself, about its blind spots, preoccupations, and religious idolatries, about the ways the church has harmed others, perhaps in the form of dogma or rigid biblical interpretation, perhaps because it lacks traditional practices of Christian hospitality that welcome the stranger, the outcast, and the despised. It will be courageous as it refuses to hide behind those things that make it feel safe and secure, be it a notion of religious favor, assurance that one's group possesses the truth, or adherence to moral principles. The repentant church is the courageous church as it seeks to be continuously reawakened to the ways it remains complicit in oppressive thought and action, in the myriad structural evils of our political, social, religious, and economic systems. It is courageous as it stands before the living God, open and receptive to divine disruption and criticism, which may be articulated through voices the church is used to dismissing and would rather ignore. The courage and honesty of Eleuthero and the Southeast White House is seen most clearly through their determination, each in their own way, to *undergo continuous conversion* as they *dwell within repentance,* as these communities remain present and engaged while being led deeper into their specific vocations. As we saw, the Southeast White House inhabits repentance as it fosters relationships among people normally divided and draws others into its communal life together. Eleuthero undergoes continuous conversion through the renewing of minds as the members honestly and courageously reflect on their own inherited and embedded theologies and invite other Christians to do the same.

While the case study of Eleuthero highlights the central role the renewing of minds plays in a nontriumphant public witness, rethinking dominant assumptions is integral to the work of both Eleuthero and the Southeast White House. Each community illustrates that a concrete implication of a repentant church demonstrating God's judgment is *the renewing of minds* . . . The triumphalistic tendencies of public witness today demand that Christians rethink dominant assumptions about Christ, the world, the church, repentance, and even the notion of witness itself. Both Eleuthero and the Southeast White House show that inhabiting repentance unsettles patterns of thinking, even those that are allegedly Christian, and both promote an education rooted in lived experience, in what Tim Clayton calls an attempt "to struggle to ask and to live what is possible."[7] As we saw, Eleuthero's confession unto repentance is inaugurated by and requires unlearning and learning anew, and the Southeast White House invites all involved in the work . . . into a transformation *fueled by experiential learning.* A guidebook meant to provoke new thinking and prompt new action reinforces the experiential learning and challenges its readers to live within difficult questions through responsible engagement with the issues and the people they affect. Continuous conversion through the renewing of minds occurs in the lives of the staff and committed "family" members as well. Louis Robertson is convicted of pride and learns from Sammie "that this is a place that welcomes everyone"; Hilary Barnett learned "how ignorant I was and how privileged I am . . . that the quality of my life is due almost entirely to the heritage I have"; Kristi Kiger shifts her understanding of poverty in the developed world and "realizes the mistake of saying, 'well, this isn't real poverty.'"[8] A posture of openness toward divine disruption, as exemplified by Louis, Hilary, and Kristi, requires that one remain within the difficult questions of faith and discipleship, that one practices a faith-seeking-understanding open to continuous conversion, even and especially when the process of rethinking is painful. God's spirit awakens and convicts, shatters conventions, and searches out hidden traces of racism, sexism, or blinding stereotypes in a church-community inhabiting repentance. In turn, the repentant community witnessing to divine judgment in this way cannot help but disavow any claim to goodness. It cannot lift itself up as a model of moral righteousness because it deems itself responsible for sin.

CHARACTERISTICS OF ECCLESIAL WITNESS DEMONSTRATING CHRIST'S RECONCILIATION

We have seen that it is precisely by belonging wholly to the world by accepting guilt and taking responsibility for sin that Christ has reconciled humanity to God and has transformed the world's ontology. The world's identity is no longer narrowed to its fallen structure; rather, in its sin and in the unfolding of redemption, the world is definitively reconciled to Christ. Because the world has been reconciled to God through Christ, though not demonstratively redeemed, the church is called to witness to this already accomplished reconciliation by being a concrete redemptive presence through responsible acts of repentance. The church community demonstrates Christ's reconciliation, then, *when its repentant activity prepares the way for or leads to concrete redemption.* Restoration and

---

7. Clayton, "Eleuthero Launch Talk," October 14, 2005.
8. Louis Robertson, interview with author, October 18, 2006; Hilary Barnett, interview with author, November 29, 2006; Kristi Kiger, interview with author, October 17, 2006.

healing may be newsworthy and have a broad public reach yet more likely will be found in those "small success stories" of slowly transforming lives of which Scott Dimock speaks.[9]

The repentant community demonstrates Christ's reconciliation with the world and makes Christ's redemption concrete by *fostering right relationships* with creation and other human beings. The Southeast White House fosters mutually transformative relationships across the various boundaries that divide human beings by positioning itself as a path upon which unlikely encounters occur and relationships with diverse populations are cultivated and sustained. By cultivating unlikely relationships, it witnesses to the inclusive and expansive nature of Christ's reconciling work that encompasses the totality of humanity. The Southeast White House witnesses to Christ's reconciliation every time an improbable group of people share a meal around the dining room table and a mentor spends time with a child. As the community shares life with an "at-risk" child or a stranger who normally would not be welcome at such a gathering, the Southeast White House witnesses to the social flourishing inherent in the kingdom of God that Christ inaugurates and embodies. The House understands itself as a "bridge" connecting people normally divided, and as bridge it facilitates double movement or mutual redemption in both the neighbors and those who formerly had no impetus to come into the neighborhood. The Eleuthero Community witnesses to Christ's reconciliation by fostering right relationships as well, specifically with the earth and with a vulnerable population of African immigrants. It also understands itself as a bridge as it seeks to be a "dot connector," or "glue" between diverse people like the Sudanese refugees and the Caucasians involved in the Winter Cache sustainability project.[10]

Tim Clayton calls potential connections like the one above a "work of integration" because it gathers people together around a shared concern or need.[11] The repentant community demonstrates Christ's reconciliation, then, not only when it serves as a bridge fostering right relationships but also when it *partners with others around a common work.* Indeed, the shared work likely will be precisely what facilitates authentic and mutually transformative relationships, both within the community and with those who do not self-describe as Christian. Evan Pillsbury says, for example, that the public lectures on theology and ecology and on the spirituality of Martin Luther King offered "space for discussion to emerge" where people inside and outside the Christian tradition could "meet in the middle and allow relationships to develop through a common work and concern, through shared values such as a shared planet."[12] Similarly, Tim Clayton's meetings with environmental professionals and activists with which Eleuthero hoped to partner opened up new possibilities for reconciliation and concrete

9. Scott Dimock, interview with author, October 16, 2006.
10. Tim Clayton, interview with author, September 8–9, 2006.
11. Ibid.
12. Evan Pillsbury, interview with author, September 8, 2006.

redemption as Tim broke down barriers by beginning these conversations with confession of the church's past and present sin that has hindered ecological care. By welcoming all who seek the good of the community, the Southeast White House also exemplifies reconciliation around a common concern. As a "house on the hill for all people," it opens up participation in Christ's reconciling work to all who struggle for the flourishing of the neighborhood regardless of whether they consider themselves inside or outside the church. By refusing to view itself as specially favored and to abide by religious dualisms, the Southeast White House respects the integrity of everyone who comes to share in the work of the House; "there is room" to participate in the being and activity of Christ, according to Marilyn Dimock, regardless of religious affiliation or lack thereof.[13] Borrowing Tim's words about Eleuthero, the Southeast White House invites people into the work in "a way that is respectful to who they are and what they are about" without necessitating that they become Christian.[14] Moreover, redemptive partnerships occur not simply between the repentant community and other groups or individuals but also among the community members themselves. John Johnson's comments about the growth of interracial relationships among the full-time mentors, who are learning to trust one another as they grapple with issues affecting their mentees, exemplifies the kind of authentic reconciliation that may emerge *within* the repentant community around a shared concern.

Finally, the repentant community demonstrates Christ's reconciliation and makes redemption concrete through its *embodied life together* that grows into an ever-enlarging new humanity. For the Southeast White House this means sharing life with its neighbors and inviting into its space those who would otherwise avoid this section of the city. As the staff and volunteers "live in the spirit of Jesus," a sense of peace and love pervade the house, and the house itself takes sacramental form and thaws others into its redemptive space.[15] The House witnesses to the lordship of Christ precisely because it has become a place within which peace, love, right relationships, and a sense of belonging reign; it has become, in other words, a picture and presence of the kingdom of God. The evangelistic import of the witness lies in the fact that the repentant church's "embodied life together" shows the world the promises of God, or in the words of Tim Clayton, "some of what the future is that we are looking towards."[16] As the repentant church keeps Christ's total restoration of this world in view, its communal existence enables all who enter into the life of the community to live more in accordance with the kingdom come. Cheryl Clayton contends that the radical and alternative form of life that becomes a picture and presence of God's kingdom must be built into the very structure of community, which would necessitate rethinking the constitution of local churches. "What we are talking

13. Marilyn Dimock, interview with author, October 16, 2006.
14. Tim Clayton, interview with author, September 8–9, 2006.
15. Marilyn Dimock, interview with author, October 16, 2006.
16. Clayton, "Eleuthero Launch Talk," October 14, 2005.

about is such a radical way of living in America that you need support; you need encouragement; you need people admonishing you," she says, "and I really believe that Christ works [through community]. Outside of this context, I don't think it would be possible."[17] Reconsidering how United States Protestants "do church" does not necessarily mean an overhaul of denominations, . . . but it would mean resisting the insular infrastructure of most churches by structuring congregations, as suggested above, around a common work or need in the world, with worship, Bible study, prayer, and fellowship growing out of this common vocation. The repentant community ordered around a common work demonstrates the reconciliation of Christ and makes Christ's being concrete when its life together ushers forth social flourishing.

As this presentation suggests, a communal life of repentance is a life of abundance. To witness to divine affirmation, judgment, and reconciliation is to share in the life and love of Christ and thus to be truly human and belong wholly to this world. The church-community that belongs to this world has ears to hear God convict it of its complicity in social/structural sin and has the liturgy and prayers of confession to face and name that sin. Confession of specific sin leads the church into its particular vocation, into social and political action full of the significance and purpose of Christ, characterized by the disposition of repentance described above. The church witnesses in a nontriumphal manner to Christ's lordship precisely through this engagement—the form it takes in the world—which both speaks for itself and nurtures a new language, granting the repentant community a new public voice at once theological and intelligible to a pluralistic society because it constitutes words not of superiority and division but of solidarity in sin and redemption. And the public proclamation in word and deed is this: God is for human beings, for the world, and if God is for us who can be against us?

17. Cheryl Clayton, interview with author, September 10, 2006.

Chapter 15

"The Cross"

2012

Gabriel Salguero

To be radical, of course, means to seize a matter at its roots. More radical Christian faith can only mean committing oneself without reserve to the "crucified God." This is dangerous. It does not promise the confirmation of one's own conceptions, hopes and good intentions.[1]

Crux probat omnia.[2]

My intimations on the cross are marinated in the reality of a Jersey-born Puerto Rican. I am a hybrid who is a child of both colony and empire. My hybridity, *mestizaje*, or *mulatez*, speaks to beingness, ontology, and identity. My hyphenated U.S.-Latino existence is affirmed by my struggle to follow the one who also lived a hyphenated existence: Jesus, the God-human. Because I take both the gospel and my context seriously, I continuously struggle with the crucifixion of Jesus, the divine hybrid, and what it means for the globalized world in this present manifestation of empire. My postcolonial hybridity informs my unrelenting struggle of *fides quaerens intellectum a justitia*, faith seeking understanding and justice.[3] Indeed, my theological and spiritual yearnings do not just seek understanding; they also seek justice.

---

1. Jürgen Moltmann, *The Crucified God: The Cross of Christ as the Foundation and Criticism of Christian Theology*, trans. R.A. Wilson and John Bowden (New York: SCM, 1974), 39.
2. Attributed to Martin Luther.
3. I feel that theology is not just as Saint Anselm of Canterbury argues, "faith seeking understanding," but good theology is also "faith seeking justice." I have made these comments elsewhere in sermons and lectures.

In the last few years as an educator, pastor, and Christian activist, I have recognized how much of my theological and spiritual reflection has been done from a postcolonial perspective. As a Jersey-Rican I constantly examine the relationship of the United States and Puerto Rico, the Caribbean, and Latin America. I was born in the U.S. mainland because of economic push-and-pull factors that brought my parents from Puerto Rico to the heart of empire. The dominant messages I heard from U.S. evangelicalism(s) were not speaking to or from the reality of many Latinos and Latinas at the peripheries of empire. The realities of neocolonialism, economic dependence, the failures of developmentalism were often ignored. The interconnectedness between empire and colony, Rome and Jerusalem, Caesar and the cross, was never a part of the canon of theological reflection. These intimations are an effort to speak from that nexus, that place of in-betweenness where the cross meets all children of empire and colony.

A postcolonial hybridity is allowing the cross to speak from its context. By postcolonial I mean a theo-ethical resistance to the methods, ideologies, and modalities of empires that negate the flourishing of life. The cross rejects the dehumanization, homogenization, and humiliation of people who seek another way. The way of Jesus saves, includes, and redeems. My postcolonial vision of the cross sees the broken body of Jesus as the inevitable end of a selfish empire. In the end the cross shouts, "Empire in its endless hunger to be God kills God daily." God is crucified in a first-century Jewish colony and in colonies in every generation since. It is only in a sadly racialized empire, where being Roman is superior to being Jewish, that we can legitimize crucifying the Divine. My postcolonial vision of the cross forces me to ask, "When has my nation, culture, and power called itself supreme at the expense of the other?" Wherever the racialized imperial impulse to classify the other as less-than arises, we see Christ being crucified anew.

I am acutely aware that my struggles with empire are not comparable to those of the thousands of people, particularly women and children, who have fled political and religious persecution that tortures and kills the body and soul. As a hybrid I recognize both my privilege, as an educated U.S. male citizen and ordained clergy, and the prejudices against me as a U.S. Latino. My postcolonial imagination and hybridity are in the context of the privileges and challenges of living in the United States, one of the richest and most powerful countries in the history of the world. Admittedly, we all gaze at the cross from a distance of time and space. Still, the cross speaks to me. My reflections on the cross begin with the confessions of a postcolonial hybrid living in one of the centers of modern power. I am both a citizen and casualty of empire.

Recently, as I looked out at the multicultural and multiethnic congregation that I pastor, I was reminded that we are all exiles. We who follow the Crucified One always live in an in-betweenness, *aquí pero no de aquí*—here but not of here. We are all following a cross that announces a kingdom not of this world. Every time I lift up the cross, it is an announcement of our Christian exile and a denouncement of the abuses of empires, powers, and kingdoms of this world. In this way the cross calls me again to the scandalous nature of the Christian message. The scandal of the cross that calls a colonized and crucified subject, Lord and God. Here I kneel, I can do no other!

So I come to the cross owning my prejudices, privileges, strengths, and limitations. Hybridity and postcolonial imagination are the *locus theologicus* that I embrace unashamedly. My *Sitz im Leben* is not a better or worse position from which to do theological reflection; it is simply my reality. My hope is that these lenses provide a space for postcolonial hybrids in the broad mosaic of global evangelical theology. In my wrestling I remember that I speak from both inside and outside the gates.[4]

"En la cruz, en la cruz, do primero vi la luz"[5] is one of the first songs I learned at Spanish Pentecostal Church where I was raised. Implicit in the theology of my childhood's hymnody is that there is something deeply revelatory about the cross. *Vi la luz* is translated "I saw the light." What light have I seen in the cross? The cross tests, in every generation, our conceptions and intentions. As a child I also sang the Spanish translation of "The Old Rugged Cross": "O yo siempre amaré esa cruz."[6] I find myself asking, "What is it exactly that I am clinging to in the cross? Have I fallen into the snare of romanticizing the cross at the price of diminishing its significance?" My reflections here point to just a few of the radical implications of the cross that are worth highlighting for our increasingly globalized context.

The cross of Jesus has too often been co-opted, domesticated, commodified, and depoliticized. How sadly ironic that the crucifixion of a colonized subject, on a cross outside the gates, continues to face the threat of co-optation. Nevertheless, the cross of Christ resists co-optation, domestication, and commodification.[7] In short, despite efforts of domestication, the cross still speaks. The fundamental query is, "What is it saying?" Saint Paul speaks of unearthing the message of the cross: "For the message of the cross is foolishness . . . , but we proclaim Christ crucified, a stumbling block to Jews and foolishness to Gentiles" (1 Cor. 1:18a, 23 NRSV). From the earliest of Christian writings until this day, the cross continues to be a scandal *(skandalon)* to both the nations *(ethnos)* of the world and religious insiders. The cross is a critique of both power and wisdom in an age where the exile, the stranger, the colonized, and anyone labeled as "other" are continuously trampled by imperial ambitions. In the cross's critique of power and wisdom I began to more fully appreciate the scandal of the

4. I borrow this phrase from Orlando E. Costas, *Christ Outside the Gate: Mission beyond Christendom* (Maryknoll, N.Y.: Orbis, 1999). What I mean here is that as a U.S. Latino, I speak from the context of empire while being relegated to its margins.

5. "En la Cruz," in *Himnos de Gloria y Triunfo* (Miami: Editorial Vida, 1961), 53. This is translated as "At the cross, at the cross where I first saw the light . . . "

6. This is the Spanish version of "The Old Rugged Cross" I sang as a child in church. Literally it can be translated "I will always love that cross" rather than the classic "I will cling to the old rugged cross."

7. For a more thorough treatment of the "resistance of the cross against its interpretations," see chapter 2 of Moltmann, *The Crucified God.*

Christian gospel. It challenges me still as a citizen of empire to recuperate this anti-imperial dimension of scandal. God's salvific project in Christ embraces both the personal and the political and their interstitial nature. The cross of Christ speaks not only to saving our souls but also about imperial power and its dehumanizing effects on the bodies of colonized and crucified subjects.

Theological reflection in the West has focused overwhelmingly on the mystical individual soul-saving implications of the cross. The anti-imperial message of the cross is in danger of disappearing. For in the cross is a prophetic judgment against oppressive nationalisms and imperial ambitions that trample the colonized subjects. I often wonder if this scandalous layer of the message of the cross has been overlooked. Can it be that the message of the cross of Christ transcends one simple definition? Opening the dimensions of the cross is not saying that this is the only way to understand the message of the cross. Rather, the argument is that alongside the repeated interpretations of the cross and the multiple atonement theories exist other layers of meaning. If I am to claim with Christians of every age, *crux sola nostra theologia,* these layers of interpretation must be examined. It is precisely here at the nexus of empire and the cross that hybridity and exile are useful lenses. Through these lenses we can see anew the radical message of a colonized and crucified Jewish Savior.

Several years ago I went to a Christian memorial service at Madison Square Garden for the victims and volunteer heroes of the September 11, 2001, tragedies in New York, Pennsylvania, and Washington, D.C. The service had worship in song and dance, prayer and meditation, as well as a sermon of comfort. What was most memorable and indeed deeply troubling to me was a hologram of the cross on the big screen throughout the memorial service. It was not the image of the cross that bothered me. What I found profoundly inconsistent with the cross of Christ was that superimposed on the cross was a waving United States flag. While I have deep respect and admiration for the U.S. flag, and the flags of any country, the flag and the cross should never be confused. Patriotism has its place, but any confusion of national pride (that means any nation) with the cross of Christ is a clarion call to revisit the cross and its interpretations for our time and place.

The cross is never the flag, any flag, U.S., Russian, Venezuelan, English, etc. The cross always remains outside the gates and resists collapsing into the state. Collapsing the cross with any symbol runs the idolatrous risk of subverting the radical message of the theology of the cross. The crucified Christ who is executed in the outskirts of an imperially occupied city reminds us that the cross is not the state. The cross is not synonymous with any nation, including mine. Jürgen Moltmann warns against the nefarious implications of this religio-political cocktail: "The Pax Christi and the Pax Romana were to be bound together by the providential Dei. In this way Christianity became the unitive religion of the unitary Roman state. Recollection of the crucified Christ and his followers retreated into the background. As often happens in history, the persecuted became the rulers."[8]

---

8. Moltmann, *The Crucified God*, 325.

When the cross of Christ becomes the emblem of the emperor, the cross has lost both its true power and its wisdom. The cross of Christ is neither Caesar's throne nor his seat of power any more than Caesar is Lord. The Christ hymn in Philippians reminds us that the death of the cross was the death of a slave *(doulos).* The message of the cross reminds us that Christ is a *Doulos-Kurios,* a Slave-Lord, not Augustus Caesar. The cross challenges a consciousness informed and formed by empires in the first century and throughout Western history. The crucified God is a prophetic critique of xenophobic nationalisms that crucify the subjugated and conquered other.

Black and Latin American liberation theologians have reminded us that the cross of Christ cannot be divorced from the real deaths of black slaves and the poorest of the poor in the Two-Thirds World.[9] Suffering people have warned that the mystification or, worse, glorification of suffering in the cross often leads to a disempowering message for abused women and children.[10] The cross is not the glorification of suffering; it is the recognition of the horrors of suffering particularly for the innocent and most vulnerable. The solidarity expressed by the crucifixion of Christ is not an affirmation of violence but God's "emphatic no" to the horrors of the torturing, othering, and execution of the least of these.

The crucifixion of Christ occurred in the context of the *Pax Romana.* The crucifixion cannot be understood outside the context of a power that established peace through war and intimidation. Crucifixions were common in the Roman Empire. Several thousands of Spartacus's followers who rebelled against the Roman Empire were crucified in the Via Appia in 71 B.C.E. Mark Lewis Taylor is correct: crucifixion was an execution, state-sponsored terrorism, to keep rebels and conquered peoples in their place.[11] Jesus was a Jewish, colonized "other" and part of an occupied territory governed by Pontius Pilate. This governor was not above using violence to secure compliance and "peace."[12]

How then do I see the cross when I remember this context? The cry is God crying with the "underside of history." Crucifixion is an instrument of keeping

9. See, for example, Leonardo Boff, *Passion of Christ, Passion of the World* (New York: Orbis, 1987); C. S. Song, *Jesus: The Crucified People* (New York Crossroad, 1990); James H. Cone, *God of the Oppressed,* rev. ed. (Maryknoll, N.Y.: Orbis, 1997).

10. See, for example, Delores S. Williams, *Sisters in the Wilderness: The Challenge of Womanist God-Talk* (New York: Orbis, 1993); JoAnne Marie Terrell, *Power in the Blood? The Cross in the African American Experience* (New York: Orbis, 1998); Rita Nakashima Brock, *Journeys by Heart: A Christology of Erotic Power* (New York: Crossroad, 1988); Jacquelyn Grant, *White Women's Christ and Black Women's Jesus: Feminist Christology and Womanist Response* (Atlanta: Scholars, 1989); Ada María Isasí-Díaz, *En La Lucha/In the Struggle: Elaborating a Mujerista Theology* (Minneapolis: Fortress, 1993).

11. Mark L. Taylor, *The Executed God: The Way of the Cross in Lockdown America* (Minneapolis: Augsburg Fortress, 2001). See also the seminal works by Martin Hengel, *Crucifixion in the Ancient World and the Folly of the Message of the Cross* (Philadelphia: Fortress, 1977); *The Atonement: The Origins of the Doctrine in the New Testament* (Philadelphia: Fortress, 1981).

12. I am not arguing here for a strict pacifism. While I am aware of just war theories and the arguments of many of its proponents, this is not what empires past and present practiced but rather genocide, and crusades were the modus operandi.

the colonized and the least of these under the boot of empire, but God is there with us. We do not see God in Rome at the seat of empire. Rather God in Christ is at the cross. God is a Jewish subject crucified by power. God is the racialized "other," not a citizen but a resident of an occupied country. The cross reveals the sinister nature of empire that uses its power to determine all of life. Empire classifies everything: citizens and slaves, Romans and barbarians, wise and foolish, life and death. The cross reminds me that when empire calls me alien, noncitizen, occupied, it does so also to Christ.

Empire seeks *biopower,* the power to define all of life.[13] Similarly, the cross of Christ also puts all things to the test, *Crux probat omnia,* and lays its claims on all of life. Just as the Roman imperial regime sought to define all of life, relationships, sexuality, and even the cosmos, the cross of Christ stakes its claims on the created order in anti-imperial ways. While empire claimed dominion over the sea and skies, the crucified Lord claims solidarity and emancipation. Virgil's *Aeneid* declared, "For these I set no bounds in space or time; but have given empire without end. . . . The Romans, lords of the world, and the nation of the toga."[14] At the crucifixion of Jesus we have a solidarity with the earth and all of creation. The cross of the Romans seeks to dominate and subdue the earth. The crucified Christ moans and weeps with the earth. In the crucifixion even the cosmos grows dark in the middle of the day (Luke 23:44).

The radical nature of the cross of Christ is that it puts a mirror to the hostile and inhumane practices of imperial domination. While the cross of Christ cannot be divorced from religio-imperial violence, it should not be understood as an affirmation of violence. The cross as symbol functions within the liberative dynamics of mimicry. "The subversive and resistant move comes from the dynamics of mimicry—a move that is simultaneously a recognition and a disavowal of potentially dominating power. Mimicry functions as both a resemblance and a menace."[15]

The mimicry of the cross presents not just solidarity with the crucified ones under the Roman boot of imperial hegemony but a denouncement of the imperial methodology. Jesus is not Spartacus. The crosses of Spartacus's followers are an embodiment of those who try to dethrone empire by the methods of empire. The cross of Christ shows another way. The way of Jesus is not the Roman road of imperial violence but an apocalyptic unveiling of the "evil, horror, and messiness of that violence."[16]

In the messiness and horror of the crucifixion it is not Jesus who is stripped naked; the Roman imperial ideology is laid bare for all to see the hypocrisy of

---

13. A term used to define the sphere of power of empire as defined for our contemporary time by Michael Hardt and Antonio Negri, *Empire* (Cambridge: Harvard University Press, 2000).

14. Virgil, *Aeneid* 1.278–283, as cited in John Dominic Crossan, *God and Empire: Jesus against Rome, Then and Now* (San Francisco: HarperSanFrancisco, 2007), 16.

15. Wonhee Anne Joh, *Heart of the Cross: A Postcolonial Christology* (Louisville: Westminster John Knox, 2006), 55.

16. Joh, *Heart of the Cross*, 102.

the *Pax Romana*. These imperial saviors *(soteris)* are no saviors at all but selfish occupiers and colonizers who seek their own expansion. The cross in all its tragedy and horror has "disarmed the rulers and authorities and made a public example of them" (Col. 2:15 NRSV). In the cross, instead of Jesus being made a public spectacle, the Roman Empire and co-opted religion are on public display. The crucifixion puts in the naked public square the cruel hoax of an imperial theology and a religious imperialism that pretends to save by subjugation, humiliation, and homogenization. When I read this my heart is affirmed. The cross of Christ ironically and powerfully brings to light the shame of imperial aspirations.

Christians all over the world should revisit the cross. This visit should challenge us to a reinterpretation of the cross of Christ. This cross exposes imperial power with the power of love that cries for justice and transformation. Christians should continue to preach a cross that scandalizes imperial, and predatory, power and affirms the power of those who are too often the marginalized, the stigmatized. Yes, a power that affirms the stigmata in such a way that it brings all empires to their knees before a reign of a God who resurrected the colonized outsider and crowned him Lord of all. In our proclamation of the Christ we are affirming that we are not complicit citizens of empire but anticolonial followers of the Crucified One. We must once again preach Christ crucified as a denouncement that shakes all the empires of this world and awakens the church to be a welcoming community to all the crucified.

Chapter 16

"Justice"
2012

Helene Slessarev-Jamir

My reflection on justice has been shaped by the multiple streams of ideas and experiences in which I have been swimming since relocating from Wheaton, Illinois, to southern California several years ago. More than ever, I now live in the U.S. borderlands, on land that once belonged to Mexico that has become home to millions of people from around the globe. I recently organized a series of "listening meetings" in preparation for a new Doctorate of Ministry in Urban Ministries at the Claremont School of Theology where I now teach. I invited religious leaders from the region's diverse ethnic and geographic communities to tell me what they wanted in the program. Consistently, they responded by saying, "Don't teach theology from the perspective of dead white men." They want to study theology and ministry paradigms that are emerging from the context of their lived experiences of diaspora and marginalization. Those same realities have become more concretized for me as I now worship in a predominantly immigrant congregation in a city that is 76 percent Latino. The realities of the United States having again become an immigrant nation are now deeply personal as we pray with members who are appealing Immigration and Customs Enforcement (ICE) rejections of their petitions for permanent residency, or with a young woman without documents who desperately wants to attend college, or with a Filipino woman who cannot go home to see her beloved mother who is dying of cancer. I too search for a God who speaks into these realities. I too need to be grounded in theologies that lift up God's expectation that nations will treat "the stranger" with justice. I too need to feel Jesus' presence in the edgy, tough places at the margins.

During my last sabbatical I worked on a book on prophetic activism in a time of empire. I spent a couple of months working on one chapter that explores the meaning of the "prophetic." I found myself deeply immersed in current scholarship on the Old Testament prophets, which left me with a profound sense of connection to the Jewish prophetic tradition. In the Hebrew Bible, I encountered a living God who is dynamically engaged in history. This is not a static, unchanging God of power. Instead, the uniqueness of Yahweh's expectation that his covenant relationship with Israel would entail care for the weak and the marginalized became clearer than ever. I was deeply moved by the beauty and power of the prophets' use of metaphor and poetry to communicate their anger at Israel's transgressions of that covenant.

Without a doubt my recent explorations bring me into deeper tension with mainstream evangelicalism. Rather than being grounded in an organic theology that seeks to discern God's presence in an infinite variety of contexts, evangelicalism remains too deeply committed to a set of truth claims that are grounded in an ahistorical reading of Scripture. This leads to a reification of Anglo-European theological constructions that support various forms of Christian triumphalism. It becomes an exclusive religion that cannot tolerate engagement with difference, with the *other*. The result is a religion fearful of boundary crossers, visionaries, and prophets who are always calling for a stretching of the gospel that evangelicals are trying to contain.

My theological explorations in recent years have been possible because I decided to leave Wheaton College, where I had served on the faculty and directed the urban studies program for fifteen years. Admittedly, as a woman from an urban, immigrant background, I was on the religious-cultural margins of what is one of the leading academic bastions of evangelicalism. Yet, being there had made me cautious, never certain when I might touch one of the electric trip wires set up to protect evangelicalism's borders. Leaving has given me a renewed sense of freedom to write and speak prophetically as the spirit leads me. I offer this reflection on justice out of my newfound spiritual freedom.

Christian justice activists ground theological understandings of their work in the concrete realities of life faced by the people with whom they are working. Their theological framework emerges in response to the unjust conditions of life found in the slums of the world; among exploited poultry, garment, and hotel workers; among AIDS orphans, gangbangers, illegal immigrants, and countless others who are abused. Confronted with pain and exploitation, they ask how God would speak to these myriad forms of human suffering. This is theology done from the bottom up, which is less concerned with doctrine and more concerned with hearing Christ speaking in the midst of suffering. Having grown up amidst the poverty of the Puerto Rican barrio in the South Bronx and having himself lived on the streets, Harold Recinos's writing embodies this form of prophetic theologizing. In *Jesus Weeps* Recinos writes, *"I knew from experience* that the broken, the oppressed, the poor, the sick, the elderly, women, sojourners, and all such persons found in large numbers in the city are special in the sight of God."[1] His own life experiences of suffering integrated with his Christian faith led him to theologize about justice for the poor.

Today, many younger American evangelicals are also coming to recognize the centrality of doing justice to the life of Christian discipleship. This new-found understanding is leading them to challenge the older generations' singular emphasis on personal piety. Since many younger evangelicals come from more privileged backgrounds, embracing justice requires that they consciously align themselves with disenfranchised people in the United States and around the world. Such experiences give them new eyes with which to read the Scriptures, which in turn pushes them to a still-deeper embrace of the gospel's message understood as liberation for and by the least of these. The search for Christ in the midst of the current context of global poverty and hunger opens the door to a reexamination of how God has responded to suffering within earlier historical contexts.

Against the backdrop of suffering and poverty, the gospel message becomes a prophetic call for spiritual, social, and economic renewal that will bring wholeness and peace not just to individuals, but also to whole communities, and to nations. At the same time, an embrace of the centrality of justice within the gospel message forces a stretching and fresh reading of the gospel, moving it beyond the traditional boundaries of American evangelical piety. Thus, the contours of contemporary Christian understandings of justice are most dynamic in those places where the lived realities of the marginalized intersect with the biblical narrative of God's interactions with humanity throughout history.

As prophetic evangelicals, we seek to respond to God's call to *shalom,* seeking to improvise collaboratively in establishing the presence of justice in all dimensions of human community. To fully understand *shalom* it is necessary to take a few steps back to examine the meaning of justice found in the Old Testament. According to Abraham Joshua Heschel, the renowned Hebrew Bible scholar, the God of the Israelites was unique in placing justice at the very center of the covenant with the people of Israel. Justice was so important to God because "righteousness is not just a value; it is God's part of human life. *God's stake in human history."*[2] This is the very God who liberated the people of Israel from slavery in the Egyptian empire, sustained them in the desert, before leading them into the land they were to inherit.

---

1. Harold J. Recinos, *Jesus Weeps: Global Encounters on Our Doorstep* (Nashville: Abingdon, 1992), 36, italics added.
2. Abraham J. Heschel, *The Prophets* (New York: Harper Perennial Classics, 2001), 253, italics in original.

Yahweh's justice as embodied in the Mosaic law was designed to maintain a relatively egalitarian society among the early descendants of the twelve tribes of Israel who were each given a portion of the Promised Land. Since access to one's inherited land was the primary means of ensuring well-being in a subsistence economy, the Mosaic law erected an elaborate set of laws protecting inheritance rights. Since land was inherited through the male, the law gave specific rights to those most in danger of marginalization—widows, orphans, and resident aliens—each of whom were at risk of being cut off from their inheritance rights. Generosity, not profit, was regarded as a central economic principle. Israelites were instructed not to withhold wages from their laborers and not to charge interest when lending money to those in need. Since the poor were not just economically poor, but also lacking in social status, the law sought to protect them from abuse by the courts, prohibiting judges from perverting the justice due to the poor in their lawsuits (Exod. 23:6). Resident aliens were to be treated as citizens (Lev. 19:33). Yahweh repeatedly reminded the Israelites that the rights of the marginalized were to be protected as an act of reciprocity for Israel having been given refuge in Egypt during a time of famine. Following these laws would ensure not only collective well-being, but also God's continued blessings of the people of Israel, as is stated in Deuteronomy: "There will . . . be no one in need among you, because the LORD is sure to bless you in the land that the LORD your God is giving you as a possession to occupy" (Deut. 15:4).[3]

These relatively egalitarian practices remained intact until the emergence of a monarchy in Israel. At that point, the land was no longer seen as Yahweh's gift, but as the king's possession. The new hierarchical social structures provided the wealthy with increased leverage over the poor. The monarchy taxed its citizens; those who could least afford to pay were at the mercy of the wealthy. Credit was available, but borrowers were required to pay high interest rates. Without regulation and with a corrupted judicial system, creditors could demand payment of a debt at any time, leading to the creation of a permanent class of very poor people.[4] In response to the growing inequality and marginalization, God spoke out through the prophets. Beginning with Amos, followed by Hosea, Micah, First Isaiah, Zephaniah, Jeremiah, Nahum, and Habakkuk, the prophets condemned the myriad forms of injustice and warned of Israel's eventual destruction if it continued to ignore its covenantal relationship with Yahweh. For the Hebrew prophets, learning to act righteously was one of the principal means by which humans served God. The value of all forms of worship, including sacrifice and prayer, was contingent upon moral living. The prophets believed that humans principally served God through the practice of love, justice, and righteousness. Anything else was regarded as hypocrisy. When first the northern kingdom and

---

3. Biblical quotations in this chapter come from the New Revised Standard Version.

4. Leslie J. Hoppe, O.F.M., *There Shall Be No Poor among You: Poverty in the Bible* (Nashville: Abingdon, 2004), 10–11.

later the city of Jerusalem itself were destroyed, the prophets interpreted the events as God's punishment for Israel's misdeeds. God, who judges individuals, cities, and nations, will not indefinitely tolerate those nations that oppress the weak and the poor.

In the earlier, Mosaic period, the people of God had been narrowly defined to include only the descendants of the twelve tribes that Moses had led out of Egypt. In fact, Yahweh gave the people of Israel permission to commit acts of genocide against a foreign people, the hated Canaanites, who were already living in the land promised to the Israelites. While the Mosaic law required that resident aliens be treated as citizens, they were restricted from full participation in worship. By the time of the exile, after the people of Israel had been scattered to live among many other ethnicities, Yahweh, speaking through the prophets, unfolded a more inclusive vision of who constituted the people of God. Although the prophets' words were still primarily directed at the people of Israel, there was an emerging recognition that foreigners could under certain circumstances become part of the covenant people. A passage from Second Isaiah declares that

> foreigners who join themselves to the LORD,
>   to minister to him, to love the name of the LORD, . . .
> all who keep the sabbath, and do not profane it,
>   and hold fast my covenant—
> these I will bring to my holy mountain,
>   and make them joyful in my house of prayer; . . .
> for my house shall be called a house of prayer
>   for all peoples.
>   (Isa. 56:6–7)

Significantly Jesus repeated the last portion of this passage after he had driven the money changers out of the Jerusalem temple. Jeremiah, conveying God's counsel to the exiles in Babylon, advised against isolation. Instead, Yahweh called on them to "seek the welfare of the city where I have sent you into exile, and pray to the LORD on its behalf, for in its welfare you will find your welfare" (Jer. 29:7). Now the Israelites would thrive only by seeking the welfare of their enemies. This new, more inclusive understanding remained intact after the exiles returned to Jerusalem. Ezekiel, a postexilic prophet, for the first time incorporates resident aliens who have had children into the new division of land among the tribes so that they too would now receive an inheritance of land.

Jesus articulated a still more radically new, inclusive understanding of who is included among the people of God. Jesus' message is a universalizing one; it is a boundary-crossing vision. He breaks down the boundaries of ethnic exclusiveness. The old assumptions of religious purity were cast out as Jesus embraced friends and foes alike, clean and unclean—outcasts of all sorts, including prostitutes and lepers, who were the people with HIV/AIDS of his day. He embraced women, including those who were single, unattached to a male head of household, which had been the only circumstance under which women had status under the Mosaic law. In his words and actions he conveyed a vision of who can enter the kingdom of God that defied the religious establishment that functioned as the boundary preservers within postexilic Jewish society. For Jesus, the act of healing was more important than maintaining the Sabbath— Jesus improvised in his interpretation of the Sabbath law to bring restoration and healing to the hurting. At every turn, Jesus was challenging the religious establishment that was seeking to protect old, outdated understandings of who can be holy. Now the people, by their acts of faith, determine holiness. To the temple priests and the guardians of the religious institutions charged with protecting the status quo, Jesus was a heretic and therefore a threat that had to be eliminated.

Jesus stood in the long line of Hebrew prophets who had railed against the religious and governmental powers for their violations of the covenant with Yahweh. He had come not to abolish the law or the prophets but to fulfill them (Matt. 5:17). He situated himself directly within the prophetic tradition by reading from Isaiah in his first public address to his hometown synagogue and then proclaiming to the audience that "this scripture has been fulfilled in your hearing" (Luke 4:21). Jesus' goal was to bring about a renewal of the covenant for a new historical period, for the circumstances faced by the people of God in the context of a brutal Roman Empire and the impending destruction of the Second Temple, which would send the Jewish people into permanent exile. For Jesus, the central criterion for inclusion was faith, not ethnicity or gender. This new inclusivity is embodied in Jesus' willingness to respond to the pleas for healing from people who are clearly outside of the traditional boundaries of the people of the covenant. He healed the Roman centurion's servant even though the soldier belonged to the Roman occupying army. Afterward, to emphasize the significance of this single act, he declared, "Truly I tell you, in no one in Israel have I found such faith. I tell you, many will come from east and west and will eat with Abraham and Isaac and Jacob in the kingdom of heaven, while the heirs of the kingdom will be thrown into the outer darkness" (Matt. 8:10–12). The healing of the Canaanite woman's daughter, the feeding of the crowd of 5,000, the parable of the Good Samaritan, the inclusion of women among his closest followers, his intervention on behalf of the adulterous wife are all examples of this new inclusivity.

Justice was to now define all human relationships, not just those among friends or people of the same nationality, ethnicity, gender, or religious identity. Justice was also to define the actions of whole cities, which were the centers of administrative power and wealth under Roman rule in the ancient Near East.[5] The same was true of nations, since the extended passage in Matthew 25 concerns the judgment of nations based on whether they have fed the hungry,

5. Bruce J. Malina, *The Social Gospel of Jesus: The Kingdom of God in Mediterranean Perspective* (Minneapolis: Fortress, 2001), 26–27.

given the thirsty something to drink, welcomed the stranger, clothed the naked, visited the sick and those in prison. For, "just as you did it to *one of the least of these who are members of my family,* you did it to me" (Matt. 25:40). Here again Jesus is following the earlier Hebrew prophets who had spoken of Yahweh's judgment on Israel as a nation, not just as individuals. Justice is ultimately the responsibility of those with authority and power. While the old Mosaic law had once mandated that Israel protect its own people who were at risk of economic and social marginalization, Jesus universalized the law by holding all nations responsible for the task of doing justice for the least of these.

Unlike the prophets of the Old Testament, Jesus established a community of followers that would embody this new covenant in their relationships with one another. He created an alternate community that was to live by radically different standards in the present, not just at some point in the future. The community was a place of radical hospitality, in which there was no distinction between Jew and Gentile, slave and free, and no one was in need.

To be present-day followers of Jesus requires that we see the world through Jesus' eyes; it requires us to be radical boundary crossers and not to allow a religious or political establishment to dictate who is "inside" and who is "outside." Daniel Smith-Christopher uses the image of Jesus as a "coyote," who is the person who makes sure that people crossing the borders are fed, taken care of, and given safe passage. "Jesus is a good coyote because he invites us to cross borders—often violating for the sake of the gospel, the loyalties we humans have built to separate us from one another."[6] It requires that we embrace theologies that emerge from below, theologies that grow out of the lived experiences of marginalized people to whom God is speaking in this age. It requires an ability to hear prophetic voices as they emerge around the globe, be it in the form of Dr. Martin Luther King, who spoke not only of racial justice but also of economic equity, and peacemaking, or Elvira Arellano, the undocumented immigrant whose faith led her to take sanctuary in a church in Chicago. It also requires hearing the voices of Mahatma Gandhi and Thich Nhat Hanh, a Hindu and a Buddhist respectively, who have called for an end to global violence, to be replaced by an ethic of love modeled on none other than Jesus of Nazareth. Christian justice work must be done with the recognition that "the religious is not an exclusive terrain of Christianity, because different spiritualities, forms of worship and cosmos visions are a source of meaning for millions of people." This conclusion was reached by an International Conference on Religion, Development and Cooperation held in Guatemala City in May 2008 that brought together evangelical, Catholic, and Mayan groups to discuss cooperation on development projects.

The challenge for those who are engaged in the work of justice today is indeed to allow the powerful gospel message to take forms accessible to those

6. Daniel Smith-Christopher, *Jonah, Jesus, and Other Good Coyotes* (Nashville: Abingdon, 2007), xvii–xviii.

who are standing on the margins of society. For example, is it possible for the Virgin of Guadalupe, who is revered by the mestizo people of Mexico, to bring healing and comfort to those whose land has been occupied and who are forced to leave their homes and go into exile in El Norte? Can the thief on the cross next to Jesus be reimagined as the young gangbanger in south Los Angeles? Can the Canaanite woman be reimagined as the young single mother forced into prostitution to feed her family in Zimbabwe or in Harlem? Would Jesus perhaps turn water into wine at the marriage of a gay couple? These are just a few of the present-day places at the margins that cry out for justice to be done. Might God not also curse a nation that without provocation has invaded another nation while allowing one of its own cities to lie in ruins? Is this an unpatriotic notion or might it be also a form of God's justice upon a present-day nation? Hopefully, more Christians will open themselves up to hear the call of the good coyote, the one who continuously crosses the boundaries we seek to erect.

Bibliography

Bebbington, David W. "Evangelicalism in Its Settings: The British and American Movements since 1940." In *Evangelicalism*, edited by Mark A. Noll, David W. Bebbington, and George A. Rawlyk, 365–388. New York: Oxford University Press, 1994.

Bebbington, David W. and Mark A. Noll, ed. *A History of Evangelicalism: People, Movements and Ideas in the English-Speaking World*, 5 volumes. Downers Grove, IL: InterVarsity Press, 2003–2013.

Blair, Leonardo. "Ex-Evangelical Pastor Jerry Dewitt to Host Atheist Church Service in Louisiana." *The Christian Post*, June 13, 2013. Online: http://www.christianpost.com/news/ex-evangelical-pastor-jerry-dewitt-to-host-atheist-church-service-in-louisiana-97963/.

Colson, Charles. *Against the Night*. Ann Arbor, MI: Vine Books, 1989.

Dayton, Donald W. "Some Doubts about the Usefulness of the Category 'Evangelical'." In *The Variety of American Evangelicalism*, edited by Donald W. Dayton and Robert K. Johnston, 245–251. Downers Grove, IL: InterVarsity Press, 1991.

Dorrien, Gary. *The Remaking of Evangelical Theology*. Louisville, KY: Westminster John Knox Press, 1998.

Eskridge, Larry "Defining Evangelicalism." Institute for the Study of American Evangelicals, Wheaton College, 2012. Online: www.wheaton.edu/ISAE/Defining-Evangelicalism/How-Many-Are-There.

Evans, Rachel Held. "What Now?" Online: http://rachelheldevans.com/blog/what-now-world-vision.

Gushee, David P. *The Future of Faith in American Politics: The Public Witness of the Evangelical Center*. Waco, TX: Baylor University Press, 2008.

Gushee, David P. and Dennis P. Hollinger. "Toward an Evangelical Ethical Methodology." In *Toward an Evangelical Public Policy: Political Strategies for the Health of the Nation*, edited by Ronald J. Sider and Diane Knippers, 117–139. Grand Rapids: Baker, 2005.

Henry, Carl. *Twilight of a Great Civilization*. Westchester, IL: Crossway Books, 1988.

———. *The Uneasy Conscience of Modern Fundamentalism*. Grand Rapids: Wm. B. Eerdmans, 1947.

Marsden, George M. *Understanding Fundamentalism and Evangelicalism*. Grand Rapids: Wm. B. Eerdmans Publishing Co., 1991.

McKnight, Scot. "The Ironic Faith of Emergents." *Christianity Today*, September 26, 2008. Online: http://www.christianitytoday.com/ct/2008/september/39.62.html?start=1.

Newport, Frank and Joseph Carroll. "Another Look at Evangelicals in America Today." Gallup, December 2005. Online: www.gallup.com/poll/20242/another-look -evangelicals-america-today.aspx.

Noll, Mark A. "What Is Evangelical." In *The Oxford Handbook of Evangelical Theology*, edited by Gerald R. McDermott, 19–34. New York: Oxford University Press, 2010.

Pannell, William E. "The Evangelical Christian and Black History." *Fides et Historia* 2, no. 2 (Spring 1970): 4–14.

Patterson, James A. "Cultural Pessimism in Modern Evangelical Thought: Francis Schaeffer, Carl Henry, and Charles Colson." *Journal of the Evangelical Theological Society* 49, no. 4 (December 2006): 807–820.

Perkins, John. *With Justice for All*. Ventura: Regal Books, 1982.

The Pew Forum on Religion & Public Life, "Religious Landscape Survey." The Pew Research Center, February 2008. Online: religions.pewforum.org/pdf/report -religious-landscape-study-full.pdf.

Schaeffer, Francis. *How Should We Then Live?* Wheaton, IL: Crossway Books, 1976.

Skinner, Tom. *Words of Revolution*. Grand Rapids: Zondervan, 1970.

Weber, Timothy P. "Premillenialism and the Branches of Evangelicalism." In *The Variety of American Evangelicalism*, edited by Donald W. Dayton and Robert K. Johnston, 5–21. Downers Grove, IL: InterVarsity Press, 1991.

List of Contributors

David P. Gushee is the Distinguished University Professor of Christian Ethics and Director of the Center for Theology and Public Life at Mercer University.

Carl F. H. Henry (1913–2003) was the founding editor of *Christianity Today* and taught at both Northern Baptist Seminary and Eastern Baptist Seminary.

Jennifer McBride is the Board of Regents Chair in Ethics and Assistant Professor of Religion at Wartburg College in Waverly, Iowa.

Stephen Charles Mott was Professor of Christian Social Ethics at Gordon-Conwell Theological Seminary for twenty-five years before his retirement.

William E. Pannell is Special Assistant to the President and Senior Professor of Preaching at Fuller Theological Seminary.

John M. Perkins is the founder of the Christian Community Development Association (CCDA) and is the president of the John M. Perkins Foundation in Jackson, Mississippi.

Soong-Chan Rah is the Milton B. Engebretson Associate Professor of Church Growth and Evangelism at North Park Theological Seminary in Chicago.

Gabriel Salguero is a pastor, activist, author, and president of the National Latino Evangelical Coalition.

Francis Schaeffer (1912–1984) was an author, theologian, pastor, and founder of the L'Abri community in Switzerland.

Ron Sider is the Distinguished Professor of Theology, Holistic Ministry & Public Policy at Eastern University's Palmer Theological Seminary.

Helene Slessarev-Jamir is the Mildred M. Hutchinson Professor of Urban Ministries at Claremont School of Theology.

Glen H. Stassen (1936–2014) was the Lewis B. Smedes Professor of Christian Ethics and the Executive Director of the Just Peacemaking Initiative at Fuller Theological Seminary.

Allen Verhey (1945–2014) was the Robert Earl Cushman Professor of Christian Theology at Duke Divinity School.

Eldin Villafañe is Professor of Christian Social Ethics and was the founding director of the Center for Urban Ministerial Education at Gordon-Conwell Theological Seminary.

Jim Wallis is a writer, activist, and founding editor of *Sojourners* magazine.

Nicholas Wolterstorff is Noah Porter Professor Emeritus of Philosophical Theology at Yale University.

John Howard Yoder (1927–1997) was Professor of Theology at Notre Dame and a fellow of the Institute for International Peace Studies.

Index of Ancient Sources

Index of Names and Subjects

Dawson, John, 127–29
Dayton, Donald W., xvn1, xvi, xviin6
democratic, xxv, 3–5, 45, 121
demonic, 10, 40, 72–79, 99–100, 109. *See also*
    power: evil
denominations, xvii, xviii–xx, 3–4, 115,
    123–34, 145
Detroit, 18
developmentalism, 147
Dewitt, Jerry, xvn2
DeYoung, Curtiss Paul, 133–34
dignity. *See* image of God, human dignity
Dimock, Marilyn, 144
Dimock, Scott, 138, 143
disestablishment, xvii, 89, 120. *See also* confessional state
Dobson, James, xxii
Dodd, C. H., 71
Dorrien, Gary, xvi
drugs, 25–27, 32
Duberman, Martin, 17–18
DuBois, W. E. B., 21
Dunn, James D. G., 101

economics, 5–10, 19–20, 34–46, 51, 56,
    58, 62, 64, 69–74, 77, 86n6, 98,
    117–18, 128–30, 133, 141, 147,
    155–56, 159
ecumenical, 4, 7, 10, 15
Edwards, Jonathan, 61
egalitarian, 102, 116, 156
Eleuthero Community (Portland, ME),
    138–44
elitism, 32–33, 87n9
Elizondo, Virgilio, 130
Elvira, Synod of, 32
emperor/caesar, 10, 57, 105, 105n7, 106–12,
    110n26, 147, 150
    imperialism, 110, 147–52, 157
Empire, xxix, 104–5, 107, 150n12, 151n13,
    146–52, 154
    Babylonian, 109, 157
    biopower, 151–52
    Egyptian, 109, 155–57
    Persian, 109
    Roman, 13, 32–33, 104–5, 107–8, 112,
        147, 149, 150–52, 158
    U.S., xxix, 146–52, 148n4, 150n12
    See also colony/colonialism
end times, xx, xxii, 75
England, 15, 30, 37, 43, 59, 82, 120, 149
Enlightenment, xxii, 29, 41, 108, 119

Episcopalian/Anglican, xviii, 15
eschatology, 12, 18, 95–96, 108, 119. *See also*
    kingdom/reign of God/Christ
ethics as way/walk, 49, 54–57, 56n12, 77,
    94–95, 94n2, 102, 105, 116–19, 122,
    127, 147, 151
Euro-Americans, 73
Europe, Western, xxviii–xx, xxvii, 8–9, 15, 19,
    26–27, 33, 36–37, 39, 41, 43, 51, 82,
    87, 89, 119, 125, 131, 134, 154
evangelical right/left/center, xxii–xxvi, 14, 118,
    120, 141
evangelism, xvi, xvii–xviii, xviin9, xxi–xxii,
    xxviii, 9, 21, 44, 49, 57n14, 58–59,
    76, 88, 97, 101, 121–22, 127, 133,
    144
Evans, Rachel Held, xvn2
evolution, xvii, xix, 79

faith seeking understanding and justice, 142, 146
false/alien gods, 51–52. *See also* idolatry
Falwell, Jerry, xvi, xxii, xxvi
fidelity/infidelity, 14, 51, 104, 110
Finney, Charles, xxii
flag, country, 149
following the Spirit/Jesus, 15, 47, 49, 52n9,
    53–59, 66, 78, 78n28, 89, 94–95, 99,
    114, 121, 146–49, 152, 158–59
Fox, Louise, 60
France, 29, 126
Francis of Assisi, xvii, xxvi
free church, 15–16
freedom, xxi, xxix, 14, 20, 25–29, 23–33, 49,
    58–59, 62, 64, 74, 86n6, 88, 92, 102,
    105, 108, 111–12, 121, 131, 154, 159.
    See also liberation (theology)
free love, xxi
Fuller, xxi
fundamentalism, xvii, xix–xxii, xvii, 2–5
fungible (people), 72–73

Gandhi, Mahatma, 159
Geneva Catechism, 83–84
genocide, 127, 150n12, 157
Germany, xvii, 9, 15–16, 27, 37, 43, 114
Gibbon, Edward, 33
Ginsberg, Allen, 25
GNP, 36–42
Goethe, Johann Wolfgang von, 29
González, Justo L., 96, 97n7
Gordon College, xviii
Gospels, 56

CPSIA information can be obtained
at www.ICGtesting.com
Printed in the USA
FFOW02n0947110915
16801FF